1942

THE REFERENCE SHE

Volume X

Volume XI. $6

Volume X. $4.20

THE REFERENCE SHELF

Vol. 15   No. 8

WARTIME CENSORSHIP OF PRESS AND RADIO

COMPILED BY
ROBERT E. SUMMERS

THE H. W. WILSON COMPANY
NEW YORK   1942

PREFACE

This volume is planned to tell the story of the development of censorship in World War II, with reference to its operation, its origin, its problems, and its purpose.

The field is an important one and covers many phases of activity in wartime America. Since censorship is closely linked with so many separate fields, this discussion is limited to news control alone as it affects radio and the press. No attempt is made to discuss the problems of propaganda, of suppression of freedom of speech, of the constitutional or legal aspects of censorship, or of the situation abroad, although perhaps these problems rightfully belong to the overall censorship picture.

In wartime censorship of radio and the press however, there have been greater developments and more direct evidences of news control than in any other field which the subject might possibly include. News control, after all, most directly concerns the average citizen as he listens to his radio or reads his daily paper.

Comparatively little has appeared on the subject in the newspaper columns or the nation's periodicals. Almost exclusively, the news relating to the developments in the field of censorship has been limited to leading trade journals of the news industry: *Variety* and *Broadcasting* for radio; *Editor & Publisher* for the press.

This book represents an attempt to bring together materials relating to every phase of censorship of news on the radio and in the press and to present a well-rounded picture of the situation as it exists today. Both sides of the question are presented as fairly and with as little partiality as possible.

The writer wishes to express his appreciation, for permission to reprint certain of the materials used in this book, to the Council for Democracy, to the American Civil Liberties Union,

October 26, 1942 - Published - 1.25

the National Association of Broadcasters, to the Office of Censorship, and to the Princeton University Press; and to the editors of *Advertising Age, Broadcasting, Collier's, Editor & Publisher, Fortune, Harper's, Modern Industry, Newsweek, New York Times, Public Opinion Quarterly, Redbook, Saturday Evening Post, Tide, Time, United States News, Variety,* and *Vital Speeches.*

Robert E. Summers

New York City,
   July 5, 1942

CONTENTS

CONTENTS
7

INTRODUCTION

The United States is once more engaged in war. Organizing a nation for war has always meant drastic changes in the lives of a freedom-loving people. Today, more than ever before, war touches the life and habits of every individual engaged in it, whether directly or indirectly. The concept of "total war" as practiced by the Nazis, according to historians, is nothing new. But this concept, long understood by the Axis nations, is one to which democracies have become unaccustomed.

Here in the United States, and in each of the other United Nations, people are beginning to understand the meaning of war as the German, the Italian and the Russian populations have known it for a number of years. "All out" war means that every single action of every single individual living within the nation at war must have a meaning and a purpose—that of victory!

The American people are learning about "all out" war by giving up refrigerators, radios, tires, stopping their Sunday joy rides and beginning to wear cuffless trousers and buying war bonds. This is only the beginning. Americans will soon understand the "total war" philosophy—how every action must contribute something toward victory.

The process will be slow, but already the editor and the broadcaster have found their place in the war effort. For just as in the Axis nations, this country too has learned that news is a vital instrument of war! The result—Censorship! Although eternally dedicated to the ways of democracy and with it to freedom of speech and of the press, 130,000,000 Americans today are accepting philosophically the fact that one must fight fire with fire—that against a totalitarian aggressor, a nation must adopt the most effective means of combatting that aggressor, even though the means may be completely alien to the ideals of its people.

This war finds a far different America than the America
of 1917 and 1918. Fanaticism and patriotic hysteria are absent.
Flag waving and mass-meetings "in the name of holy patriotism"
are frowned upon. As much as possible, America at war today
is maintaining a businesslike, impersonal grimness which carries
over into every phase of every day living. Maudlin sentiment
has no place in World War II, whether among the citizen
soldiers making up the largest army this nation has ever known,
or among the civilian workers and their families at home who
must support the military machine with increased production,
purchases of war bonds, and curtailment of customary pleasures,
luxuries, even liberties. America has no time for nonsense in
this war.

And perhaps it is this very change in attitude and spirit which
is responsible for the whole-hearted acceptance of any and all
regulations imposed by the government. A year before Pearl
Harbor who would have believed that the government could
"get away with" registering all men from eighteen to sixty
for the draft, or that the government could ever safely and con-
fidently issue orders for all men in non-essential industries to
start looking around for war jobs? No one would then have
believed that overnight the isolationist would disappear and
return the next day demanding a "second front" and drafting of
labor for greater production.

But all that *has* happened, has even been demanded by the
public itself. And an important part of this whole structure
of government mobilization for war, "regimentation" as it used
to be called, is censorship of radio and the press. Yet for the
first time in history, the American people seem united in one
idea—to accept any sacrifice if it will help win the war.

So, today, in the United States we are applying a strict wartime censorship over radio and the press.

What has caused this change of belief on the part of a
people savage in defense of what it considers its "unalienable

rights"? The whole story is part and parcel with the history of the United States since 1930.

When the post-war heyday ended and the beautiful bubble of everlasting prosperity broke, America was plunged into the most serious depression within recent history. Its effects reached so deeply into the economic and social structure that few if any individuals escaped its ravages. Workers, who had previously been willing to accept conditions as they found them, began to realize just how much the entire economic pattern concerned them. They learned how a company two thousand miles away could cause them days of idleness, even unemployment. People generally began to look at the world with new eyes—to see how close they had come to disaster—and the thought that it was not ended frightened them.

Franklin D. Roosevelt came into power as a result of a wave of hysteria, elected by a people frantically trying to save themselves. The early days of the New Deal and the Brain Trust seemed to be the beginning of a new order. But eventually the public awakened to the fact that the old days of peace and plenty were gone, and still the problem hadn't been solved. The New Deal collapsed, but a new factor had appeared on the scene—a wave of nationalism began to sweep across Europe and Asia. American business, which depended primarily upon its foreign trade for profits, awakened to the fact that an insignificant Austrian house-painter and a former Italian Socialist were fast becoming more dangerous to their prosperity than the generation-old menace of communism. Throughout the world, the depression had brought about great changes in the social and economic order. A new ideology sprang into being. Even in the United States, changes were taking place daily. While the New Deal may have been a failure, it had proved its point—that government action was necessary to keep the nation together in times of emergency.

And when war broke out in Europe, it was a different sort of American public who faced the prospect of having to fight again to defend their freedom. Each month saw the Nazi war machine blotting out democracy in a score of nations on the European continent. Each day, American readers saw in the papers, listeners heard over their radios, of the destruction of freedom in Nazi-held states. They learned of a new word in this world of fast communication—"censorship." Of course, they had experienced it in World War I. Orators and radical editors had ranted and raved of being denied their constitutional rights of freedom of speech and freedom of the press during the '20's. But this was different. Propaganda, in its infancy during World War I, suddenly assumed major proportions. And gradually, the public in this nation learned how the jig-saw puzzle of total war fitted together, how every news item, every radio speech had a rightful place in the war effort.

The facts were a little slow in presenting themselves, but with the struggle of England for survival, people began to see for the first time that whatever they had learned about war, and about censorship and propaganda in the past, had to be relearned this time. It was through no subtle propaganda of the American government or the British government that the American public awakened to the truth. One had only to read his daily news-paper, listen to the accounts on the airwaves—and the story was plain to see. And with this revelation, the public grew more thoughtful. Before, even after Dunkirk, this had appeared only as another war, another distasteful mess that (with native conceit) the United States would have to go over and settle eventually.

But now the picture had changed. If a man couldn't believe what he read in the papers or heard on the radio, the situation was downright serious. Everyone soon grew to understand that nothing from the war zone was released except after careful survey by a government censor. From the Axis-dominated nations, news as often as not was invented to fit the needs of the propaganda ministry. Even England learned to play this new game of power politics, of news suppression and propaganda. At first her attempts were pretty crude and transparent to the whole world.

But the realization that England was fighting to survive and that her censorship and her propaganda were means of survival stopped the bitter jibes in the American press at "British incompetence." A new respect for propaganda and its agencies began to take the place of the former suspicion in the minds of most Americans. While as yet, perhaps, the picture isn't too clear, still the public of this nation knows that communications play a tremendous role in the total war effort.

It is this realization, brought about partly by understanding of the situation, partly by belief in the necessity of any measure the government feels necessary for victory, that has permitted censorship of the press and radio in the United States today. And not only that, it has been this realization which has forced newspapers and radio stations to comply with the government's voluntary program.

Early in the war, Americans were told by their press and by the broadcasters that news from the European battlefronts could not be relied upon. Before many months the importance of knowing *where* news originated became almost self-evident. And with the understanding that news from abroad was censored, the American public began to understand the role of news control in wartime.

The effects of this control were brought forcibly to view during the Russo-Finnish War, when a controlled Finnish press painted a glowing and almost fantastic picture of Finnish victories over insurmountable odds. But the public over here was taken in. The story struck a chord in the hearts of every American, as we read how a tiny handful of Finns smashed a Russian army of 300,000 men. Then the United States slowly began to hear the real story. It seemed hard to believe that the friendly, courageous Finns had lied. But there were the facts. And Americans learned the importance of controlling the news, the value of censorship in total war strategy.

We have only to look at the record to see just how the nations at war have seen to it that the United States learned only what they wished us to learn. A proper understanding of the chief sources of the news of the world is an excellent introduction into the subject of wartime censorship and its chief reason for being.

AN UNDERSTANDING OF CENSORSHIP

DISCUSSION

What is censorship? Is it legal? Why is it necessary? What is being censored? These are only a few of the many questions one might ask about censorship. And where are the answers? They come from a handful of authorities, men who dealt with censorship in the last war or worked with it or studied its problems and operation, men such as George Creel, James R. Mock, Byron Price, General Douglas MacArthur and others.

From them comes practically the only real knowledge of the subject. And yet even they, as few in number as they may be, can't agree on the extent, the value, or the purpose of censorship in wartime. Creel is opposed to censorship. In this he voices the opinions of a large proportion of the newsmen in America today. Mock sees the problem from the viewpoint of a historian, and advises only that the mistakes of the past be avoided in the future. Other authorities have conflicting opinions: some want even greater censorship, others want less; some demand completely official regulation, others a strictly voluntary policy to be followed as discretion demands. That is the situation, and through it all, Byron Price, chief censor of World War II, wades in this maze of theories, strengthening the censorship structure under his control, selecting what he considers the best of each man's suggestions.

An understanding of the subject of censorship in this nation at war is essential before any analysis of the problems and operations of news control can be made. In the following pages an attempt has been made to correlate a number of these different views and as much other information of a general nature as possible into a comprehensive survey of wartime censorship of radio and the press today. In some degree one can see the over-

all picture of the problems concerned with the operation of
censorship, its weaknesses and contradictions, as well as its value
and importance to the successful conclusion of the war effort.

A DEFINITION OF CENSORSHIP [1]

For several years now Americans have read regularly in their
free press how the Nazis and Fascists suppress freedom of expression drastically; how they flood their countries with blatant
propaganda; and how they permit to be published or broadcast
or even merely uttered only information favorable to themselves.
Thus when the average American thinks of censorship, he thinks
of it these days in terms of the totalitarian variety. And often
he assumes, without thinking, that application of censorship in
this country means, or will mean, the same drastic restrictions
here as it has meant under the dictators. We shall see.

What *is* wartime censorship? Lowell Mellett, director of the
Government Reports at Washington, describes military censorship by saying that under it the army and navy have control over
such information as they have to disseminate. That is always
accepted in time of war as it is in time of peace, and "nobody
questions the propriety of such censorship." Also, in wartime,
Mr. Mellett goes on, there has to be censorship of outgoing
communications—the mail, and the telegraph and the cable
messages going abroad, and "I believe nobody would seriously
question the propriety of such censorship." Furthermore, in
wartime, he continues, "definite control of radio is necessary.
Radio, by its very nature, requires such control. I believe there
can be no argument about that. And I think that will be the
extent of censorship during the war."

His first point—that the army and navy have control over
information at their disposal—is elaborated further by army and

[1] From "Censorship," pamphlet in the Democracy in Action series, no. 10.
p.11-12. Council for Democracy. New York. 1942. Reprinted by permission.

navy officials, who explain that under standard military regulations, "there automatically devolves upon the commander *in the
theater of operations* the duty of imposing a certain type of censorship, covering the actions of newspaper correspondents, photographers, radio commentators and even visitors." The degree
and extent of this censorship in the field of operations of course
depends on the controlling factors in each particular theater.
The responsibility devolves upon the commander, and he has
wide latitude in its application.

So there you have the official explanation of what strictly
military censorship is. To sum up, it consists of control of war
news at the source of war news, plus control of outgoing communications, including especially radio. And all this control
is exercised with but one objective in view; to keep from the
enemy any information which might be valuable to the enemy.

But in addition to these censorships listed by Mr. Mellett,
there is another censorship now in effect. It is described best
by John Sorrells, present Assistant Director of Censorship. According to Mr. Sorrells, there is in effect now a "voluntary"
censorship of press and radio—a "gentlemen's agreement" that
they will not publish or broadcast certain types of information
which might give aid and comfort to our enemies.

A SUMMARY OF THE SITUATION [2]

The American public, which has long been used to a press
with freedom that Congress may not "abridge" (the word of the
Bill of Rights), seems to be taking deep interest in the restrictions of information that the real perils of war have imposed.
The interest is partly revealed by the fact that reader letters to
correspondents and editors deal steadily and often with the
matter of censorship, wherefore, an occasional summary such as
the following is indicated.

[2] By Arthur Krock, Washington correspondent for *The New York Times*.
From "A Summary of the Censorship Situation." *New York Times.* 91:18.
January 13, 1942. Reprinted by permission.

The situation at present is compounded of confusion, co-operation and uncertainty on the part of authorities and the press alike. The confusion can in part be traced . . . to "too much machinery." The cooperation stems from a sincere desire on both sides to have nothing published that will lend aid to the enemy. The uncertainty has its source in government's attempt to link mandatory with voluntary censorship and then determine what the rules of voluntary censorship should be.

Since the experiment is young, and every one in the United States is inured to democratic ways, it is not strange that this uncertainty should not yet have been resolved. Censor Price is working on it earnestly and the belief continues to prevail among Washington newspaper writers that in so far as he and Mr. Early design and control the censorship pattern it will be sensible, efficient and honest.

The press's ancient freedom has gone in several respects, some of which are dictated by considerations of public safety. Its foreign dispatches are being censored with that objective, and such mistakes as are being made in this editing are traceable to the youth of the system, terrors of subordinate individuals and several bites at the same cherry. Editorial comment and news expository departments have been left so far to the self-restraint and sense of responsibility of their authors—which may or may not be an enduring arrangement—, but the value of exposition necessarily has been reduced by the growing censorship of the facts on which such exposition must be based.

This censorship of these facts at the source is also a measure of public safety, and as to policy there can be no quarrel with it. Until or unless concealment is used to shield official incompetence or weakness of organization it is an essential evil of war. The enemy, for example, should not be informed of the details of the production designed to defeat him. But if all the important facts concerning it are withheld, even as confidential, not-to-be-published guide for exposition, then it will not be possible to know whether production is being competently administered and the stream of billions is being turned into material at the best possible rate.

That is a problem which war has posed both for the government and for the press. Freedom in its Bill of Rights definition having vanished for the duration of the war, it remains to be seen how greatly the restrictions will affect those areas of information where censor and press may honestly and patriotically differ over what will give aid to the enemy, and those items which are annoying to officialdom rather than of military value to the foe. Some time must pass before the whole effect of censorship can be calculated.

Censorship is always a two-way street. From one direction comes the news that is independently gathered by the press, and the comment and exposition based on that news. From the other comes the news over which the government has control. For the first time in recent history, the government is regulating the flow in both directions. The result, of course, is a greatly abridged press, and the public should do its reading with this clearly in mind.

AN EXPLANATION OF CENSORSHIP [3]

There is no question of whether or not we are to have censorship; we have some censorship today and will unquestionably get more. But by far the most crucial question remains yet to be decided—namely, what kind of censorship are we to have, and how will it be applied?

Officially the answer has been given—not just once but repeatedly, and not by the President alone but by his aides, his Cabinet members, his wife, and the highest ranking officers of army and navy. Of censorship in principle their avowed attitude

[3] From "Censorship," article. *Fortune.* 23:88+. June, 1941. Reprinted by permission.

can be summed up as Calvin Coolidge summed up the preacher's sermon on sin: "He's against it." Steve Early, the President's press secretary, summed up for everybody: "I don't believe the country as a whole or the newspapers as a whole want a government censorship. The President doesn't want it, I don't want it, and Lowell Mellett doesn't want it. I don't believe there is going to be any." . . .

On military censorship "to which no one objects," Major General Robert Charlwood Richardson Jr., broad-minded head of the army's Bureau of Public Relations, has stated: "The present attitude of the War Department toward censorship is that there shall be no censorship, even in time of war. . . . Censorship should be restricted to censorship in the theater of operations, which is solely the responsibility of the commander in the field. . . . No one . . . will object to that type of censorship in the theater of operations if intelligently conducted."

Thus, by official promise, there is only one basic censorship problem: to keep valuable information from the enemy—a simple matter for regulation by army and navy. And thus, as officially contemplated, there is one censorship trend only—that of "voluntary censorship." And by official definition "voluntary censorship" is not censorship at all. Precisely what it is and why the official definition has not been accepted will be explored later. For the moment let us pursue further the Administration line.

First governmental sanction for "voluntary censorship" appeared on December 31, 1940, in a "confidential" letter mailed by Secretary of the Navy Frank Knox to 5,000 press, radio, and picture editors, requesting "avoidance of publicity—unless announced or authorized by the Navy Department—on virtually all navy news except recruiting." . . .

After the Knox letter the next censorship pronouncement came from President Roosevelt himself, at his press conference on February 21. He specifically suggested voluntary censorship, declaring that it worked well in the last war. Occasion for his comment was publication of secret testimony given by General Marshall before the Senate Military Affairs Committee regarding the strengthening of Pacific air fleets. Pointedly absolving working reporters, the President raised what he said was an interesting problem which he thought the American people ought to be thinking about. The question, in two parts, was: whether congressional committee members ought ethically, morally, and patriotically to talk outside of executive sessions; and if they do talk, whether the sending and publication of that information was a reflection upon the ethics, morals, and patriotism of publishers, editors, and heads of Washington news bureaus. . . .

So much for censorship as Washington sees it—with one more notation. In censorship discussions throughout the Capital there is a marked tendency to look to the last war for precedent and experience. There is much to learn from the 1918 archives but to be brief if not original, this is not the last war.

From the experience of France and Britain in this, a total war, it is clear that there are some serious misconceptions in democratic thinking about the functions of the press in wartime. The press in a democracy is still the fourth estate; it is almost a fourth branch of government. It is not, as in Germany or the U. S. S. R., a branch of *the* government, but a part of our constitutional system. There is the legislative, the executive, and the judicial branch—and there is the press. It is impossible to imagine governmental processes in the United States without a press. Its first function is to inform, its second to criticize. Censorship is a direct threat to both functions and hence a direct threat to effective democracy. Without information there is no basis for criticism, and without criticism there is, as the saying goes, tyranny. Even democratic governments tend to forget that the press is the critic of government, not the government of the press. War's chief danger is not that press criticism will obstruct the war effort; the chief danger is that because of its very sensitivity to national crisis the press will yield too readily to criticism from the government. To illustrate, consider France.

France tackled censorship with no subterfuges. Every word published was censored and much that was written was never published. French papers appeared regularly splashed with great blank white spaces. Under French theory anything was censorable—and nearly anything of interest was censored, including statements and documents released by other branches of the government. Except for a brief period after Reynaud came to power, the political censorship was absolute, meaning that anything in any way critical of the government or anyone in it was suppressed. Not only as a critical and constructive public force but even as a channel for the communication of information the French press failed utterly. There was less news in the French press than in the German or Italian, with the result that the hiatus was promptly filled with all kinds of destructive enemy rumor and misinformation.

What the French lacked was the skill and experience of a Goebbels in applying totalitarian techniques. They never developed a plausible propaganda that could be used as ersatz news. The French notions of propaganda were infantile. It was routine French practice to kill news pictures or dispatches because the censors suspected—sometimes quite rightly—that they showed France or the French in a ridiculous light. With equal freedom they killed material of inestimable value to France in its efforts to sell its war to the world as well as to its own people. In doing so, of course, the military was arrogating to itself the civil function of the propagandists. Pictures of soldiers drinking in cafes were absolutely forbidden. An innocent Kodachrome of a soldier quietly fishing in the Seine was censored on the absurd ground that Dr. Goebbels might use it to show that the French soldiers were so underfed that they had to fish for their dinner. . . .

That is by no means an exaggerated statement of the case. It is inconceivable that the French Army or the French Government or French morale could have sunk to the levels they did had the people of France been adequately informed by an honest, aggressive, critical press, left free to perform its democratic duties. And the lesson to learn from France is simple and significant; totalitarian principles cannot be applied successfully to *parts* of a democracy. By definition they must be "total"—or they will in all probability be botched.

British censorship is frequently as stupid as anything in France. The classic is about the censor who refused to allow a correspondent to mention the Thames Estuary. In exasperation the correspondent substituted "Amazon" for "Thames"—which was passed forthwith. And then there was the censor who, at the time of the Russian invasion of Finland, took a correspondent to task for repeated use of what he thought was a code word, "Helsinki." The sorry chronicle of the British Ministry of Information is worth a special mission to London to study how not to handle censorship and propaganda.

Nevertheless the British press, working though it is against great bureaucratic odds, has managed to retain some power. During the early months of the war there was the usual tacit understanding among the press lords of Britain that it wouldn't do to rock the boat, i. e., no effective criticism. Hence the failure to turn editorial guns on the Chamberlain government—in spite of widespread conviction that Chamberlain was leading to disaster. The British press helped turn out Chamberlain, though it failed to use its power until a terribly late hour. Even so, self-censorship, both of information and criticism, must be held accountable for many of Britain's errors, most serious of which has been the never-ending effort to kid the public into believing that things were better than they actually were. Much information has been kept from the British public, but whether it has been kept from the enemy is something else again.

As may have been gathered by now, censorship is no fourth-grade subject. Stated at its simplest the problem is to keep from the enemy information of value. The first area of confusion centers about what is valuable. Now, all information is of value to the enemy. The population of a country, the location of rivers, cities, ports, its resources, its government, its ethnic and linguistic composition are all of value to the enemy. These, of course, the enemy already possess. Plants and facilities can be located from standard reference works. Naval and aircraft registers, army organization manuals, officer rosters, congressional hearings contain 95 per cent of the material that the military considers secret, confidential, or restricted—or will when hostilities begin. As General Richardson has admitted, there is only a handful of truly vital military secrets—mostly highly technical. Next come troops, ship, and plane dispositions and movements. Here the information must be fresh to be valuable, yet it is undeniably valuable. Mere delay (which is apt to be the most that censorship accomplishes) may be all that is necessary.

Beyond true secrets and army and naval movements and dispositions lies endless disputed territory. Secrets may be deduced from isolated bits of apparently innocent information. (Navy's deductive classic is their cracking of the dark secret of Japanese naval guns by checking the export of a special kind of steel from a small middle western steel plant.) Disclosures of production lags may tip off the enemy to vital weaknesses. But it may also be more important that the people at home should know the weakness than that the enemy should not know. There is in all censorship a strong unconscious tendency to cut off the nose to spite the face. On technical grounds of secrecy, the army say, may show good reason to conceal the failures of a new tank, though such censorship may lead to false optimism with consequent reaction of dispair. A German deputy after the last war declared before the Reichstag that military censorship had done more harm—militarily—than all the papers in Germany could have if the censorship had been lifted entirely.

It may be argued that in total war the military spreads over ever widening areas of civil life and that hence censorship must spread with it. Followed to its logical end we thus get total censorship, which as we have seen in France is fatal for a democracy. The only thing is to cut it short, straining at all times to confine the definitions of valuable information to the shortest possible list of taboos.

Having decided what information is in fact valuable to the enemy, the next question is how to prevent him from getting it. It is in this area that the worst confusion exists, and the ultimate confusion, the question that lies at the heart of the whole present censorship debate in the United States, is the confusion of the press with the enemy. They are not one, Fortune insists, and the same. To keep information from the press is not necessarily to keep it from the enemy.   *16762*

In the case of the "Malaya," if President Roosevelt and Secretary Knox be granted their position—that the press should not have reported and photographed the ship's arrival—then the assumption must be that the Germans get their information directly or indirectly from newspapers, newsreels, photographs, and broadcasts. Since American publications and American newsreels get to Germany very late, if at all, it must also be assumed that German agents in the United States gather their information upon publication and relay it to Berlin. If this be true, then the logical approach is to intercept the flow of information from German agents to Germany. All that requires is censorship of cables and radio messages, censorship of outgoing mail to Germany and neutral countries, monitoring for illicit radio stations, the active cooperation of our good neighbors on the same lines— and some ingenious method of delaying the diplomatic pouches.

However, the assumption that German agents depend for information on the morning paper, the radio, and their neighborhood newsreels seems a bit ingenuous. The arrival of a British warship in a United States port is impossible to conceal from the people who live around that port. Identity can be established with a spyglass. Departure can be learned by walking down to the waterfront and having a look. Does Secretary Knox believe that the Germans don't have agents in all United States ports? Does he believe the German consulate relies on published reports of plane production or tank production or the location of new smokeless-powder plants? It is too easy to get accurate information directly—by having agents right in the plants if they want to. Does anyone believe that in a plane plant employing 10,000 men it is possible to keep much secret? In Germany it is. There they quarantine whole districts. In the United States, where freedom of movement and communication still exists, it is folly to think that information is disseminated only by the press. It is much more difficult for a reporter to get into a defense plant than for a foreign agent, who has simply to apply for a job.

For weeks the landing of British troops in Greece ("worst-kept secret of the war") was kept out of the British press. Meantime the German military attache at Athens sat dangling his legs over the side of disembarkation docks, counting the British troops as they came down the gangplank. The problem is not to keep information from the press but to keep it from longshoremen, waiters, barbers, barkeeps, sailors' sweethearts and officers' wives —and the enemy.

The case for radio censorship has more validity because broadcasting transmits information instantly beyond our shores— that is, beyond reach of peripheral censorship (mail, cable, wireless). And it may be that radio for this reason should be subject to censorship in some degree. But if censorship is applied to radio it should be applied for reasons of communication, not of dissemination.

To sum up, all information is valuable but the enemy possesses virtually all of it anyway or can get it if needed. Press censorship is not going to curtail or hinder the flow of information to the enemy because the enemy is not dependent in important measure on the press. It is nonsense to think that dispatch of troops or ships can be kept from the enemy merely by forbidding the press to publish it. The small amount of information that is truly vital—technical secrets and dispositions, movements, and other information of real military value—must *be kept secret at the source.* A secondary check through peripheral censorship can then be established when necessary.

Inept and shortsighted censorship at the source can, of course, frustrate completely the efforts of a free and critical press to keep the public properly informed. Military censorship, by a law as forceful as that of gravitation, tends toward political censorship, becoming a means for stifling criticism of official ineptness and incompetence. The principle that must be established and adhered to strictly is that military censorship is confined to military secrets. Censorship for other reasons—"public interest," for instance, or that easy out, "national morale"—is a direct and intolerable interference with a free press. Army and navy censors are not the judges of what makes good—or bad—propaganda. It is too easy for them to be influenced by what may be good or bad propaganda for themselves, their particular outfits, or their commanding officers. It is too easy for them to censor unfavorable revelations about, say, poor housing conditions in an army camp on the ground of "public interest." Censors are very human. The difference between getting a dispatch on the presses or having it censored in full often hangs on the condition of the censor's liver—and the life of a censor, caught as he is between pressure from his superiors and the wily and resourceful members of an embattled press, indubitably makes for liverishness.

Though intelligent and liberal censorship at the source is the ideal censorship—if any censorship can be ideal—some voluntary censorship is required to cover circumstances in which the press happens upon truly vital information such as technical secrets or troop dispositions. What is needed are a few clear definitions of what is and what is not of value to the enemy. On any such basis the press will cooperate. The press will never cooperate . . . if the rules are wholly lacking in reality.

By far the loudest censorship complaints have been against voluntary censorship. Ostensibly the least oppressive because it appears to be the freest, in practice it is extremely hazardous. The press cooperated in self-censoring all news of the navy not official-ly authorized. But three weeks after Secretary Knox's "confiden-tial" letter, full details of navy construction were put into the *Congressional Record* by Congressman Vinson. When *Aviation* magazine carefully suppressed all details of new American combat planes, the British aviation magazine, the *Aeroplane,* appeared a few days later with all the facts. What should be the decision of the press on news that the State Department wanted in print and the navy did not, or on news that the navy wanted in print and the O.P.M. did not? How decide to what extent criticism would spur the national defense, and to what extent give comfort to the Nazis? More often than not the editor who plays ball loses out to more aggressive competitors. He may, at worst, withhold information that would aid his country by exposing vital weaknesses. Meanwhile, lacking any clear and realistic definitions of valuable information, he may run afoul of the Espionage Act with its elastic powers, or post office control of second-class mailing privileges. Most vicious of all is indirect pressure, at which the British excel. The possibilities here are foreshadowed in Secretary Knox's attempt to get the pilot who flew the photographer over the "Malaya."

The one hard and indisputable fact about censorship is that there is nothing, absolutely nothing, to be said in its favor. In-sofar as it is necessary, it represents a bitter compromise with the unpleasant facts of an imperfect world. It is a deliberate retro-gression, an admission of defeat, temporary at least, in the ageless fight for freedom and truth. And more unfortunately, censorship is only half the battle. The other, which here can only be noted in passing, is propaganda. Censorship is defensive, propaganda offensive. To change the figure, it is just as serious to publish untruth as to suppress truth. But whereas the case against censor-ship is overwhelming, there is a case for propaganda—good propaganda, of which the best *is* the truth.

CENSORSHIP AND THE PRESS [4]

From its beginnings, the American press has lived amid recurring crises.   Only by courageous struggle was it able to establish its place in New World Society, and to attain financial stability and intellectual freedom.   In later years it has seen all of these possessions threatened again and again.   It has survived wars and depressions and has come of age a vigorous American institution, rich in ideals and liberties, unmatched anywhere in the world.   But in spite of all they have endured and all that they are, the newspapers of the United States may well find the year 1942 a period of supreme trial and judgment.

We are engaged in a desperate war—a war not only for existence but for that better existence for which we have yearned during long years of doubt and apprehension.   No industry and no individual can expect to escape the tribulations and the sacrifices of such a war.   I have faith that you as editors, and the newspapers you represent, will not flinch or whimper on the firing line.

I would be the last to discount the sacrifices which are inherent in censorship, even voluntary censorship, in a free country.   It has been said many times that news is the lifeblood of journalism and that the stoppage of news is the one unforgivable crime.   So I begin this discussion, as we must begin any discussion of censorship, with a recognition of certain basic truths.

The first of these is that you will never like censorship. Everything the censor does, from opening private letters to keeping Page One stories out of print, is contrary to all we have been taught to regard as right and proper.   Because you are Americans you resent this sort of interference.   No one

[4] Address by Byron Price, Director of Censorship, prepared April 16, 1942 for delivery to the American Society of Newspaper Editors and for broadcast over the Blue Network.

need doubt where a censor would wind up in a popularity contest.

Second, voluntary censorship will never be an exact science. No mathematical formula can be devised to determine in all cases whether certain news should be withheld from the public. So long as each editor is his own censor, there will be differences of judgment and some confusion and disappointment. Nor should it be forgotten that censorship can make no guarantee against the publication of exclusive stories. It happens even in normal seasons that one newspaper will print a story and its competitors will not. That will happen, too, under censorship.

Third, some of the operations of censorship will always appear nonsensical to the individual, particularly if he is among the censored. It is human nature to agree to a restriction in the abstract, but to become resentful when that same restriction strikes home. Censorship is, therefore, highly vulnerable; it often is unable to defend itself without disclosing the very information it is trying to withhold. In short, censorship is God's gift to the dyspeptic editor and the lackadaisical columnist. Whenever all other inspiration fails, it takes no effort to attack censorship.

The Code of Wartime Practices for the American Press was a pioneering venture. It was far from perfect, and even now is undergoing a revision in the light of experience. But it had this underlying quality which I believe deserves to endure: It put newspapers and other publications on their honor. It enlisted every writer and every editor in the army of the republic. That, I think, is not only a challenge but an opportunity. If the newspapers of the country will do their duty on the home front, if they will be watchful of their respective communities and will speak the language of victory, the job will be so much the easier for our armed forces, whose sacrifices are incalculably greater than any of ours.

But under a system where each editor is his own censor, why do we need an Office of Censorship? The answer is that in

every endeavor which enlists the cooperation of many participants we must have certain ground rules. It is neither possible
nor necessary that every participant agree as to the wisdom of
all of these rules. The essential thing is that the rules shall
be understandable, that they shall be evenly and justly administered, and that they shall be followed uniformly. If there
are those who think they should be allowed to make their own
rules, I remind them that in the highly competitive newspaper
field, only chaos could result from a situation where a few,
among many, refused to take part unless they could run the show.

The vast majority of editors have understood these requirements, and I present the appreciation of the Office of Censorship that the results have been so good in so many communities.
But in the conduct of a war, majority support is not enough.

I know of no editor who has deliberately attempted to
sabotage the experiment, but there are some editors who are far
too forgetful of their responsibilities. More than once we have
had occasion to wonder whether the news that we are at war
has penetrated some of your city rooms. There still are too
many apologies, after the damage has been done. If the physical
situation were different, if we could see the whites of the
enemy's eyes, and if any one of these editors had a pistol in
his hands and was defending his home and his family, he
would not be forgetful, and he would not be taking chances.
Yet, everyone of you actually is defending his home and his
family, even though some of you do not seem to know it;
and the weapon you have at your disposal is more powerful than
any firearm.

After four months of war we should be at the end of
apologies and excuses. We should be at the end of forgetful-
ness. No editor who is conscious of his responsibilities and
worthy of the title he holds will expect any longer to continue
business as usual.

It must be conceded that any editor who desires can "beat
the censor." There are plenty of ways to evade the spirit of

the code while appearing to observe its letter. This is not, however, a contest between the government and the editor; it is a contest where the government and the editor are on the same team. The results are what count; and in the results each of you has just as large a stake as any of your fellow-citizens who happen to be serving in official capacities.

Nor does your part of the teamwork end entirely when you have squared yourself with the specific terms of the code. The responsibility of a newspaper in wartime goes far beyond superficialities and formulas. Either you are going to help win, or you are not. If you are not, then you should not parade as a member of the team.

By way of one specific example I should like to speak to you on a subject about which you have heard from me often enough before. It is the subject of accuracy and responsibility in journalism. You are all aware that we are in the midst of psychological as well as physical warfare. Rumor and misinformation march to battle under the same command with tanks and planes. However good your intentions may be, you are doing your readers and your country a great disservice if you permit your columns to be used for rumor-mongering and inaccurate drivel, whether is comes from one of your own reporters or from a writer hundreds of miles away. Irresponsible journalism is reprehensible anytime, anywhere; in wartime it may easily become a crime against national security. Authenticity is the number one priority of wartime journalism.

During the past three months I have heard many complaints from editors that the Office of Censorship foolishly requests the nonpublication of information already known to thousands of ordinary citizens. Well, I would like to make a test of that. In the case of a ship sinking or the erection of a new war production plant I would like to inquire exactly what the public really knows. You as newspapermen are well aware that the stories told by those present at the scene of action never fully agree. Instead of one story, the public hears a dozen stories.

But the newspaper is a fact-finding mechanism, and the American press as a whole is the greatest fact-finding institution in existence in the world today. You as editors have had long experience with rumors and contradictions. You are trained in the art of arriving at the truth, and you have built up contacts over many years for that specific purpose. Surely there are reasons why these expert facilities should not be placed at the disposal of enemy agents.

I do not mean to touch at all upon the question of what military news the government itself should make public, or the reasons why certain news should be withheld officially. That does not come within the purview of the Office of Censorship, and discussion of it is much better left in the more expert hands of General Surles and Admiral Hepburn, who are to appear on this program. In passing I hope I may be permitted nevertheless to remind you that the responsibilities which rest upon these officers are tremendous; and to give you my word, as one newspaperman to other newspapermen, that those responsibilities are being discharged with a thoughtfulness, a sincerity, and a courage unexcelled in these serious times either within or without the government.

What I am dealing with here, however, and what the Office of Censorship is dealing with every day is a separate matter. It is the basic principle of the code. It is the principle that upon certain important topics news which may come into your possession should not be published unless and until the government makes it officially available. I repeat from the code itself: "In war, timeliness is an important factor, and the government unquestionably is in the best position to decide when disclosure is timely."

I have said that only results are important. In the general scheme of national censorship, how important are the results from voluntary censorship of the domestic press? In my opinion these results come near to being all important.

Once information is printed in newspapers, it is extremely difficult to withhold it from broadcasting. Once it is broadcast, it will be heard abroad. And once it is known abroad, there is little point in censoring it from outgoing news dispatches, or private cablegrams, or communications by mail. The more we learn about the philosophy of censorship, the more the Code of Wartime Practices for the American Press emerges as the heart of the whole far-flung operation, and the more apparent it becomes that the only place where information can effectively be withheld is at the source. On many fateful occasions, the key to the complicated mechanism of publicity and world communication will lie in your own hands.

It is natural that this should be so. For within the broad salient of world struggle there are encompassed many individual struggles, and one of them involves a particular liberty which is especially prized by all of us here today. Once more freedom of the press is on trial. You know as well as I do that there are even some Americans who have no confidence in voluntary censorship, but believe that compulsory censorship alone can do the job we have to do.

Upon what will success or failure depend? Under the exceptionally capable captaincy of John Sorrells we have assembled at Washington as able and patriotic a staff of seasoned news executives as the country has ever seen together. They are devoting long and difficult and largely thankless hours to the task of making voluntary censorship work. But even so, we all must realize that the results of this experiment will not be determined in the Office of Censorship. They will be determined by the publishers and editors who control the policies of individual publications.

It is a happy circumstance that the President of the United States has put his confidence in your patriotism and your understanding, and has turned his back on those who argue that only compulsory censorship can be effective. It will be an unhappy day for all of us if it is found that that confidence was misplaced. I personally do not believe that such a day will come. Whether it does is up to you.

RADIO: A NEW WEAPON [5]

For a century and a half the American press has been a militant and successful guardian of our constitutional freedom of speech. This defense has not been accomplished without sacrifice. Our history books record the stubborn determination of editors and publishers to maintain free speech, often at the expense of their own security, even at the expense of their lives.

Now, in this critical hour of our history, the American press has a new partner—radio, going into world battle for the first time. It is radio's first major test. The nation's broadcasters, like the nation's editors, are called upon to prove their capacity for defending freedom by appraising it properly and observing clearly its legitimate boundaries. The experience involves sacrifices; but you are a young and virile industry, and you have shown that you can take it. Day in and day out, your cooperation with the Office of Censorship has given us many reasons for encouragement; and as the war goes on I know you will perform more and more effectively your allotted share of the common effort.

It is a very large share indeed. Some of us go back far enough to remember our first contact with radio through the agency of headphones and a crystal set. In those dim days, by patience and determination and a little imagination, we could sort out of the spitting and crackling a foggy barber shop quartet, or perhaps a piano solo, or a nervous announcer extolling the virtues of a new snake oil. From such a beginning broadcasting has become today the greatest form of mass communication known to man. Its responsibilities have increased accordingly.

[5] An address by Byron Price, Director of Censorship, prepared for the annual convention of the National Association of Broadcasters, Cleveland, Ohio, May 11, 1942.

To those who are trying to keep information from the enemy, the magnitude of radio as a facility of communication is appalling. Its scope can be measured only in terms of oceans and continents. We cannot forget that our stations number among their listeners the trained agents of our enemies. They sit attentively at loud speakers both inside and outside the United States. Within a matter of hours, statements broadcast by American stations come rolling back, with characteristic distortion, over the shortwave facilities of the Axis propagandists.

These facts are not new. They are known to all of us. But they are repeated here because none of us can afford to forget for one moment the dangerous power of the instrumentality known as radio. They explain why the Office of Censorship is requesting constantly and repetitiously that the interview type program be rigidly supervised against last-minute insertions and thoughtless questions, and that every item of broadcast news be weighed with care before it is put into the lap of the enemy. They explain why we have asked stations to process news before they broadcast it, and to recognize that responsibility for disclosing dangerous information cannot be passed on to the man on a news service desk, perhaps hundreds of miles away.

A great responsibility rests also upon commentators and news analysts, and that responsibility extends—as in the case of news dispatches—to you who make them available to the vast audiences here and abroad. There is no circumstance growing out of the war which cannot be so interpreted and appraised that its true significance is lost. Honest, constructive analysis of the war effort is one thing, but speculation and prediction which makes itself the vehicle for smuggling of dangerous information is another thing entirely. If you operate a station, I think it is only reasonable that you should bear the responsibility for the use to which that property is put. It will be our purpose in the Office of Censorship to deal with responsible management, not with individuals.

In fact, it is not too much to say that the success or failure of voluntary cooperation in broadcasting will depend upon the degree of control which patriotic broadcasters exercise over the operation of their stations. There will be errors of judgment, of course; such confusions are inevitable under any voluntary system. What we should be more deeply concerned about, however, is the error which results, not from faulty judgment, but from thoughtlessness or carelessness. We have now been at war for five months. Surely no broadcaster can any longer plead unpreparedness.

By the very nature of radio you are in the front line of combat, literally as well as figuratively. You are in actual contact with the enemy, whose submarines are listening near our shores. If you have careless employees, or employees who find clever means of evading the Broadcasters Code, then your own investment is being used against you. It is like cheating at solitaire. National security is not an abstract term, used to signify something intangible and remote. National security means your security, and the national interest is your own interest.

Now you will begin to suspect that censorship sees only the potential evil in radio. Far from it. This is not a cry of calamity, but rather a call for vigilance—vigilance as studied and deliberate as that of American sailors scanning the waters for the periscope of a submarine. That is the price of victory.

If radio has a tremendous potentiality on the side of evil, it has an equal potentiality on the side of good. The affirmative aspects of your war contribution—and it has been a very great contribution—may not be the direct responsibility of censorship, but censorship has a strong interest in it. For one thing, the more militantly you take up the torch, the sooner the war will be over, and the job of censorship ended. Of more immediate import, however, is your ability to both entertain and inform the American people. It would be a tragedy for all of us if, under the pressure of war requirements radio resigned that facility for public entertainment which gave it birth. It would be a still greater tragedy if in an over-zealousness of self-censorship, radio ceased to be an effective instrument of public information.

The American people must be given comprehensive news about the war. Not only are they entitled to this news in their own right, but if it were denied them, they would not be so likely to give the war their full support. From the standpoint of censorship it must be recognized that if the curtain were drawn too tightly, in the name of national security, all efforts to maintain voluntary cooperation by press and radio would be put to serious hazard. If the press and radio themselves carried their voluntary enterprise to the point of strangulation, the public would intervene.

It all becomes a question of where the line is to be drawn. On the one hand there are agencies of the government which, because of the particular responsibilities assigned to them, are naturally skeptical of every disclosure. On the other hand are the press, the radio, and the public, anxious for a maximum of news. Each of these groups is eager to help the other; in fact the consoling and encouraging element is that no one worthy of the name of American, be he broadcaster, reporter, navy officer, buck private, or plain citizen, wants to endanger a single life by disclosing something which should be kept secret.

You can only resolve such situations by the rule of reason. Narrow thinking, on either side, can lead only to ridiculous results and national harm. The fact is, for instance, that knowledge of almost everything which happens in the United States might conceivably be of some value to the enemy. Anyone who desires to do so can find justification to withhold almost any piece of news whatever. It could even be argued with force that the broadcasting of time signals might give information to the enemy. All his clocks and watches might have stopped!

Such a conclusion would go far afield. Yet in other instances it can be shown convincingly that real danger arises from disclosures which on their face appear perfectly harmless. For example, there is the subject of casualties. Those who have expert knowledge tell us that casualties among officers in a naval engagement provide an excellent index, not only to information as to which ships were engaged and damaged, but in what part of the ships the damage occurred, and how serious it was. The battle stations of officers aboard any ship are well known to the navies of the world and thus, it is maintained, the enemy would know what happened to a ship if he had prompt access to the lists of the wounded.

We receive in the Office of Censorship many letters from radio listeners. A large proportion of them complain that too much detail is disclosed in broadcasts. Some point out that broadcasts in enemy countries make no similar disclosures; that in fact such broadcasts disclose nothing at all about many subjects which are freely discussed by the American radio. The corollary of that is, of course, that in totalitarian countries the people themselves are kept in ignorance and must be kept in ignorance if dictatorships are to be maintained. I believe that many of those who make these criticisms would be the first to protest if a similar philosophy were followed here and if they themselves were deprived of essential information.

Some listeners are concerned particularly about disclosures of progress in war production. They feel that broadcasters have gone too far, not only in indicating the location and character of production plants, but in programming some of the actual operations of these plants. That is a large question, about which it would be difficult ever to arrive at general agreement. The practices of foreign governments who have had longer experience in the war differ greatly. In England, for instance, only the most cautious disclosures are made, but in Canada war production is put in the show window as an encouragement to morale. No other question has been more continuously or more carefully considered by the Office of Censorship. We have sought to follow a reasonable middle course but I suppose no one can say with certainty whether it has always been the wise course.

Another subject which agitates many listeners is the continuing availability on the dial of foreign language broadcasts emanating from American stations. Not being able to understand these broadcasts, some have reached the conclusion that things said in a foreign tongue have no place in wartime radio. It is not always realized that these programs all come from stations owned and controlled by American citizens and operating under license of the Federal Communications Commission. Many likewise do not understand that the programs are carefully supervised and that they constitute in some cases the only means of reaching by radio large groups of loyal Americans, so that they may be informed of what their government is doing and encouraged to help in such ways as by purchase of war bonds. Seditious broadcasts, naturally, will not be permitted to continue, whatever the language; but there is no disposition to interfere with any broadcast merely because it is not an English-language broadcast.

About all of this we must be practical and reasonable, remembering that often when the enemy is kept ignorant, so inevitably are our own people. The question of relative importance between these two considerations deserves, in every case, the most earnest and patriotic attention.

The Code of Wartime Practices for American Broadcasters attempted to set up certain guideposts, somewhere between the extremes of viewpoint, somewhere along the pathway of common sense. It is by no means a complete solution of the problem, but we hope it will help. We in the Office of Censorship stand ready always to give such additional help as we can and if you would come to us more often with your specific problems, we might mutually contribute more fully to the end we all desire.

There is only so much, however, that the Office of Censorship can do. . . . In the language of the code: "The American broadcasting industry's greatest contribution to victory will be the use of good common sense. Radio is one of the greatest liaison officers between the fighting front and the people. Its voice will speak the news first. It should speak wisely and calmly."

THE IMPORTANCE OF THE TRUTH [6]

There has been nothing more astonishing in the progress of war, which is really the application of the mechanics of force to human nature, than the position that public opinion occupies. One cannot wage war under present conditions without the support of public opinion, which is tremendously molded by the press and other forms of propaganda.

Men will not fight and men will not die unless they know what they are fighting for and what they are dying for. Considering the enemy systems, you may think that a threatening statement; but the care with which the enemy keeps the truth from the people, the care with which he endeavors to incline their minds to certain channels and to implant in their concepts certain ideas, shows the great weight he lays upon it.

In democracies it is essential that the public know the truth. In the old days they used to call that control by the military in time of war censorship, and it embodied a method of control whose complete emphasis was placed upon the prevention of leakage of certain information of military value. Censorship in these days, however, has gone infinitely beyond that. That is almost A B C; it is expected by everyone. There is almost voluntary censorship now; no one wants to help the enemy, and the moment the public knows that any thing printed has inadvertently or unwittingly helped the enemy, they themselves will demand that such aid be stopped.

The reason for the efforts made by the United States and this Commonwealth to inform the public and keep the public informed of what is going on is that if the public do not know the truth, their imaginations at once come into play. If they do not know, their confidence is reduced. Silence will begin to react against you.

[6] From a statement by General Douglas MacArthur, in command of Allied forces in the Southwest Pacific, issued at his first press conference in Australia, March 23, 1942.

It is therefore of prime importance that the public be instructed so they can summon all their confidence, all their determination, and all their purpose in support of the war effort. . . .

What I have said does not mean that what we give out here you have to take and use. It does not mean that you have to limit yourselves to "canned news" and that you cannot use your own brilliance. It does not mean that you have got to abstain from criticism, but I hope that before you criticize you will avail yourself of all the facts, and if you do you will find that most criticism disappears.

When you start to tear down, to destroy public confidence in the leaders of a military movement, you practically destroy an army.

THE OPERATION OF CENSORSHIP [7]

The government's system of keeping war secrets out of the news is a two-part operation.

First, the War, Navy and all other departments issuing military information cut out of official announcements anything they believe would help the enemy. This is censorship at the source. It means that part of the truth is withheld. The navy and the army announce their losses of ships. The navy announces American merchant ship losses and neutral shipping losses in American waters. The army and navy announce total casualties, but do not give out casualty lists. They do not reveal their aircraft losses. They have kept the press well informed of their expansion programs. The army has made public all it could of the facts about General MacArthur's remarkable stand on Bataan. Neither the army nor the navy has used the word "victory" in any communique announcing operations in this war.

[7] From "Threat to Freedom of Press?" newsstory. *United States News.* 12: 13-14. March 6, 1942. Reprinted by permission.

While army and navy communiques give only part of the truth, they are meticulous statements of fact so far as they go. Moreover, they are models of completeness compared to the war news from Tokyo, which has yet to admit even one of the many sinkings of Japanese ships, with their tremendous losses of life. The United States Army and Navy say that the time element in disclosing facts about the war is vital, that, as quickly as information loses value to the enemy, it will be given out, and that ultimately all significant facts will be disclosed.

The second part of the government's two-part system is self-censorship by the press and radio. The purpose of this is to get voluntary co-operation of the 2,000 daily and 6,000 weekly newspapers, the 900 radio stations and the magazines in withholding information which would be helpful to the enemy, until it is officially announced.

Byron Price, appointed by President Roosevelt as director of censorship, is handling this job smoothly and efficiently. A code has been drawn up for guidance of editors and broadcasters. Information asked to be withheld pending official announcement includes reports of movements of troops, ships, planes and supplies; pictures or maps of fortifications; specific information about war contracts and production schedules; unofficial weather reports; casualty lists; reference to military objectives in this country, exact routes taken by enemy vessels or planes, and counter measures by American defense forces. Mr. Price reports that co-operation of editors and broadcasters is patriotic and widespread. The system of voluntary censorship is working.

Checks upon the tendencies of military men to go far in the direction of secrecy are found necessary in this war as in the last one. Woodrow Wilson looked upon public opinion as a major force and insisted that it be kept informed regardless of what the generals and the admirals might say. George Creel, President Wilson's war information chief, declared in *Collier's* that "a free people are not children to be humored, cajoled and lollipopped with half truths for fear that whole truths would frighten them."

Today laymen having a deep interest in maintaining freedom of the press are given important places in President Roosevelt's information organization. One is Mr. Price, who sits as a member of the Censorship Policy Board, headed by Postmaster General Frank C. Walker and including the Vice President and five members of the Cabinet. Another is Archibald MacLeish, Director of the Office of Facts and Figures, who is Chairman of the Interdepartmental Committee on War Information and is in charge of working out broad policies of public information. The influence of these and others tends continually to strengthen the hand of public relations officers in the army and navy who see the need of getting more information to the public.

These influences seem to cluster around the present voluntary system of censorship. President Roosevelt is asking that censorship be kept in harmony with American institutions. Mr. Mac-Leish calls for a "strategy of truth" as against the Axis "strategy of terror." "It is our hope," says Mr. Price, "that the columns of American publications will remain the freest in the world, and will tell the story of our national successes and shortcomings accurately and in much detail." . . . All are agreed that full information should be given out so far as compatible with public safety. The differences of judgment arise as to the dangers and benefits of suppression.

Military men are inclined to give greatest weight to the disasters that happen in war as a result of carelessness in handling vital military information. They emphasize that a ship may be sunk, a munitions plant blown up, or a regiment wiped out through slips of editing. They urge caution above all else.

Laymen agree on the need for discretion, but some point out that suppression may cause disasters, too. At Pearl Harbor, secrecy did not deprive the Japanese of knowledge of the location of a single ship or plane. But it did conceal the real situation from the American public. It deprived the army and navy of the public criticism that would have awakened them. At Singapore, the British censors muzzled Cecil Brown, radio com-

mentator, and choked his warnings that the port's defenses must
be strengthened or lost—and it was lost. . . .

"We do not need less criticism in time of war," believed
Woodrow Wilson, "but more. It is hoped that the criticism will
be constructive, but better unfair attack than autocratic suppression."

THE IMPORTANCE OF NEWS [8]

It says much for the powers of self-discipline in a free and
willful people that liberty of the press very willingly submits to
putting itself in a strait jacket for the duration of the war. Everyone uncomplainingly takes it for granted that communications
will be censored and that news will be controlled at the source,
and that this will be done not as the law says it may be but as
military judgment says it shall be. Censorship on those terms
requires a pledge of unlimited confidence to be exchanged between the government and the people; and so, happily, it
begins. But we shall do well at the same time not to underestimate the difficulties.

The government lays down what appears to be a very legible
rule to govern the release of news. The conditions are two.
First, the facts must be fully verified; second, publication of
them is forbidden if they tend in any way, direct or indirect,
to give aid and comfort to the enemy. But you could not invent
a general rule that would leave more to arbitrary discretion in
its application to a particular case.

News is of two kinds—good and bad. Any bad news at all
tends to give aid and comfort to the enemy. Then what will
you do with it? Withhold it from the people until it is certain
that the enemy already has it?

Take the communique. In its daily report to the people the
government cannot tell everything that has happened, and the

[8] From "Censorship," editorial. *Saturday Evening Post.* 214:26. January 24,
1942. Reprinted by permission.

more critical the situation is the more this will be true. Why? Because the enemy is reading it too. You cannot have two reports—one for the people and one for the enemy.

In the business of bombing, for example, the enemy's only firsthand knowledge of his hits is from his own pilots, who tend naturally to exaggerate what they think they have done and are liable in any case to be mistaken. The enemy, therefore, anxiously watches the news on the other side in order to check the claims of his own pilots; and one of his artful tricks is to put forth fantastic claims in his own communique with intent to provoke on the other side a denial, on the chance that the denial will be informing. Thus, it was very important for the Japanese to know whether or not they had got an aircraft carrier at Pearl Harbor, as their own pilots said they had.

The communique, indeed, now is one of the weapons of strategy. The Russians in theirs were most despondent just on the eve of the unexpected counteroffensive that forced the German war machine suddenly into reverse. The purpose was probably twofold. One part of it was to deceive the Germans; the other was to hasten American and British aid.

On the free Anglo-American side there is no likelihood of bad military news being suppressed or long withheld for fear the people cannot take it. The British are extremely the other way. They are nourished by bad news. "It must be remembered," said Mr. Churchill, in a recent review of the war before the House of Commons, "that here at Westminster and in Fleet Street"—newspaper row—"it has been sought to establish the rule that nothing must be said about the war that is not altogether discouraging. Although I must admit the British people seem to like their food cooked that way, a military spokesman addressing a large army might do more harm than good if he always put things at their worst, and never allowed buoyancy, hope, confidence and resolve to infect his declarations." He was defending the military spokesman at Cairo, whose reports on the North African campaign, the English people thought, had been disgustingly optimistic, and they were complaining of him on that ground.

But there is another kind of bad news which, although it is not strictly military in character, does tend nonetheless to give aid and comfort to the enemy; and the question about it is not whether the people can take it but whether the government can, because it is news of the government, of its own blunders and failures and mistakes of political judgment. What will the censor do with facts of that order? What ought he to do with them?

This is the kind of news that free criticism tends to reveal; and here it is that censorship faces what is perhaps its most unruly problem. For all the aid and comfort it may afford the enemy, shall criticism be free? In England it is. Mr. Churchill has at times complained of it, yet very mildly and with grim understanding. Suppression of criticism would be incomprehensible in England. So it would be here. Free criticism is troublesome. It does present a problem. Nevertheless, it is one that will solve itself if let alone. A government in the popular principle, being trusted by the people to control their news at the source and censor their communications for military reasons, must in turn trust criticism to censor itself. And this it does much more than can be realized by those who know only when it errs and have no idea how many times it makes the right answer when it asks itself this question: All things considered, will the saying of this truth do more good than harm? And if, in a given case, it comes too often to the wrong answer, then people themselves by their extreme disapproval will extinguish it, with no aid from the censor.

Good news, you might suppose, offers the censor no problem at all. Nevertheless, good news can be a liability. People may make too much of it. Bad news moves them to greater exertion, whereas good news may tempt them to relax. . . .

To be on the safe side, we must expect a long hard war. News tending to belittle the resources of the enemy or to make us complacent about our own must be discounted. How? Not by suppression and certainly not by distortion, but by mixing bad news with good, by emphasis, by keeping the facts in perspective. Thus you come to censorship policy, touching the handling, timing and spacing of the news, for its effect upon public morale.... The censor has no policy of his own. He executes the government's policy, and when he fails to do that, there is a new censor.

Censorship is unavoidable. Although it may be authorized by a wartime statute, and is in that sense lawful, it cannot be administered by any rule of law. You may read in the Constitution that the Congress shall pass no law to abridge freedom of speech or freedom of the press; but when drums beat, the law flies away, says the proverb. Moreover, censorship entirely innocent of propaganda belongs to some faraway realm of the ideal. The subtle power of propaganda that is implicit in control of the news is bound to be exercised, because, first, a government is human, and for the reason besides that every government is obliged to believe that it knows what is best for the total good.

This is our second experience. In the war before, it was the Committee on Public Information. Now it is the Office of Censorship, which has a more honest and a more severe sound and, we suppose, a more severe intention. Even so, there will be, we think, forbearing to almost any point, no want of cooperation and no unfair criticism, so long as the government holds free of hurt and trespass that confidence with which people, both the believing and the unbelieving, have suddenly overwhelmed it.

HISTORY OF AMERICAN CENSORSHIP

DISCUSSION

Logically, a study of the experience with censorship in the past comes before any real analysis of the situation at the present time.

Censorship has existed since the founding of the nation. It came ashore with the Pilgrim fathers at Plymouth. And in one form or another, censorship has annoyed various elements of American society throughout our history, both in time of war and in time of peace.

As in Europe, lack of communications between the pioneer communities made censorship relatively unimportant until very recent times. Even during the Civil War, the question was not so much how much a newspaper could print, but how much it could *get* to print, and then whether or not that information was used patriotically. The situation which existed during the War Between the States couldn't exist today. News coverage is much more complete. Communications are almost instantaneous. There is no divided allegiance of editors in the matter of loyalty to the United States. So the situations are not comparable in any way.

In any case, until the First World War the United States had never experienced any *official* censorship, by the government itself, of all means of communication. James R. Mock points out that the World War of 1917-18 offers practically the only example of wartime censorship in this country. And through careful analysis of its mistakes, something can be learned about the practicability of "all-out" censorship in this war, what to avoid, and what to expect along certain lines if the mistakes of World War I are copied in World War II.

As Mr. Mock has stated, "The present is too early to evaluate or judge the efforts of Mr. Price and his censorship. The year 1965 should be about right for that study. Today, however, is the proper time to notice the only official wartime censorship this country has had."

This chapter concerns America's past experience with censorship in wartime. How much attention should be paid to the historical side of censorship depends a lot on the developments of news control in the future. One thing, however, is certain. The situation has changed greatly since the days of Mr. Creel's censorship activities. The whole complexion of news has changed. Foreign correspondents are now accredited, even necessary, adjuncts of the military arm. No army fights without having a newsman on the spot to write up the progress of the battle for the folks at home. In Washington, the public relations staffs of the War Department, the Navy Department and all the other wartime news sources are larger than ever before. This has but one purpose: to keep the public informed. History has no parallel for the "total war" coordination of information. It can only show when and what news was forbidden in the past.

Furthermore, radio hadn't entered the picture in 1917-18. Today it assumes a role which is almost more important than the newspaper itself. The result is a completely new and different problem which censors of twenty years ago never knew.

Yet the history of the control of news in the United States is important, if for no other reason than the fact that much of our present regulation of news is based upon these experiences of the past. From history alone can we find precedents which have stood the test of time and which were suited to the American way of life.

CENSORSHIP IN AMERICAN HISTORY [1]

In times of crisis, our liberties have always disappeared to some degree. Freedom of speech and freedom of the press have been the sectors in which the greatest losses have occurred. Just before the beginning of the Revolution, spoken or printed expressions of opinion had to agree with the prevailing taste of the neighborhood or suffer restraints amounting, in many instances, to mob violence.

During our War for Independence, minorities had few privileges. In regions controlled by Americans, Tories were driven from their homes, were deprived of their votes, and were prohibited from holding any public office. Regions dominated by British sympathizers saw English generals having the mails searched for rebel matter, or even forcing prominent rebels to flee the neighborhood. . . .

With the supporters of the Constitution, the Federalists in power, and with the nation at peace, personal liberty had to fear only the Indians and the English common-law principle of seditious libel. This doctrine rendered King and Parliament immune to criticism. Despite the fact that in the United States the people were the government, political factions invoked the doctrine on this side of the Atlantic to punish their opponents.

This guerrilla type of politico-judicial warfare was brought into the open by the Alien and Sedition Acts of 1798, when war with France threatened. The Alien Act was not enforced by President Adams, but the Sedition Act was used against editors and others whom he and his party wished to silence. It provided:

That if any person shall write, print, utter or publish . . . any false, scandalous and malicious writing or writings against the government of the United States, or either house of the Congress, . . . or the President . . . with intent to defame the said government or to bring them

[1] By James R. Mock, co-author of "Words That Won the War." From "Censorship 1917." p.6-23. 1941. Princeton, N.J. Reprinted by permission of Princeton University Press.

. . . into contempt or disrepute; or to excite against them . . . the hatred of the good people of the United States . . . he shall be punished by a fine not exceeding two thousand dollars, and by imprisonment not exceeding two years.

Armed with this legal instrument, the Federalists, with Secretary of State Pickering in the vanguard, used the courts to put to flight their political opponents. Under that short-lived statute —it expired March 3, 1801—not more than twenty-five persons were arrested and ten were found guilty of violating the law. . . .

The storm of protest these measures aroused has not been obscured by the passage of time. Madison accused the federal government of exercising a power not delegated to it, and one which, "more than any other, ought to produce universal alarm, because it is levelled against the right of freely examining public characters and measures, and of free communication among the people thereon, which has ever been justly deemed the only effectual guardian of every other right."

Opposition to these acts led to the passage of the Virginia and Kentucky Resolutions in 1798, which declared that a state had the right to nullify an Act of Congress. This question of states' rights continued to trouble the nation until the Civil War provided an answer.

Those odious Federalist measures brought about the downfall of the party and the election of Jefferson. In fact, it is said that it was the vote of the first victim of the Sedition Act, Matthew Lyon of Vermont, "that broke the tie in the House of Representatives in 1800 and elected Jefferson president."

Never again has a political party attempted to destroy its chief rival by a sedition law patterned after that of 1798. No matter how sorely tempted a political party was to resort to such measures, growth of sectionalism, the rise of the slavery issue, and America's absorption in American affairs after 1815, together with the memory of the fate that overtook the party championing the Alien and Sedition Acts—all these factors worked against the reenactment of such measures.

When our next great crisis came after 1798, mobs and a general accounted for the negation of individual liberties during the War of 1812. That there were so few instances of repression in the Second War for Independence may have resulted from the fact that public opinion about the struggle differed from section to section, but only rarely within a given section.

In New Orleans after the defeat of the British there, Andrew Jackson was upon one occasion more than censor. *The Louisiana Gazette,* on February 21, 1815, announced that Jackson had received word of peace between the United States and England. The general demanded that thereafter the editor secure his permission to print news of such nature; and the bickering began. It ended with Jackson imprisoning a writer who protested the censorship, turning out of the city a judge who issued a writ of habeas corpus in favor of the imprisoned writer and therewith trying the offender by a court-martial. The incident was closed when peace was proclaimed. . . .

Freedom of speech and of the press is measured by tolerance of the public, not of the law. For instance, in 1812, a person could safely object to the war with Britain only if he lived in New England, rather than in regions where the struggle was popular. This was likewise true during the Mexican War; expressions that would have brought punishment in 1798 were applauded half a century later. On Sunday, June 7, 1846, the noted minister, Theodore Park, preached "A Sermon of War" in Boston; referring to the heads of the government, he said: "The political authors of a war on this continent, and at this day, are either utterly incapable of a stateman's work, or else guilty of that sin. Fools they are, or traitors they must be." Try to imagine what the officials of other times would have done with Parker for uttering these words: "In regard to this present war, we can refuse to take any part in it; we can encourage others to do the same; we can aid men, if need be, who suffer because they refuse. Men will call us traitors, what then? . . .

We can hold public meetings in favor of Peace, in which what is wrong shall be exposed and condemned."

The Civil War saw the first great threat of destruction of the republic and of personal liberties. With a nationwide struggle involving nearly all citizens as fighters or as producers of material, with a long, shadowy, and fluctuating boundary between the rival factions, and with southern sympathizers in the North and northern sympathizers in the South, freedom of speech and of the press was greatly curtailed. To all intents and purposes the Constitution was placed in cold storage. After all the successful efforts of Marshall to assume powers for the judiciary, that part of our government did not assert itself effectively until after the war. The writ of habeas corpus was suspended in the North and in the South.

Inroads upon personal liberty from 1861 to 1865 were not made wholly under statutory enactments. One must look to sources other than the results of the application of the Confiscation, Indemnity, and Treason Act, in order to explain the great number of cases in which arbitrary arrest, imprisonment without trial, and release without explanation were meted out to individuals. The number of persons treated in this fashion is variously estimated from 13,000 to 38,000.

Those citizens lost their liberties at the hands of army officers, United States marshals, and state and local authorities acting under instructions from federal officials. Although the President, according to the historian James Ford Rhodes, did not direct a single arrest, "he permitted them all." Lincoln would have had time for nothing else, had he attempted to keep watch against the raids upon constitutional guarantees that his Secretaries of State and of War, and his generals were making. The War Department established a censorship over telegraph lines, while the Postmaster General denied the use of the mails to newspapers charged with being disloyal. In some instances, newspapers reached towns for which they were destined only to be confiscated by the authorities there. . . .

A Washington paper incurred the displeasure of Stanton by publishing information of military movements. On March 7, 1862, the day following that violation, Stanton ordered Brigadier General Wadsworth, the military governor of the District of Columbia, to take immediate military possession of the printing office in which the paper, *The Sunday Chronicle,* was printed, to destroy all the papers that could be found there, "and hold the parties in custody that they may be dealt with according to the rules and regulations of war." . . .

Editors . . . seemed especially to suffer loss of their constitutional rights. Missouri provided the setting for such an occurrence. Although it was not among the eleven seceding states, southern sympathizers and supporters, under the leadership of Claiborne F. Jackson and General Price, had necessitated the continued presence and the active intervention of Union troops. In that state of affairs, Edmund Ellis had published in his *Boone County Standard,* from October 1861 to February 1862, pro-Confederate articles under such headings as, "Root, Abe, or Die," "News from General Price," and a pamphlet, "To the Patriot Army of Missouri."

A military commission convened at Columbia, Missouri, and found Ellis guilty of publishing information for the enemy and of encouraging resistance to the government and laws of the United States. He was ordered to be placed outside the lines of the state of Missouri for the duration of the war, and the presses, type, furniture, and material of the offending editor were ordered confiscated and sold for the use of the United States. The finding and sentence were approved by command of Major General Halleck.

The fate of the *Boone County Standard* was harder than that which overtook the *Chicago Times* and the *New York World.* The Illinois paper was suppressed by General Burnside, the commander of the Department of Ohio, "on account of the repeated expression of disloyal and incendiary sentiments." In spite of an injunction issued by Judge Drummond of the United

States Court restraining the military forces from carrying out the order of the general, a captain and his men seized the office of the *Times,* and prevented the morning issue of June 3, 1863.

This procedure, far removed from the threat of rebel armies, caused articulate opposition. In Chicago, a meeting of prominent citizens, presided over by the Mayor, sent a request to Lincoln to rescind the order. A resolution by the state legislature at Springfield denounced the action. In response to these expressions of public sentiment, Lincoln rescinded that part of the order which suppressed the *Times,* and the Secretary of War informed Burnside that he was to arrest no more civilians and to suppress no more newspapers, until the President had been consulted.

Less than a year after the Chicago paper had been penalized, a similar fate befell the *New York World.* It had published a false proclamation of the President, "gloomily recalling recent disasters, setting a day for public humiliation and prayer, and calling for 400,000 men." An order, signed by Lincoln, . . . directed General Dix to arrest the persons involved and to imprison them until they could be tried by a military commission. Three days later, however, they were released, and the military forces were withdrawn from the printing establishment. . . .

Opposition to these Civil War attacks upon our constitutional guarantees has been largely ignored, as much by the historian as by the agents who made the attacks. The attitude that the military took toward Judge Drummond's injunction in the *Chicago Times* affair was typical. In most instances in the North, a clash between civil and military jurisdiction resulted in the civil giving way. Army officers refused to answer writs of habeas corpus, and the courts, seemingly, could do nothing to carry their writs into effect. Seizing and holding persons without trial was condemned by more than one judge, but it was "carried on with a nonchalant disregard for either courts or Constitution."

Several powerful voices were raised in protest against the curtailment of free speech and free press. . . . But such outbursts were mere whispers drowned in the roar of popular approval that greeted the extra-legal silencing of the dissenters. . . . Thus, in the final analysis, the people themselves, by their own inattention, if not their downright approval, made it possible to set aside the Constitution during the Civil War and in the era that followed. . . .

In the years that immediately followed the Civil War, the First Amendment to the Constitution had little meaning for a large minority of our citizens. The southern states were reconstructed by their enemies in and from the North, who saw to it that generations of intelligence and leadership were penalized in favor of the ignorant and the amenable. For the first few years after Appomattox, the states that had seceded were divided into five military districts with a general at the head of each. With them in control, constitutional guarantees existed only at their whim. With so much power in their hands, and with Civil War animosities still rankling, the wonder is that more acts of oppression were not committed. . . .

As far as the federal government is concerned . . . no liberties . . . were threatened again until World War I. In fact, during our War with Spain, the public at large was hardly aware that any censorship existed. The yellow journals of the time had played their part in bringing on the struggle, and they were not going to be denied any news that could be secured in any manner. The methods they used, which in some instances included their own dispatch boats, made it almost impossible for the government to withhold any information relating to affairs in Cuba. This situation was partly met by General Greeley of the Signal Corps, who succeeded in securing the cooperation of the Western Union Telegraph Company in Florida. As a result, by May 1898, censors were employed at Tampa, Miami, and Jacksonville. This meant that any confidential information correspondents might learn in Cuba could reach the newspaper only by dispatch boat or by mail. By the time the boat or letter could get to New York or to other places outside Florida, the news was stale. Seemingly, the only protests about that censorship were lodged with the Secretary of War by the *St. Louis Post Dispatch* and the *Pittsburgh Dispatch*.

In the meantime, similar arrangements had been made in Porto Rico . . . messages detrimental to the welfare of the United States were forbidden.

Thus matters stood when peace was concluded, and we received the Philippines from Spain. In those islands, "the little brown brother . . ." did not look with favor upon a change of masters. More than two years of fighting were to ensue before the United States gained complete control. . . . The Secretary of War directed General Otis, the commanding general, to censor press dispatches. Complaints arose from the American press almost at once, not because of the suppression of news, but, according to the *New York Herald*, because of discrimination. On January 31, 1899, the *Herald* carried a cable from London to the effect that the censorship at Manila was giving an opportunity for Spaniards abroad and the anti-expansionists at home to promulgate the wildest kind of fairy tales about deplorable conditions under the Otis regime. When the Associated Press representative at Manila also charged that preference was being given to other press representatives, the War Department informed Otis that there was no desire to interfere with his censorship of matter sent from there, but that it was necessary for all to be treated alike.

Otis' activities continued, and the criticism of the press for his handling of the news of our operations in the Philippines went on. . . . This controversy finally led him to the point where he was willing to remove the censorship and let them cable anything. . . . On October 10, the *New York Times* carried the news that press censorship had been removed, and that the Manila correspondents had been unrestricted since September 9.

The Philippines were to receive the attentions of a censor during the time of the Military Governor. On December 18, 1900, censorship instructions were given to the Manila office of the Eastern extension of the Australasia and China Telegraph Company. . . . These regulations were in force when Aguinaldo was captured in March 1901, and the backbone of the insurrection was broken.

Beginning with 1914, some form of censorship of communication and of news existed in this nation under the sanction of the United States Government, until such supervision had been recognized by a formal legislative enactment during the time we were at war with the Central Powers.

When this country sent troops to Vera Cruz in 1914, some news that the War Department thought unsatisfactory was printed in our papers. The Secretary of War asked General Funston at Vera Cruz if he had a censorship over the cable from that city. Funston replied that the censor was Captain Charles W. Wells who had succeeded Naval Constructor Gatewood at that job. . . .

By March 13, 1916, some members of the Fourth Estate who had heeded the request of the War Department to refrain from printing information of use to the enemy in Mexico began to feel that they were losers. James Keeley, editor of the *Chicago Herald* and later European head of all of the Creel committee propaganda against the Central Powers, asked the War Department to define the limits of censorship. . . .

The Judge Advocate General could offer no suggestions. He observed that under the circumstances the patriotism of newspaper editors and their cooperation for the success of the expedition in Mexico had to be relied upon with respect to such matters as Keeley pointed out.

Brigadier General Macomb, Chief of the War College Division of the Chief of Staff, held that censorship of the press functioned only in theaters of operations or where martial law existed, and he had no information that the latter had been declared in the United States. The general pointed out that the way to handle a problem . . . was through the exercise of forethought, that all steps should be taken before the occasion arose for the application of censorship. Nothing was done with that recommendation. Instead, the commanding general of the Southern Department appointed a censor with whom copies of all dispatches sent out by correspondents were to be filed.

Through all this controversy, the people at large had been concerned only indirectly, and had been interested even less. Their attention was centering more and more upon America's connection with the European struggle. . . . By April 1917, most Americans had evolved a simple pattern out of the complex European situation. There were only two sides, one black, one white, the former pro-German, the latter pro-Ally. And we were resolved that in this nation we would be all white.

In our excited state of mind, in 1917 and 1918, divided counsels or opinions were discouraged. The demand was for a united nation, and to achieve it the American people cheerfully surrendered—sometimes knowingly, sometimes unknowingly— their constitutional liberties under a stream of city ordinances, and of state and federal laws.

MILITARY CENSORS IN THE CIVIL WAR [2]

Let us remember what was originally behind censorship. In the struggle of politically organized society with kin-organized society and later with religious organization of society for the paramountcy in social control, the dignity of the political sovereign was a very important consideration. Criticism of public

    [2] By Roscoe Pound, former Dean of Harvard Law School. From "Government in Time of War." *Vital Speeches.* 7:375-6 April 1, 1941. Reprinted by permission.

officials and discussion of public affairs was thought dangerous
to the security of political institutions. The dignity of the
political organization of society was of itself something to be
guarded. Any infringement of it might bring government into
less esteem and threaten its existence. In a democracy where
the force of politically organized society is wielded by a majority, it is easy for a majority to feel that what it does has sufficient
justification in its doing so; that everyone should hold to the
views for the moment of the ruling majority and profess its
beliefs. Anything less, it is easily persuaded, is subversive of
the paramount social organization. It is as easy for King Demos
to feel that want of conformity to his will on any serious subject is dangerous sedition as it has been for King Rex to hold
the same doctrine.

When, however, we come to consider censorship in war or
emergency from the standpoint of the relation of the reasons
behind it to the scope to be allowed it, I submit we must make
a distinction. We must distinguish between censorship to prevent military information and other information useful to the
enemy from reaching the enemy, on the one hand, from, on the
other hand, censorship to prevent criticism or discussion of
governmental acts and of past military operations and the general
conduct of the war. The excuse for the latter is that such criticism and discussion encourages the enemy. But where a democracy is at war the enemy must know that a ruling majority is
behind the war and can derive no real comfort from the critical
publication of even a clamorous but politically powerless minority. It is not as if an autocrat, holding down a people with an
iron hand, was waging war and any published dissent indicated
he was losing his grip and faced with revolution at home. When
armies were dependent upon volunteering, there was some excuse for assuming that criticism of the government or of its
conduct of a war might operate to hold back enlistment. No
such ground can be set up where armies are raised by conscrip-
tion. James Russell Lowell's "Biglow Papers," published during

the Mexican War, probably had no effect whatever on the prosecution of the war by the government.   But such publications
would be dealt with drastically if extreme militarists could have
their way today.

In the summer of 1863, when Lee was moving on Pennsylvania, Morgan was preparing to invade Ohio, Rosecrans was
stalled in middle Tennessee, and Johnston was collecting an
army in Grant's rear behind Vicksburg, there was an emergency
if our government ever encountered one.   But General Burnside's order suspending the *Chicago Times* for "repeated expression of disloyal and incendiary sentiments" was at once revoked by President Lincoln.   In the summer of 1864, after Cold
Harbor, after the operations about Petersburg seemed to have
reached a standstill, when Sherman seemed to be making little
headway toward Atlanta, and Early was in the Shenandoah Valley, a great political party was allowed to hold a convention
which in its platform pronounced the war a failure.   Joel Parker
at the Harvard Law School was allowed to attack the legality
of important items of the administration's policy.   Throughout
the Civil War the committee on the conduct of the war examined
generals and witnesses as to military operations, and newspaper
controversies went on as a result—notably the controversy between Meade and Sickels as to the second day at Gettysburg
and between the adversaries of Meade and his partisans as to
the whole conduct of that battle.   After Shiloh, during the long
struggle to get a foothold back of Vicksburg, and after Cold
Harbor, Grant was persistently attacked in the press.   But the
attacks were without effect on his imperturbable pursuit of his
duty, and neither helped the South nor hindered the military
operations of the North.   I have never thought that our conduct
of the last war was aided by the imprisonment of Mrs. O'Hare
or that it was impeded by the excited query of an obscure journey-
man cigar maker as to why we were aiding Czarist Russia.

It is worth while to consider whether, instead of relying upon
our own experience, we have not, since 1917, been going on

ideas taken from continental Europe, seeking a coerced outward unity, and importing a censorship which belongs to and has grown out of the exigencies of a very different type of government from ours. The problem is to find some adjustment between the war powers of the government under the Constitution and the constitutional guarantee of free speech and a free press. To the extreme militarist who would abrogate all guarantees in time of war and set up a military absolutism in the supposed interest of efficiency, one must answer that military efficiency in a democracy is not endangered by things that threaten it under an autocracy. Even in time of peace the autocrat is sensitive about criticism and public discussion of his acts. Neither in peace nor in war, as was shown in our Civil War, need a democracy fear criticism or discussion. What gives aid to the enemy is something very different, namely, information as to armaments, movements, plans, the whereabouts of troops and ships of war, and the like. As to these things undoubtedly there is another story and a rigid censorship may be necessary in any time of serious war.

Only an overwhelming necessity can justify the setting aside of one of the fundamental guarantees in our constitutional polity. All that I have seen urged for so doing proceeds on an assumption that American Government cannot wage war and stand up under criticism. But our government has proved it can do so in the crisis of a great Civil War. Moreover, a democratic government presupposes free criticism and free discussion. If the people, and that means any of them, cannot be suffered to criticize and grumble and argue pending war, does it not follow that they ought not to be suffered to vote pending war? But in the Civil War we held a congressional election in 1862, and a presidential election in 1864 with no untoward results.

Cautious doling out to the press of news from the front is no doubt a necessity of effective conduct of war. Suppression of information as to plans and movements, movements of vessels, and the like, is clearly necessary. Here is the legitimate field of censorship in time of war. American experience contradicts the assumption that more than this is required in the nature of things or that the very exigencies of war demand more.

In a time of rise and establishment of absolutism all over the world, in a time when the bigness of everything and the economic unification of the land continually add to the power of the central as against the local government and increasingly concentrate power in the person of the chief executive, we must be vigilant to preserve the fundamental guarantees on which our federal government rests. This means in practice that the press must be vigilant for us. Only if the press is free to perform this function in our polity can we be sure that wars to maintain democracy do not in result become wars to establish autocracy.

CENSORSHIP 1917 [3]

Certain groups in the United States had not waited for our declaration of war on April 6, 1917, before they began agitating for some federal wartime restrictions of freedom of speech and of the press. Foremost in that assemblage were the army and navy. As early as 1907, the former was considering "The Press in War" as it applied to (1) illustrations of the mischievous effect of unrestrained publication, (2) laws of the other countries restricting publications, and (3) constitutional guarantee of "freedom of the press." There is no evidence that any measures were recommended for legislative enactment as a result of that study, at least at that time. But the subject was not likely to have been forgotten, since the British were continuing studies of like nature down to the outbreak of war.

In 1915 the War Department considered the subject again. This was a result, in part, of communications the department received from Americans in England pointing out the weak-

[3] By James R. Mock, co-author of "Words That Won the War." From "Censorship 1917." p.40-72. 1941. Reprinted by permission of Princeton University Press.

nesses of censorship there and stating that those weaknesses came about because no provisions for censorship had been made before hostilities began. Another reason for resuming this study was the Mexican situation that has been noticed in the preceding chapter. With Europe and Mexico presenting concrete problems of censorship, our Chief of Staff directed a consideration of legislation "necessary to control the press in time of war," and at the same time ordered a study of methods employed by the English to control the press. To those members of the General Staff who were engaged in this work, the Act of March 3, 1911, "To prevent the disclosure of national defense secrets," seemed too limited in its operation. After considering the expanse of territory our country embraced, the chance of irresponsible publication by periodicals and newspapers in wartime, and the fact that telegraph, telephone and cable lines were privately owned, the officers submitted a tentative draft of legislation that they recommended be sent to Congress for action. The measure they proposed would have conferred upon the President the power to restrict the publication of certain information inconsistent with the defense of the country.

Again, no legislation came directly from this work of the General Staff, but the next year, 1916, saw the army and navy working together on the problem of censorship. A joint board of the two services recommended a bill empowering the President, in time of national emergency, to issue a proclamation prohibiting publication of news relating to our armed forces, matériel, or to the means and measures contemplated for the defense of the country. . . .

When this measure was proposed by the joint board, it found a similar idea expressed in Senate Bill S-5258. This latter was designed to prevent the disclosure of national defense secrets. It did not satisfy the War, Navy and Justice Departments, and a conference of representatives from those three agencies proposed amendments that dealt specifically with control of the press. The Attorney General, however, thought it would not be wise to include censorship in S-5258. And censorship was to wait until 1917 before it became a law.

In the meantime, the Secretary of War, with no prospect of any legislation on the subject close at hand, was trying to prepare for any emergency that might arise in connection with censorship or the need for it. . . . In order to establish such censorship of the press, telegraph, cable and other means of communication as might be necessary, and might "now and hereafter" be authorized by law, he requested Daniels [Secretary of the Navy] to designate a navy officer to cooperate with an army officer, appointed for the same purpose, to draft the necessary rules and regulations for the effective control of publications and means of communication. Those two officers were to consult with representatives of the press associations residing in Washington regarding rules and regulations to be adopted. Daniels approved the suggestion.

Secretary of War Baker also foresaw another use to be made of those officers. They were to be required, from time to time, to recommend officers of the army and navy, preferably from among those on the retired list, "to act as censors at the various places where such services may be required."

So far as Baker's department was concerned, it may be said to have gone under censorship to the common citizen, June 9, 1916. At that time a temporary division of the office of the Secretary of War was established, to be known as the Bureau of Information with Major Douglas MacArthur in charge. It was to be the only source of information given to the press from the War Department, except that of a routine nature that did not bear upon the contemporary military situation.

To encourage the establishment by law of a more extensive censorship, Secretary Baker wrote Edwin Y. Webb, chairman of the House Committee on the Judiciary, August 11, 1916. He invited Webb's attention to the lack of any law authorizing the President to restrict the publication of certain vital defense information. Baker observed, "In this country the proper legislation authorizing such control of publication should be adopted when, as now, the country is at peace." ... Webb assured Baker that the matter would have his prompt attention.

Although no legislation resulted immediately, the censorship ball had been started rolling. And, on February 5, 1917, Webb is found introducing a bill that proposed to punish with life imprisonment any unauthorized person who, in wartime, should collect, record, publish, or communicate certain military information, or who should communicate or publish reports or statements that were false, or that were "likely or intended to cause disaffection in, or to interfere with the success of, the military or naval forces of the United States."

The next day, opinions that were opposed to this espionage bill began to find their way to Washington. ... Undismayed ... Daniels and Baker continued perfecting their censorship plans. The former was more active than the latter in this respect. On March 1, 1917, he proposed to Baker that the Navy Department continue the censorship of radio stations and begin to censor all cable stations. At the same time, according to the plans of Daniels, the War Department would look after communications via telephone and telegraph at our international boundaries, "and elsewhere if necessary." Nine days later, he was requesting a voluntary censorship by the newspapers with regard to shipping news. ...

Before Congress assembled, the press received another check upon its privileges. On March 24, regulations relative to censorship were announced after a conference of the State, War, and Navy Departments. The newspapers of the country were asked to follow them voluntarily, pending enactment of a press censorship law. Five of the six regulations, according to the *New York Times,* had been drawn at the Navy Department. The sixth, presented by the State Department, was the one that editors regarded as objectionable. It read: "It is requested that no information, reports, or rumors attributing a policy to the government in any international situation, not authorized by the

President or a member of the cabinet, be published without first consulting the Department of State."

While these departmental censorship activities were in progress, with War, Navy, Treasury, and State taking the lead, the extra session of Congress reassembled. After hearing President Wilson's war message, the bills began to be introduced, and among them was one by Congressman Webb that was destined to become the Espionage Act of June 15, 1917.

Before that bill became a law, however, the first of three executive orders dealing with censorship, had been issued. On April 13, the Secretaries of State, War, and Navy, in a joint letter to the President, had recommended the creation of a Committee on Public Information in which the two functions of censorship and publicity could be joined. This suggestion followed rather closely many ideas that had been expressed previously . . . by leading newspapermen and publishers. . . .

The day following the joint letter from the three cabinet members, Wilson created the Committee on Public Information. It was composed of newspaperman George Creel, chairman, and the Secretaries of State, War, and Navy. . . .

Creel's group merely supervised a voluntary censorship of the press, which left the matter of news suppression up to the newspapers themselves. Of course, the army and navy censored the information they gave out, but news, for instance, about troops moving from the one camp to another was at the mercy of the papers in the vicinity of those camps, if they chose to use it. Approximately 99 per cent of the press observed the rules of this voluntary censorship, and since it was voluntary they made little complaint about the denial of the freedom of the press.

The President's second executive order No. 2604 of April 28, 1917, relating to censorship, went into effect four days later. That order related to all cable and land telegraph lines leading out of the United States. . . .

Section 3d (the Trading-with-the-Enemy Act), together with Title VII of the Espionage Act, was the basis for the first censorship board in the history of the United States.

The subsection mentioned above read: "Whenever, during the present war, the President shall deem that the public safety demands it, he may cause to be censored under such rules and regulations as he may from time to time establish, communications by mail, cable, radio or other means of transmission passing between the United States and any foreign country he may from time to time specify, or which may be carried by any vessel or other means of transportation touching at any port, place or territory of the United States and bound to or from any foreign country. Any person who willfully evades or attempts to evade the submission of any such communication to such censorship or willfully uses or attempts to use any code or other device for the purposes of concealing from such censorship the intended meaning of such communication shall be punished" with a fine of not more than $10,000 or imprisonment for not more than ten years, or both.

Six days later, the President deemed that the public safety demanded it, and established the Censorship Board, together with other agencies of a wartime character. Section XIV to XVI of executive order No. 2729-A created the board, whose personnel consisted of representatives of the Secretaries of War and Navy, the Postmaster General, the War Trade Board, and the chairman of the Committee on Public Information.

THE CREEL CENSORSHIP [4]

As many scars bear witness, I was the official censor during the World War. For two years I rode herd on the press, trying to enforce the concealments demanded by the army and navy.

[4] By George Creel, chairman of the Committee on Public Information, 1917-18. From "The Plight of the Last Censor." *Collier's.* 107:13+. May 24, 1942. Reprinted by permission.

Two long, hectic years, and at the end of the disastrous experiment I fell to my knees and offered up a fervent prayer that just as I had been America's first official censor so would I live in history as the last.

Unhappily, it turns out that fighting men are like the Bourbons. They die but they never learn. Still insisting that secrecy is as much a part of war as ships and guns, a censorship of the press is again in operation, having been initiated by the Secretary of Navy in conference with the heads of publishers' associations. Only a "voluntary" arrangement, however, as the announcement is careful to explain, lacking compulsory and punitive features. Nothing more than a patriotic pledge with one hand on the heart and the other on the flag.

Well, that is just what we had, and all we had, in 1917 and 1918. The war-making branches, to be sure, clamored for a law with teeth in it, but when Congress balked a plan was worked out that made the press its own censor. The desires of government with respect to the concealment of "military secrets" were set forth in careful detail, and sent to every newspaper in the land. On the printed card that carried them was this paragraph: "These requests are without larger authority than the necessities of the war-making branches. Their enforcement is a matter for the press itself."

Simple enough and proper enough on its face, but not only did the plan fall down in operation, but out of it came a long train of irritations that made for lasting angers and ill will. The resentments of the bedeviled press deepened into revolt, equally bedeviled officials fumed and what should have been a friendly and cooperative relationship went rancid. By way of adding to tragedy, it soon became painfully apparent that the whole business had no real point, no justification in necessity.

Secrecy is essential in connection with many activities of the war machine, although the need is often exaggerated beyond the bounds of common sense, but censorship of the press in *any* form is not the answer, never was the answer and never will be the

answer. Not in this country at any rate. Just as it failed in the
First World War, so will it fail again, for the causes of failure
are inherent in the plan. I was a fool not to have seen it, but
the "shush-shush" campaign impressed me, and "voluntary" was
a magic word that soothed away all suspicion of trouble.

The physical difficulties of enforcement, for example, should
have been plain, for European countries presented no such problem as the United States with its stretch of 3,000 miles from
coast to coast, its forty-eight states and scores of great cities.
Administration, therefore, had to be broken down to every
metropolitan center, for it was obviously absurd to assume that
San Francisco, Dallas, Minneapolis, New Orleans and Miami
must telephone Washington whenever a ruling was required.

This huge machine, even when created, did not function with
automatic precision, for "information of value to the enemy,"
or "definitely damaging to the progress and maintenance of the
national defense," and "compatible with the national security"
were phrases subject to as many interpretations as there were
interpreters. Oftentimes generals and admirals were in sharp
disagreement as to what should be suppressed or passed, so that
rulings flatly contradicted each other. One group of high officials, with some appreciation of publicity values, would urge
pictures and features stories, while another group would not want
to admit that we had either an army or a navy. It took me two
months to get permission for correspondents to visit the Grand
Fleet.

Quite naturally, this confusion at the source had its effect
on junior officers in the field. In cases of doubt they "played
safe," ruling against publication even when suppression was
patently absurd. There were many instances where papers
were denied permission to give the location of aviation plants
although the information was to be found in every telephone
and city directory. A powder factory was being built in plain
view of a large city, an enterprise lauded by the Chamber of
Commerce, but reporters were ordered to ignore its existence.

Printing of ship news was forbidden, although notices of arrivals and departures were posted in hotel lobbies.

Now and then, however, some field man would go off the deep end. One very rigid prohibition was against the photographing of tanks, and although the papers implored, the rule was enforced. Imagine, then, our dismay when a newsreel concern burst forth with a complete set of tank pictures. The press raged, generals thundered and an investigation disclosed that a young captain had given the required permission, thinking it a help to recruiting. After much stewing around, everybody came to the conclusion that there was no good reason why tank pictures should not be taken.

By way of adding to the magnitude of the task, it was not only the news columns that had to be watched. What good for the city desk to suppress transport sailings and troops movements when the society columns contained every detail in the account of the wedding of an army lieutenant or a navy captain? Nor was the rural press any less important than the metropolitan, for country editors, going down to the depot to see "the boys" off, rarely failed to report their destination.

With the best will in the world on both sides, violations soon came to be daily occurrences. New York censors would kill a story to which Chicago officials offered no objection. A paper in Kansas City or Milwaukee, asking for an interpretation, would be told not to print a story. A rival paper, exercising its own judgment, went ahead and slapped the story on the front page. Straightway a scream from the city editor who had telephoned for a ruling and had abided by it. A lieutenant would bar one newspaper from taking plane pictures and the next day a colonel would give the right to a rival sheet.

Along with unintentional violations there were many bold and open breaches of the agreement out of the average editor's sheer inability to resist an "exclusive story." The publication, for example, of testimony given by army or navy men before supposedly secret sessions of a congressional committee. As a

that would reach the Germans unless he kept close watch on his tongue. Virtually everything we asked the press not to print was seen or known by thousands, making secrecy a joke. . . .

Secrecy is an essential, but it is not going to be provided by any censorship of the press, for if the information comes to the ears of a reporter, most certainly it will have been learned by any spy worth his pay. Concealment of new inventions and technical developments, along with war plans, is the business of the military authorities. Secrecy at the source is the one and only answer. That is where enemy agents are going for their information—peeping, prying and bribing.

This was the conclusion forced on me back in 1917, and at a date when the "voluntary censorship" had been in operation less than two months. Although convinced in my own mind that the plan was both unworkable and useless, I felt the need for making sure, and before taking any action had a heart-to-heart talk with a man high up in one of the intelligence units.

"Tell me," I asked him, "do you honestly believe that the enemy is stupid enough to rely for its information on something as slow and haphazard as the indiscretions of the press?"

"I do not." The answer came without a moment's hesitation. "Speech in transmission is the essence, and it takes a day, not minutes or hours, for newspapers to reach the enemy or a neutral country in direct communication with the enemy."

"Then common sense," I insisted, "indicates the employment of spies, and the use of cables?"

"Of course."

As a result of this conversation I went to President Wilson, and in July, 1917, he issued an executive order subjecting all cable communications to rigid censorship. This done, what the newspapers printed ceased to be of importance. Even when enemy agents succeeded in getting hold of military secrets, they could not get the information out of the country, and attempts to do so resulted in their detection and arrest.

PRE-WAR VIEW OF CENSORSHIP [5]

Because democracies are not given to unanimity, the strictest regimentation of print, speech, and thought must be imposed on the people in time of war, when the entire energies of the nation must be harnessed to prosecute the war to a victorious conclusion. Perhaps the most dramatic manifestation of the suspension of civil rights during a conflict is the censorship of published matter. We are already made aware, through the ominous little boxes to be found on the front page of today's newspapers and by the announcements by American radio commentators that their dispatches have been censored, of the existence of a stringent foreign censorship of news. In the event that the United States is drawn into the war what will be the nature of the control of the press inside our own country? Will censorship be one of facts only or will it also become a censorship of opinion? What will be considered dangerous opinion? What agencies will be set up by a wartime government to implement the censorship? By what means will such agencies enforce their control?

While it may be conceded that military censorship is a necessity in time of war to prevent information of military value from reaching the enemy, has the government the right to censor publications on the ground that the opinions expressed might possibly interfere with the success of the war? If so, what are the criteria of judgment concerning such opinions?

It is impossible to conjecture what the specific answers to these questions will be in the event that the United States becomes involved in the present war. However, some reasonable suppositions can be formulated on the basis of the censorship activities of the government during the [First] World War, and on existing documents containing plans for the administra-

[5] By Lucille B. Milner, Secretary of the American Civil Liberties Union, and Groff Conklin, free-lance writer. From "Wartime Censorship in the United States." *Harper's Magazine*. 180:187-95. January 1940. Reprinted by permission.

tion of public relations in the next war. An examination of what happened here during the last war will serve to show to what extent the thoughts of American citizens can be controlled by a vigilant censorship. It will also reveal the fact that once a war hysteria has been spread by official propaganda, intolerance for spoken or written criticism is likely to be greater among the people themselves than in the government.

The whole question of censorship is not simply one of laws dealing with what may or may not be printed. It is a question of those laws, plus an organized effort on the part of the government to persuade the people of the righteousness and justice of the war plus the hysteria engendered by the government's propaganda. Of course efforts toward this end have long been employed in wars, but it was not until the First World War, when the Committee on Public Information was set up with George Creel as chairman, that an organized effort to enforce a draft of public opinion got under way. . . .

Censorship of publications in this country was of two distinct types, pre-publication or preventive censorship, and post-publication censorship. The pre-publication variety, though universal in days before the Revolution in America, when the governors appointed by the British Crown had the right to ban any written material from publication if they so desired, has never since then existed in this country, with one major exception which occurred during the World War. This was the pre-publication surveillance exercised over the foreign-language press. However, an organized but voluntary preventive censorship also existed during the [First] World War among the newspaper editors of this country. Both the official censorship of the foreign-language press and the unofficial control of newspaper copy are more fully described further on in this article.

Post-publication censorship power during the war was vested largely in the Post Office Department, although methods of dealing with dangerous publications which were distributed by hand rather than through the mails were developed by the

Department of Justice. Legislation defining what should be censored and how the censoring should be accomplished was part of two much broader laws which dealt with all types of control considered necessary during wartime. The more important of these two laws was the Espionage Act, and the second, the Trading-with-the-Enemy Act.

The Espionage Act was chiefly concerned with the suppression of spy activity, eradication of conspiracy to defeat the armed forces, protection of military secrets, control of enemy aliens, and enforcement of neutrality in future conflicts between other nations. It was Title I, Section 3 of the Act (now Title 50, Section 33) which had to do specifically with the matter of sedition. This clause reads as follows:

> Whoever, when the United States is at war, shall willfully make or convey false reports . . . with intent to interfere with the operation or success of the military or naval forces of the United States or to promote the success of its enemies (2) and whoever, when the United States is at war, shall willfully cause or attempt to cause insubordination, disloyalty, mutiny, or refusal of duty, in the military or naval forces of the United States, (3) or shall willfully obstruct the recruiting or enlistment service of the United States . . . shall be punished by a fine of not more than $10,000 or imprisonment for not more than twenty years, or both.

This clause defined the crime for which freedom of speech and press could be abrogated during the last World War or during *any subsequent war,* as the phrase "when the United States is at war" indicates.

The section of the Espionage Act which made commission of the crimes in print subject to censorship was Title XII, empowering the Postmaster General to bar from the mails any literature which was deemed in violation of any part of the Espionage Act. However, first-class mail was declared to be inviolate from opening by any save the clerk of the Dead-Letter Office, or other person authorized by search warrant. Actually this clause meant that the Postmaster had the right to bar anything from the privilege of the second-class mail rate, and gave him ample authority to suppress any publications which contravened the provisions of the Act, since without the privilege of the less expensive second-class mail rate few publications could be distributed.

Before the Espionage Act became law, on June 15, 1917, a powerful struggle against its censorship provisions was conducted by the newspapers. The fight began in February of the same year, when they protested against the Webb-Overman Bill. As introduced, this bill threatened with life imprisonment anyone who should publish information which might be useful, directly or indirectly, to the enemy. The Webb-Overman Bill passed the Senate but died in committee in the House.

However, by the time the final Espionage Act was passed, the attention of the press and the country at large had been diverted by the campaign to raise the first Liberty Loan, and by the enforcement of the Draft Act. The censorship provisions of the 1917 law received but little attention in the press.

Over half of the nearly two thousand prosecutions, and a similar proportion of the one hundred and more censorship cases brought under the Espionage Act, were conducted under the authority of these 1917 provisions of the Act. Individuals, organizations, and publications alike were prosecuted on the grounds of "intent" to persuade disloyalty. In most cases the actual substance of the speech or the literature involved criticism of the government, the war's aims, or the draft, rather than any concrete or proven interference with the operation of the war. In one case a man was sentenced to a long term of imprisonment for stating his belief that the Supreme Court would declare the Draft Act unconstitutional. . . .

Congress decided to revise the Espionage Act. In recommending the amendments the Attorney General stated that the original law had proven inadequate to meet individual utterances which, though not in violation of the original act, were still creating much trouble, and had resulted in numerous horse-whippings and tarrings-and-featherings, and in two known lynchings. The Attorney General then suggested certain amendments to cope with this situation, and Congress added more amendments, until the final revised legislation, which soon became known as "The Sedition Act," made criminal the following ten new offenses: Saying or doing anything with intent to obstruct the sale of United States bonds; uttering, printing, writing, or publishing any disloyal, profane, scurrilous, or abusive language, or language intended to cause contempt, scorn, contumely, or disrepute as regards the form of government of the United States; or the Constitution; or the flag; or the uniform of the army or navy; or the armed forces of the United States; or any language intended to incite resistance to the United States or promote the cause of its enemies; urging any curtailment of production of anything necessary to the conduct of the war with intent to hinder it; advocating, teaching, defending, or suggesting the doing of any of these things; and any words or acts supporting or favoring the cause of any country at war with us, or opposing the cause of the United States in that war. The penalties which applied to the original clause of the Espionage Act dealing with "sedition" were made applicable to these new crimes. Thus in order to protect outspoken citizens from threatened mob violence, the new laws made them subject to twenty years imprisonment, or ten thousand dollars fine, or both. . . .

No legislation remotely approaching this in its infringements of the rights of freedom of speech and press had existed in this country since the famous Alien and Sedition Acts of 1798. Those acts were passed by the Federalist Party to combat the propaganda of the French Revolution, and to preserve their party in power. So unpopular were the Acts that they were largely instrumental in bringing about the defeat of the Federalists in 1800, and a tradition against laws on sedition was established which was not broken until the hysteria of the World War brought the new "Sedition Act" into existence.

The Trading-with-the-Enemy Act dealt in some of its clauses with the censorship of the foreign-language press in this country, and in others with the censorship of all messages between foreign countries and the United States. Under the clause controlling the foreign-language press, the publishers of such periodicals were required to submit to the Postmaster General's office sworn translations of every article in them which dealt with the government of the United States, the war, any foreign government with which we were at war, or the policies or international relations of the United States. The section provided the instrumentality for a powerful preventive censorship of the foreign-language press.

To censor the messages between the United States and any foreign country, the Trading-with-the-Enemy Act authorized the establishment of a Censorship Board. This board took over the cable censorship function of the Naval Communications Division of the Navy Department. It was composed of representatives of the Secretary of State, the Secretary of War, the Secretary of the Navy, the Postmaster General, the War Trade Board, and the famous Committee on Public Information. The man who represented the Committee on Public Information on the Censorship Board was George Creel, chief of the committee.

In addition to being the formal sponsor of all the war propaganda, Creel's committee was also the "informal" agent for newspaper and periodical preventive censorship. Dealing with the papers, the magazines, and the news syndicates, it established certain categories of material which should not be printed. Most of these concerned information which might prove of value to the enemy, or information of military importance.

The newspapers did not really like this surveillance, nor could they understand a great many of the decisions of Creel's committee as to what constituted military information, but they submitted to this "voluntary" self-censorship with as good a grace as possible. Actually the Committee on Public Information had only the right to approve or disapprove articles which were voluntarily submitted to it by publishers previous to publication. If it approved such pieces, they were stamped, "Passed by the Committee on Public Information."

But the Censorship Board, of which George Creel was also a member, did have the power to recommend to the Postmaster General that he bar the mails to publications containing "seditious" material, and to suggest to the Department of Justice that it prosecute the publishers of such material. This was in addition to its primary task of censoring cable and other outgoing and incoming messages.

There were several other organizations and departments busy ferreting out "seditious" material in addition to the Censorship Board and the Committee on Public Information. For one thing, Department of Justice agents throughout the country examined all kinds of printed material, and reported instances of "seditious" utterance to the Postmaster General for punitive action. The Military Intelligence Division of the army undertook similar activities.

An Executive Postal Censorship Committee, located in New York, was set up to assist in the examination of printed matter. Local postmasters throughout the nation were directed to act as local censors, reporting to the Washington office anything which they judged derogatory to the government or subversive to the conduct of the war. Numerous private organizations were engaged in hunting down seditious utterances. The Pennsylvania Press Club acted as watchman over all the State of Pennsylvania for the Post Office and the Department of Justice, and an organization known as the American Protective League received semi-official approval in its task of securing information about seditious publications and dangerous speech.

Furthermore, there were thousands of amateur censors, who reported information about individuals and organizations and about all classes of printed matter which they thought were in violation of the "Sedition Act." A great majority of such reports were the result of personal hatreds, spite, imagined injury, or attempts to gain unfair competitive advantage.

The powers of the Postmaster General to deal with this stream of supposedly seditious literature were absolute during and directly after the war. He could suppress anything he wished without citing evidence or giving reasons. Although in the majority of cases he censored only specific issues of a periodical, he had the power to suppress the periodical entirely on the ground that, because it had missed one issue, it was no longer entitled to second-class mailing privileges under the postal laws, since it was no longer "regularly" issued.

The barring of a publication from the mails by the Post Office was virtually without appeal. The Postmaster General claimed that his acts were not reviewable by any court. This claim was based on an early judicial decision that the Postmaster General's decree must be regarded as conclusive by the courts *"unless it is clearly wrong."* No one can be proved "clearly wrong" in matters of opinion. Never during the whole course of wartime and post-wartime censorship were any of the Post Office's decisions censoring publications reversed by the courts.

Finally the Postmaster General had the right to keep anyone guilty of violating the Espionage Act from receiving mail, thus blocking any activity on the defendant's part.

During the existence of this postal censorship the distribution of over one hundred publications was interfered with—the greatest violation of freedom of the press in America's history. One of the earliest and perhaps the best known of the censorship cases was that of *The Masses*. The New York City postmaster barred the August 1917 issue of this political monthly from the mails. The publishers then asked the Federal District Court to enjoin the postmaster from excluding the offending issue. Judge Learned Hand held that the portions of the magazine held seditious by the postmaster did not advocate violence, or in any way command or suggest opposition to the war, and he granted the injunction. The Post Office then appealed, and the

Circuit Court of Appeals voided the injunction. The court's construction of the Espionage Act permitted prosecution for the saying or writing of any words which had even the remotest tendency to persuade to sedition as defined under the Act. The judges held that no immediate intent to persuade and no evidence of success in the persuasion had to be proved. It was on the basis of this decision that a majority of the Espionage Act prosecutions were conducted, and most of the censorship actions were undertaken by the Post Office.

The case of the Milwaukee *Leader* was of equal importance. The Postmaster General revoked the second-class mailing privilege of the paper on the ground that it was opposed to the war. The case was appealed to the United States Supreme Court. In a decision rendered by that court it was held that the Postmaster General had authority to do this, and that conviction under the Espionage Act was not required before the Post Office could act. In other words, the Post Office under this decision was given absolute authority over the whole press of the nation, not only to ban a specific issue of a publication, but to suppress "on evidence satisfactory to the Postmaster General," the periodical as a whole, through absolute revocation of its second-class mailing privilege.

Armed with these judicially granted powers, as well as those specified by the Espionage Act and its amendments, the Post Office was empowered to act as censor of the press of the United States. A list of the periodicals and books suppressed and censored by the Post Office during and after the war reveals that the Postmaster General was not concerned only with pro-German, pacifist, anti-war and treasonable material. The interests of the department, as of other government bodies, were not only in waging the war to a successful conclusion. They extended also to the suppression of all types of criticism of the government, whether pacifist, religious, or political in origin. For example, *The Freeman's Journal and Catholic Register* was censored for reprinting a statement by Thomas Jefferson to the effect that

Ireland ought to be a republic; *The Nation,* for attacking Samuel Gompers, labor's representative on the Council of National Defense; and *The Public,* for suggesting that the government should raise more money by higher taxes and less by loans. . . .

Censorship and other suppressive acts continued long after the end of the war. The Espionage Act of 1918 was not repealed until March 1921, and it was used right up to that date. A year after the Armistice the Attorney General raided the offices of the Seattle *Union Record* and suppressed the paper because of its political views. The New York *Call* was still being barred from the mails thirteen months after the Armistice. A number of censorship prosecutions occurred during the hysteria which followed the war, which found its most virulent expression in Attorney General Palmer's notorious "Red raids."

The situation today is very different from twenty years ago. If at the end of the war in 1918 the temper of the people and of the government was such as to make the restoration of civil rights a subject for bitter struggle, what will they be today? We have ample evidence that censorship in a coming war will be more complete, more drastic, and even less concerned with the constitutional rights of freedom of speech and press than was that of the last war. Already the public is being called upon to report "subversive" acts and utterances to the Department of Justice. . . .

Government operation of the radio in the event of a "national emergency" is already authorized under the Communications Act of 1934, and while it may not now be invoked, would certainly take effect instantly on our involvement in war. It would place the most powerful medium of propaganda today in the hands of a government which would tolerate only the expression of its own views and purposes. The 1917 Espionage Act is still on the books, ready to be invoked in case of war. Although the 1918 "Sedition Act" was repealed, similar and even more repressive legislation has passed one or the other house of the present Congress and will be acted on when Congress reconvenes in January.

DEVELOPMENT OF CONTROLS

THE APPROACH TO WAR: 1941

August [1]

Recently the chairman of the Federal Communications Commission, James L. Fly, called newspaper and radio men to his office and asked them to cease mention of the Stalin Line in connection with the Russo-German fighting. He said if the newspapers and radio built up a legend about a strong Stalin Line, such as was built up about the Maginot Line, then when the Germans broke through the effect upon the American public would be all the more depressing.

Nobody paid much attention to this, partly because the idea seemed silly and partly because it wasn't Mr. Fly's business to tell newspapermen and radio men how to write their copy.

September [2]

Acting Secretary of War Robert Patterson and Acting Secretary of the Navy James Forrestal informed Congress last week that both the army and the navy are preparing plans for censorship of all communications between the United States and any foreign nation, American overseas possession or ship at sea.

According to the information submitted to Congress such control would be applied to both outgoing and incoming communications by any means of transmission and is supposedly intended to prevent espionage and entrance of foreign propaganda.

[1] By Raymond Clapper, Scripps-Howard syndicate writer. From "The Press Must Be Free." *Broadcasting*. 21:20. August 4, 1941. Reprinted by permission.
[2] From "Proposals To Censor Communications Are Told to Congress by Army and Navy," newsstory. *Broadcasting*. 21:52. September 22, 1941. Reprinted by permission.

Both Mr. Patterson and Mr. Forrestal told Congress that the current plans do not contemplate compulsory censorship of the press and that they must be approved by a "higher authority" and would have to be supported by legislation. . . .

In his letter Mr. Patterson said "the War Department has, in the past, examined into and studied the question of compulsory censorship of the press and radio, and many other problems, with a view to being prepared to offer timely solutions should the need therefore be required to the interests of national defense." However, he pointed out there were no such plans along that line now in preparation by the War Department.

OCTOBER [3]

Secretary of Navy Frank Knox said last week that plans for navy censorship of overseas communications are now well under way but emphasized that absolutely no censorship of domestic news publication or news broadcasts is involved, other than the voluntary method now in operation.

Expressing gratification over what was termed the excellent cooperation demonstrated by the various services in voluntarily avoiding publicity on restricted matters, Mr. Knox said the navy's plan to scrutinize overseas communications is in line with its policy of preparing for emergency measures.

The secretary said that supervisory control (censorship) of all communications passing out of the United States during a period of national emergency is obviously vital to the national security to prevent leakage of military, naval and economic information to enemy or unfriendly powers. As the "first line of defense," it was pointed out, the navy is charged with the responsibility of cable and radio communications censorship.

The navy's plans are being made to insure a minimum of interruption and inconvenience to legitimate business, it was

[3] From "Navy Proceeding With Censorship Plan, Possibly Conflicting With Donovan Unit," newsstory. *Broadcasting*. 21:14. October 20, 1941. Reprinted by permission.

stated. At present officer personnel enrolled from various businesses which are the heaviest users of cables and radio communications—press, banks, shipping, export and import trades—are being trained so that the traffic of these interests can be handled by experts. The training classes are being conducted under the direction of the Commandant of the Third Naval District in New York.

ORGANIZING FOR WAR

PEARL HARBOR! [4]

Declaration of war with Japan this week was promptly followed by appointment of J. Edgar Hoover to coordinate censorship of all news and communications until a permanent censor is named.

President Roosevelt's designation of the G-Man Chief . . . was merely an assignment to coordinate and plan. Mr. Hoover, a lawyer, will not be the official censor when the system becomes operative.

With the outbreak of war a modified censorship on news—at the source—came into play in Washington but swift happenings there and far out on the Pacific Ocean gave correspondents the heaviest file of copy of this generation. . . .

At his press conference Tuesday, President Roosevelt pleaded with reporters to be patient with the slow flow of news and warned that rumors will not be supported by official agencies through comment on them. Public relations staffs of the armed forces will confer with one another to establish the accuracy of reports from the theater of operations before releasing news.

Mr. Roosevelt carried that thought into his fireside chat that evening, saying:

[4] From "J. E. Hoover Coordinator of U.S. War Censorship," newsstory. *Editor & Publisher.* 74:64. December 13, 1941. Reprinted by permission.

"To all newspapers and radio stations—all those who reach the eyes and ears of the American people—I say this: You have a most grave responsibility to the nation, now and for the duration of this war. If you feel that your government is not disclosing enough of the truth, you have every right to say so. But—in the absence of all the facts, as revealed by official sources—you have no right in the ethics of patriotism to deal out unconfirmed reports in such a way as to make people believe they are gospel truth."

In New York, the navy took over censorship of outgoing communications within a few hours Sunday night. Twenty-five newspapermen commissioned as ensigns and lieutenants are among 100 censors operating on four floors of the I.T. & T. Building, 67 Broad Street, where navy censorship had headquarters in New York during the First World War.

Plans in the making for two years went into operation Sunday when M-day arrived for the censors. At 9:23 P. M. the admiral in charge got word that the official censorship on outgoing messages of all kinds was to become effective immediately.

As explained to the press through *Editor & Publisher,* the aim of the censorship "is to cooperate as fully as practicable with commercial interests so that as little interference as possible will result from censorship." . . .

At San Francisco a smaller staff handles about 10 per cent of outgoing press, another at New Orleans 5 per cent. The remaining outbound file is cleared through New York censors.

International telephone messages are handled by the navy at the source in New York and San Francisco. It is understood that stations operated by the army to censor land towns are at work at Mexican border towns. . . .

A group of English journalists appealed directly to Secretary of the Navy Frank Knox this week for relief from "very trying censorship." At the same time representatives of the Foreign Press Association conferred with the navy officials in New York.

There were three chief complaints: Delay in clearing dispatches, failure to notify correspondents of deletions from their articles, and almost insurmountable difficulties placed in the way of foreign-language messages. The latter complaint came largely from representatives of South American newspapers.

The language difficulty of South American correspondents was ended Wednesday night when the Postal Telegraph Company announced it would accept Spanish language messages to all points in Central and South America provided they are filed by well established correspondents or press associations. . . .

While Washington awaited the expected sweeping changes in regulations on communications, several agencies of the United States Government acted to protect vital information.

Addressed "To the press, radio, and other disseminators of information," was the following from Chairman Emory S. Land of the United States Maritime Commission:

> The United States Maritime Commission, in adopting a wartime policy, requests all agencies of public information to refrain from publication or announcement of anything, or the use of photographs, which contains any information, either direct or indirect, concerning the movement, position, cargos or destination of any merchant vessels in any waters. Full cooperation with the commission in the execution of this wartime policy will be appreciated.

The Navy Department announced reinstatement of the Espionage Act of 1918, imposing heavy penalties for willful exposure of information of possible value to an enemy.

From the War Department came this notice:

> On account of the possibility of sabotage, information relating to the routes, schedules and destinations of troop movements within or without continental United States is restricted, except when specifically announced by the War Department.

Rear Admiral Hepburn, director of navy press relations, told the press the voluntary censorship requested by Secretary Knox under date of December 31, 1940, will continue in effect. This system placed in the category of restricted information, unless authorized by the department, the following:

Mention of

1. Actual or intended movements of vessels or aircraft of the United States Navy, of units of naval enlisted personnel or divisions of mobilized reserves, or troop movements of the United States Marine Corps.

2. "Secret" technical United States naval weapons or development thereof.

3. New United States Navy ships or aircraft.

4. United States Navy construction projects ashore.

Short-wave broadcasts sent abroad automatically came under the surveillance of Colonel William J. Donovan's Office of Coordinator.

The Weather Bureau of the Department of Agriculture indicated that weather reports may be placed under censorship ban, marking a departure in censorial practice which is related directly to the increased use of aircraft. Germany and Great Britain already class the weather forecast as a military secret.

At least on the West Coast and in the Southwest, weather reports were clipped of their "state of weather" and "precipitation" figures, and weather forecasts for the area also were eliminated.

DECEMBER 7

RADIO JOINS UP [5]

As soon as first word was flashed of Japan's surprise attack on Pearl Harbor December 7, radio swung into action, throwing regular schedules overboard to keep the whole nation advised of minute-to-minute developments. By the end of the week, with all networks and most stations operating around the clock, news schedules had been adjusted to disturb normal functions

[5] From "Industry Takes Its Place in War Program," newsstory. *Broadcasting.* 21:7, December 15, 1941. Reprinted by permission.

least. But listener interest reached record peaks every hour of the day and night.

Following prearranged plans, the Defense Communications Board, headed by F.C.C. Chairman James Lawrence Fly, took over before the emergency was an hour old. The fruits of more than a year of planning promptly were realized, and much confusion and unrest which might have reached the hysteria stage was averted.

The brunt of operation in a war economy was felt on the Pacific Coast, from San Diego to Seattle and as far east as Idaho, because of possible air attack. All stations were silenced, particularly after dusk, in these areas, to prevent use of their carriers as "homing beacons." Blackouts also were experienced momentarily in the East.

Prearranged plans all down the line affecting communications immediately became operative. The army, charged with control of domestic communications in wartime, originated the orders for coastal blackouts and station silencing through Corps Area Interceptor Commands. Full instructions have been sent stations regarding operating procedure.

D.C.B. became the supreme communications arbiter under an Executive Order signed last Wednesday by President Roosevelt, formalizing powers granted him under Section 606 of the Communications Act. Chairman Fly promptly dispelled fears of drastic action by pointing out that the order simply delegated to the D.C.B. certain authority already contained in Section 606, and that it "does not mean that any general taking over or operation of private radio by the government is contemplated."

Pointing out that the step was procedural, he said there is no change in policy or plans; that it has long been known that the military may require certain communications facilities in connection with the national defense, and that many of these needs already have been arranged by agreement, primarily with communications companies. He emphasized no censorship factor was involved.

In every quarter, the words of President Roosevelt, admonishing radio and the press to avoid alarm and rumor and to use caution and judgment, were echoed. The bywords were "avoid rumor" and "when in doubt, don't."

Chairman Fly expressed reasonable satisfaction last Friday with overall developments. He reiterated the need for caution and use of editorial judgment. Every device should be employed, he said, to avoid a nationwide "case of jitters" and pointed out that radio could perform yeoman service in this regard.

While the bugaboo of censorship repeatedly arose, it was definitely established that aside from military censorship at the source, there is no intent to invoke purely internal censorship affecting radio and the press. Outgoing communications are being censored, both by the navy and on international shortwave broadcasts, through the Office of the Coordinator of Information.

DECEMBER 8

CASUALTY LISTS RESTRICTED [6]

Emphasizing discretion and public service, the War Department last Monday issued to broadcasters a credo for war news. The suggested pointers, included in a special war bulletin distributed by the N.A.B. cover broadcasts of casualty lists and secret information, along with advice in connection with transmitter protection, activity of radio news editor groups in each state, and establishment of a regular schedule of official communiques by the War and Navy Departments.

The War Department recommended that stations confine their broadcasts of casualty lists to "only names of persons in your immediate listening area," leaving publication of complete lists up to the newspapers. Following release of the War Department's recommendations, developed by the Radio Branch of the Bureau of Public Relations, headed by Ed Kirby, N.A.B.

[6] From "Broadcasts of Casualty Lists Are Restricted in Army Plan," newsstory. *Broadcasting*. 21:26. December 15, 1941. Reprinted by permission.

director of public relations, the N.A.B. advised stations to refrain entirely from broadcasting the names of casualties.

Responding to this action, Mr. Kirby declared:

This is deeply appreciated, as the broadcast of casualty lists would, in effect, set up obituary columns on the air when such time can be used to elevate morale rather than depress it. Because of the opportunity for mispronunciation of names, it is felt that such lists should appear in print rather than uttered over the air. No objection to mention, however, of occasional newsworthy names, or, of course, to the broadcast of numbers of casualties.

The War Department also reemphasized Secretary of War Stimson's caution against broadcasting or publishing information on the strength, positions, or movements of United States troops.

In the same memorandum station managers were advised to call for military protection of their broadcast plants where necessary, although they were later urged to request the services of federal troops only when local forces are inadequate or exhausted.

The supplementary statement indicated the primary responsibility for protecting the property of stations and public utilities lies with the owner and the local and state government, but advised that if local forces are unavailable, requests should be submitted to the Corps Area Commander after all local resources are exhausted.

District directors of N.A.B. have been requested to furnish immediately to Mr. Kirby the names of state chairmen of news editor-program director organizations set up all over the country during the current cycle of N.A.B. district meetings. The groups, cooperating with War Department officials, were set up to work together in coordinating their coverage and treatment of war news.

The War Department's original recommendations regarding broadcast of casualty lists follow:

No casualty lists will be released until nearest of kin have been notified. They will be available for immediate broadcast, upon release, from this wire (press service). To eliminate undue anxiety, however, it is suggested that only names of persons in your immediate listening area be broadcast. No network will broadcast complete lists, although newspapers will publish them. Names of casualties, when released, should be broadcast in regular newscast periods or in groups in time set aside for that purpose and not as flashes, interrupting regular program service. Rumors of casualties should not be broadcast. No surmises of persons believed to be on casualty lists should be broadcast until officially confirmed in official releases from the War Department.

DECEMBER 16

PRICE APPOINTED CHIEF CENSOR [7]

All Americans abhor censorship, just as they abhor war. But the experience of this and of all other nations has demonstrated that some degree of censorship is essential in wartime, and we are at war.

The important thing now is that such forms of censorship as are necessary shall be administered effectively and in harmony with the best interests of our free institutions.

It is necessary to the national security that military information which might be of aid to the enemy be scrupulously withheld at the source.

It is necessary that a watch be set upon our borders, so that no such information may reach the enemy, inadvertently or otherwise, through the medium of the mails, radio or cable transmission, or by any other means.

It is necessary that prohibitions against the domestic publication of some types of information, contained in long-existing statutes, be rigidly enforced.

Finally, the government has called upon a patriotic press and radio to abstain voluntarily from the dissemination of detailed information of certain kinds, such as reports of the move-

[7] Franklin D. Roosevelt, President of the United States. From his statement on censorship released at a press conference, December 16, 1941.

ments of vessels and troops. The response has indicated a universal desire to cooperate.

In order that all of these parallel and requisite undertakings may be coordinated and carried forward in accordance with a single uniform policy, I have appointed Byron Price, executive news editor of the Associated Press, to be Director of Censorship, responsible directly to the President.

DECEMBER 19

THE CREATION OF THE OFFICE OF CENSORSHIP [8]

By virtue of the authority vested in me by the Constitution and the statutes of the United States, and particularly by section 303, Title III of the Act of December 18, 1941, Public Law 354, 77th Congress, 1st Session, and deeming that public safety demands it, I hereby order as follows:

1. There is hereby established the Office of Censorship, at the head of which shall be a Director of Censorship. The Director of Censorship shall cause to be censored, in his absolute discretion, communications by mail, cable, radio, or other means of transmission passing between the United States and any foreign country or which may be carried by any vessel or other means of transportation touching at any port, place, or territory of the United States and bound to or from any foreign country, in accordance with such rules and regulations as the President shall from time to time prescribe. The establishment of rules and regulations in addition to the provisions of this order shall not be a condition to the exercise of the powers herein granted or the censorship by this order directed. The scope of this order shall include all foreign countries except such as may hereafter be expressly excluded by regulation. . . .

The Director of Censorship shall establish a Censorship Operating Board, which shall consist of representatives of such de-

[8] Executive Order Prescribing Its Functions and Duties, December 19, 1941. (Abridged).

partments and agencies of the Government as the Director shall specify . . . [and] perform such duties with respect to operations as the Director shall determine.

DECEMBER 29

RYAN NAMED BROADCAST CENSOR [9]

Acting in accord with industry suggestions, Byron Price, Director of Censorship, appointed J. Harold Ryan, . . . as broadcast censor, with the title, Assistant Director of Censorship.

The appointment had been recommended by the war-born Radio Coordinating Committee, representing the heads of the five industry trade groups, which met in Washington Dec. 22-23 at the call of George B. Storer, interim president of National Independent Broadcasters. . . .

The Ryan appointment was made by Mr. Price in an announcement last Friday—one of the first executive positions he has filled since assuming office a fortnight ago. Mr. Ryan will be the industry contact on clearance of questionable data. The theme, advocated by Mr. Price, is for self-regulation on censorship, so far as possible, in all media.

Mr. Ryan assumed his new duties coincident with announcement of his appointment last Friday. In announcing the appointment, Mr. Price said Mr. Ryan would "deal principally with problems affecting radio." Simultaneously he named John H. Sorrells, of New York, executive editor of the Scripps-Howard newspapers, as assistant director of censorship, in charge of press activities. He indicated that one or more additional assistant directors would be named. . . .

Mr. Price has not yet completed organization of his office, which undertakes one of the most important tasks in the wartime picture. With the naming of Mr. Ryan, however, he has hurdled

[9] "J. Harold Ryan Named Broadcast Censor," newsstory. *Broadcasting.* 21: 7-8. December 29, 1941. Reprinted by permission.

his first big problem. Under the Executive Order issued Dec. 19 by President Roosevelt, creating the Office of Censorship, there will be a censorship policy board made up of cabinet members and other high government officials and a censorship operating board, established by Mr. Price, to consist of representatives of "such departments and agencies of the government as the director shall specify."

This board under the supervision of Mr. Price, will perform such duties with respect to operations as the director shall determine. . . .

The operating board probably will meet frequently, perhaps daily, since it will be the active body. The policy board will meet only occasionally with Mr. Price, it is understood, for the handling of questions of transcendent importance.

DECEMBER 30

MOVE TOWARD ENFORCEMENT [10]

Possibility is seen that the F.C.C. will be the punitive agent in case of stations violating whatever censorship regulations are promulgated. Though there are no definite arrangements, it was suggested that any broadcaster flaunting the Price organization would find himself on the receiving end of a Commish citation, required to demonstrate why his ticket should not be revoked for disregard of the "public interest" requirement. Minor infractions undoubtedly will be recorded in Commish files and reviewed whenever a license renewal is sought. When asked to comment on the Commish attitude, Fly observed this problem "seems to be something for the lawyers to get their teeth into."

Fly noted that the statute does not permit the F.C.C. to undertake direct control over what is aired, but expected it to be represented on committees set up for policy determination.

[10] From "F.C.C. Will Spank Those Stations, If Any, Defying U. S. Office of Censorship," newsstory. *Variety*. 145:30. December 31, 1941. Reprinted by permission.

JANUARY 11

CENSOR BOARD ORGANIZED

Appointment of 16 representatives of government departments and agencies in the Censorship Operating Board, which will utilize the specialized activities of the governmental divisions represented, was announced Jan. 11 by Byron Price, Director of Censorship.

Those appointed were: State Department, Michael J. McDermott, chief of division of current information; Treasury, Herbert E. Gaston, assistant secretary; War Department, Maj. W. Preston Corderman, chief postal censor; Justice Department, Inspector L.A. Hince, F.B.I.; Postoffice Department, Inspector William A. Kenyon; Navy Department, Capt. H. K. Fenn, chief cable censor; Commerce Department, Norman Baxter, assistant to the secretary; Board of Economic Warfare, Allen Peyser, consultant; Board of Governors of the Federal Reserve System, Ernest G. Draper, board member; F.C.C., E. K. Jett, chief engineer; Federal Loan Agency, W. C. Costello, assistant to the Federal Loan Administrator; Library of Congress, Luther H. Evans, chief assistant librarian; Maritime Commission, Mark O'Dea, director division of maritime promotion and information; Office of Coordinator of Information, David K. E. Brunce, special assistant; Office of the Coordinator of Inter-American Affairs, Francis A. Jamieson, chief of press division; Office of Government Reports, Lowell Mellett, director.

JANUARY 15

PRICE ISSUES CENSORSHIP RULES [12]

Releasing a code of wartime practices for newspapers, magazines, and other periodicals, Byron Price today called for "some sacrifice of the journalistic enterprise of ordinary times," but promised there will be no "news or editorial blackout."

[11] From "Federal Bureaus on Censor Board," newsstory. *Broadcasting*. 22:44. January 19, 1942. Reprinted by permission.
[12] James J. Butler. From "Price Issues Censorship Rules; Promises 'No News Blackout,'" newsstory. *Editor & Publisher*. 75:5. January 17, 1942. Reprinted by permission.

"It is the hope and expectation of the Office of Censorship that the columns of American publications will remain the freest in the world, and will tell the story of our national successes and shortcomings accurately and in much detail," Mr. Price said. . . .

"If information should be made available anywhere which seems to come from doubtful authority, or to be in conflict with the general aims of these requests; of if special restrictions requested locally seem unreasonable or out of harmony with this summary, it is recommended that the question be submitted at once to the Office of Censorship.

"In addition, if any newspapers, magazine or other agency or individual handling news or special articles desires clarification or advice as to what disclosures might or might not aid the enemy, the Office of Censorship will cooperate gladly. Such inquiries should be addressed to the Office of Censorship, Washington, D. C." . . .

Meeting correspondents at a press conference following release of the code, Mr. Price said: "I don't think anybody is happy about this whole thing. Various government departments are not, newspapers are not, the Office of Censorship is not. Censorship is not something to be happy about."

Asked what would happen if a newspaper, either inadvertently or willfully ignored the requests, Mr. Price said: "We are not crossing that bridge until we come to it—if we come to it. Experience under voluntary censorship in recent months shows that 99.9 per cent of the newspapers favor withholding from publication information of value to the enemy.

CENSORSHIP CODE FOR PRESS [13]
(Condensation)

Specific information which newspapers, magazines and book publishers are asked not to publish except when such informa-

[13] From "Wartime Restraints," pamphlet. American Civil Liberties Union. March, 1942. p. 12. Reprinted by permission.
Full text of the press censorship code, revised as of June 15, 1942, appears in the Appendix.

tion is made available officially by appropriate authorities falls into the following classes:

Troops
Ships
Planes
Fortifications
Production
Weather
Photographs and Maps
General
(a) Casualty lists
(b) Damage to military and naval objectives
(c) Transportation of war material
(d) Information about the movements of United States officials

JANUARY 16

CENSORSHIP CODE FOR RADIO [14]

The censorship code for radio is divided into three categories:
1. News programs
2. Ad lib programs
3. Foreign language programs

Radio management may act as its own censor outside of the suggestions contained in the code.

News falling into the following classifications should be kept from the air except in cases where the release has been authorized by appropriate authorities:

Weather reports
Troop movements
Ships

[14] From "Wartime Restraints," pamphlet. p. 19-20. American Civil Liberties Union. March, 1942. Reprinted by permission.
Full text of the radio censorship code is included in the Appendix.

Planes
Experiments
Fortifications
Production
Casualty lists
Releases of photographs and Selective Service enrollments
Unconfirmed reports
Communications

The broadcaster is asked to remember that there is need for extraordinary care, especially in cases where he or his authorized representative is not in full control of the program. These informal types of programs fall into four classifications:

Request programs
Quiz programs
Forums and interviews
Commentaries and descriptions

Full transcriptions should be kept for all foreign language programs and it is further suggested that broadcasters take all necessary precautions to prevent deviation from the script by foreign language announcers or performers. (Foreign language is here taken to mean any language other than English.)

JANUARY 16

INDUSTRY COMMENTS [16]

Expressing complete agreement with the rules set down in the new radio code issued by the Office of Censorship, advertisers and broadcasters said today that none of the audience participation programs now on national networks would be affected by the edict. At the same time it was indicated that

[15] From "Censors Tighten Rules on Radio Audience Shows," newsstory. *Advertising Age.* 13:8. January 19, 1942. Reprinted by permission.

every effort would be made to tighten up any loopholes that might conceivably violate the code in the future.

It was pointed out in radio circles that early news reports of the code did not agree entirely with official interpretations given to broadcasting executives. For example, quiz programs involving audiences of more than 50 people are not considered potentially dangerous, especially when participants are picked by those directing the show. No volunteers are to be permitted from the audience, thus eliminating the possibility of getting enemy messages onto the air. Special attention will also be paid to seemingly innocuous remarks, such as "this is certainly a cold night," or other tips that might broadcast weather conditions.

Commenting on the censorship rules, Clarence L. Menser, N.B.C. program manager, said there was no expectation that quiz programs on that network would be canceled. Instructions have been issued to producers, announcers and masters of ceremonies to veer away from all subjects the government regards as taboo, he added. For some time these shows have been monitored with extra care in Radio City, he continued, so that if, during any so-called ad-lib programs, objectionable statements are made by audience participants, a cut will be made immediately. Mr. Menser also expressed the opinion that the code "will have a salutory effect, especially among some of the smaller stations which have overlooked the importance of strictly observing common sense censorship rules."

At Mutual, Fred Weber, general manager, declared that affiliates of the network "will recognize the practicability and soundness of the instructions, and will comply with them in all their programs." He said that since the outbreak of war Mutual and its stations have imposed many voluntary regulations applying to program operations, particularly those concerning news, musical requests and audience participation broadcasts. The latter type, he pointed out, are produced before large studio audiences and are carefully supervised. No quiz or participation shows now on Mutual originate from remote locations such as airports or railroad terminals or similar public gathering points, he added.

C.B.S. officials confined their comment to the observation that they regard the rules as both reasonable and intelligent.

The regulations issued today by the Office of Censorship called on broadcasters to ban man-in-the-street, request and other spot programs which might be used by Axis agents to communicate with their headquarters or with saboteurs through prearranged signals.

In addition, broadcasters were told that because they were being heard abroad by Axis intelligence operatives, "certain material which may appear in news service wires as appropriate for newspapers may not be appropriate for radio." It was explained that printed matter is censored at the national borders, a procedure obviously impossible with broadcasts.

Censorship Director Byron Price urged that, generally speaking, the radio industry discontinue "any quiz program originating remotely, wherein the group is small, and wherein no arrangement exists for investigating the background of participants."

A considerable number of network programs will find it necessary to tighten up their methods of operation under the new code, although it seems unlikely that any network programs will be forced off the air.

THE DEVELOPMENT OF CONTROL

JANUARY 29

PLANNING TO END CONFUSION [16]

Navy public relations chiefs are working on a plan for news release which they hope will end confusion such as existed after the "Coimbra" was sunk off the Atlantic Gulf Coast. The more

[16] From "Navy Working on Plan for News Releases," newsstory. *Editor & Publisher.* 75:7. January 31, 1942. Reprinted by permission.

recent problem arose after a navy press official at Port Arthur, Texas, disclosed to the press that submarines had been seen. The announcement was not cleared through Washington, but that fact was not pressed after press association wires carried the story. But when the press accounts expanded to include a statement that planes were being sent to track down the enemy craft, the department requested that the "second phase" of the news development be kept from print. Then it was discovered that some papers already had the story on the street, and the kill was rescinded. The story on the hunt by planes came from what the code of censorship established as an "appropriate source," yet was regarded by the department to be news which should not be printed. Commander Paul Smith at the Navy Department described the Atlantic and Gulf Coast incidents as instances of confusion which have necessitated a re-examination of rules governing regional press officers of the navy. New and more explicit regulations are in prospect.

FEBRUARY 1

PUBLICATION OF ARMY ORDERS DISCONTINUED [17]

The War Department announced, effective today, it will discontinue publication of orders to army officers on their new assignments. Such orders will be considered restricted and not communicable to the "public or the press," the Department said.

FEBRUARY 7

REGULATION OF WAR CORRESPONDENT [18]

The War Department has drafted regulations to cover the work of war correspondents and to fix their status in the theaters of operation.

---

[17] From "New Army Rule," newsstory. *Editor & Publisher.* 75:9. Feb. 7, 1942. Reprinted by permission.
[18] From "Army Lists Regulations for War Correspondents," newsstory. *Editor & Publisher.* 75:8. Feb. 7, 1942. Reprinted by permission.

The preamble of the rules recognizes that correspondents perform "an undoubted public function in the dissemination of news concerning the operations of the army in time of war," but carries this admonition:

> Correspondents accompanying troops in the field occupy a dual and delicate position, being under the necessity of truthfully disclosing to the people the facts concerning the operations of the army, and at the same time of refraining from disclosing those things which, though true, would be disastrous to us if known to the enemy. . . .

With reference to the requirement of accuracy, the report warns:

> A correspondent will be suspended from all privileges for the distortion of his dispatches in the office of the publication which he represents and also for the use of words or expressions conveying a hidden meaning which would tend to mislead or deceive the censor and cause the approval by him of otherwise objectionable dispatches.

Intelligence officers with the various commands will act as censors on the spot.

The manual provides:

> In general, articles may be released for publication to the public provided:
> 1. They are accurate in statement and implication.
> 2. They do not supply military information to the enemy.
> 3. They will not injure the morale of our forces, the people at home, or our allies.
> 4. They will not embarrass the United States, its allies, or neutral countries.

FEBRUARY 9

CABINET SPEECHES CENSORED [19]

President Roosevelt and members of Congress are virtually the only federal officials left beyond the reach of censorship as a result of an order extending news control to Cabinet members

[19] From "O.F.F. to Censor Speeches of Cabinet Officers," newsstory. *Editor & Publisher*. 75:7. February 14, 1942. Reprinted by permission.

and key officers of administrative agencies who now must submit all speeches, for clearance before delivery, to the Office of Facts and Figures.

The federal judiciary, naturally, does not come within the censorship rules since it is not a news source in the accepted meaning of the term. . . .

An example of the type or propaganda activity in which O.F.F. will engage came to light recently when West Coast newspapers were asked to give their readers editorial assurance that there is no real basis for hysteria and panic. The Department of Justice has the situation well in hand, was the suggested theme of the editorial campaign designed to allay fear of Japanese invasion or sabotage.

The results of that effort were not pleasing. Shortly afterward, Administration Senator Sheridan Downey of California carried the same message to his state via radio. Representative Leland Ford of Santa Monica, Cal., a Republican, says he sought radio time to "tell the other side," and that he was first granted time but later told he could speak only in the event his address was cleared by O.F.F.

February 14

Industry Feels Censorship [20]

Industry is also subject to the wartime rules of censorship which apply to newspapers, magazines, and radio. The specific restrictions of the code of censorship apply to advertising, house organs, catalogs, other industry publications, and interviews with the press.

The two general tests to apply to this problem are, first, don't disseminate information of value to the enemy; second, don't withhold information of common knowledge. These two

[20] From "How Censorship Affects Industry." *Modern Industry.* 3:60. February 14, 1942. Reprinted by permission.

rules are vague, subject to varied interpretation, and sometimes confusing.

In case of doubt the question should be submitted to the army or navy, if it affects either of these services, or to the Office of Censorship. Both the army and navy have public relations staffs equipped to give quick clearance to manuscripts, advertising copy, and photographs.

In giving out information to newspaper and magazine writers, company officials and plant managers should remember that responsibility for observing the censorship code rests with the publishers. This means that if a manuscript is to be cleared with the appropriate government officials before publication, the company spokesman need not hesitate in giving the writer information about production methods, labor supply, and operating problems which would be of value to the general public and to other war contractors provided this information does not come within the specific bans of the code. As a matter of fact, the Office of Censorship is somewhat concerned lest some contractors withhold information of no particular value to the enemy but which might be of great assistance to other companies in converting to war production and in speeding output.

The section of the code which covers production information directly affects industrial advertising and house organs, both as to printed copy and photographs.

FEBRUARY 23

NEW RADIO BAN [21]

Testimonials and request numbers on network programs relayed to the West Coast were banned, probably temporarily, last week as a result of a sudden order from the Fourth Interceptor Command in Los Angeles, because of possible coded espionage

[21] From "Army Command on West Coast Forbids Net Testimonials and Request Programs," newsstory. *Broadcasting.* 22:14. February 23, 1942. Reprinted by permission.

which would give aid and comfort to the enemy. Simultaneously, many stations along the Coast have agreed to forego request programs and any other "communications from the public" for the same reason and were said to have been threatened with shutdown if they did not comply.

The matter immediately was taken up with J. Harold Ryan, assistant director of censorship for radio, and the War Department Radio Branch. Mr. Ryan and Ed Kirby, chief of the Radio Branch, promptly decided to dispatch R. C. Coleson, administrative chief of the Radio Branch and a former West Coast broadcaster, to Los Angeles to adjust the matter and eliminate confusion.

Orders to stations and to the networks came from the F.C.C. inspector on the Coast, it was learned, following instructions from the Interceptor Command. The networks, it was reported, decided last Tuesday to comply promptly, but undertook steps to remedy the situation. Misunderstanding of the manner in which testimonials are handled in commercial programs was ascribed as the basis for the summary order.

From the war's start, the military establishment has felt that testimonials and request numbers might be employed as a means of coding intelligence to the enemy, either to submarines off the Coast or on direct pickup from higher powered stations. The fact that testimonials in commercial programs clear through at least three hands—advertiser, agency and network, as well as the party whose testimonial is used—apparently had not been conveyed to military authorities with sufficient clarity to preclude issuance of the order.

Moreover, the essential time lag in such presentations, which may run several weeks or months, would appear to dispel any possibility of subversive use. Request numbers on network programs are at a minimum and their deletion is not expected to cause any hardship, even though the element of danger there, too, may be entirely secondary.

With the issuance through the F.C.C. inspector of the orders to stations not to carry any announcements from the public to West Coast stations, confusion promptly was provoked. Such intelligence, in the first place, falls within the purview of the Office of Censorship, rather than the F.C.C. field force, it was pointed out.

One of the first repercussions following issuance of the order developed when a clear-channel West Coast station carried a network testimonial. This brought a prompt reprimand from the Interceptor Command and the F.C.C. inspector.

MARCH 1

OPEN CENSORSHIP BEGINS OPERATION [22]

Open censorship was established March 1 by Lieutenant-Commander J. R. Mickler, in charge of the United States Navy radio and cable censorship in New York, to speed transmission abroad of a press file of some 200,000 words sent daily by news services and about 30 special correspondents. This step was praised by the Foreign Press Association, which has pressed for an open censorship informing correspondents of deletions made.

"Lieutenant-Commander Mickler has been in sympathy with the association's request, but has informed us that open censorship would not be practicable until "additional personnel became available at the office of Radio and Cable Censorship at 67 Broad Street, New York," the association's publication said Feb. 27. "The personnel requirements are understood now to have been met."

Mickler told *Editor & Publisher* that thirty censors are now on duty on three watches daily at 67 Broad Street and the Press Wireless censorship in the Times Tower, Times Square. Most of the correspondents and editors have elected to have their

[22] From "Open Censorship Started in New York on Foreign File," newsstory. *Editor & Publisher.* 75:7. March 7, 1942. Reprinted by permission.

dispatches transmitted at once and then be notified of any deletions. Correspondents in Washington were advised of the censorship change and are now notified by collect telegram of any deletions made in their copy. A few feature writers have elected to be notified of changes before their stories are sent.

Not more than a half dozen appeals from rulings of the radio-cable censorship are received daily, said Mickler. Both the navy and the correspondents are "reasonably satisfied" on decisions reached after discussion of points at issue, he added.

The three forms of procedure open to correspondents are: (1) to have censored cables transmitted as they stand, with later notification of changes; (2) to have cables held until the writer can be reached by phone and told of deletions, or (3) to give the navy censorship discretion to transmit at once or hold the cables until an effort to inform the correspondent of deletions is made.

MARCH 9

ADVERTISING CENSORED [23]

Stating that "it is not the desire of the Office of Censorship to diminish the effectiveness of advertising" which "can help speed the industrial effort," John H. Sorrells, assistant director of the office, has given specific answers to a series of twenty-four questions concerning wartime advertising procedure, submitted by the Association of National Advertisers.

Answers reveal that in general there are no specific requirements or prohibitions but that advertisers should be guided by the principle of not disclosing information that the enemy could use in a military way. Names and addresses of officers to whom doubtful copy should be submitted are given.

Prefacing his answers to the A.N.A. questions, Mr. Sorrells outlines the general situation as follows:

[23] From "Censor Formulas Given Advertising," newsstory. *Broadcasting*. 22:36. March 9, 1942. Reprinted by permission.

I would like to say in this connection that it is not the desire of the Office of Censorship to diminish the effectiveness of advertising. We believe that the story of the American war effort is one which should be told properly by every media at hand. American industry will benefit by anything which will help accelerate the tempo of our war accomplishment. Advertising, properly conceived, can help speed the industrial effort, as it has in the past been a tremendous factor in promoting the American system of mass production.

The advertiser must realize, of course, that he shares equal responsibility with the editor and the publisher for suppressing information that the enemy could use to inflict damages on our forces, or sabotage our industrial effort.

Manufacturers of material and equipment used by our military forces should guard against specific disclosures of plant locations, either in copy or illustrations. They should not reveal specific details concerning the nature or the type of material or equipment they are producing. They should not reveal production progress in specific figures. They should not reveal their stocks and surpluses or raw materials. They should not describe new designs or new processes or even new experiments with new designs and processes.

However, advertising copy can stress the skill and the inventiveness of the engineer, of the chemist and the designer, in general terms. Advertising can describe the extent of manufacturers' facilities, without specific disclosures of plant locations, or of the nature of production or of the performance of their production, etc.

MARCH 12

AMATEUR PHOTOGRAPHY HIT [24]

Amateur photographers were reminded today by Byron Price, Director of Censorship, that they have an important part in keeping vital information from the enemy.

The government has no intention of discouraging picture-taking, [Mr. Price said] but there are many good photographic subjects besides fortifications, airports, troop transports, and equipment of the armed forces.

Even the private circulation of many such pictures domestically can do harm, and of course no military pictures can be permitted to

[24] News release from Office of Censorship, March 12, 1942.

leave the country unless they have been made under government supervision. When a photograph or a film is stopped by censors at the border it is wasted, and in these days, especially, waste is unwise.

Camera clubs have expressed a desire to cooperate in avoiding the taking of photographs of a military nature. Their patriotic understanding is highly commendable.

Detailed information about the handling of all types of films by international mail, freight, or express is being prepared and will be made public soon.

The Office of Censorship has received many inquiries as to why newspapers, magazines and news reels present pictures of such scenes as army camps, warships, and plants where war supplies are being made.

I believe there is little real cause for apprehension. These pictures normally have been approved in advance by the government for publication in order to show the American people what the armed services are doing and what American factories are producing. They have been closely inspected to make certain that they contain no details which the enemy might like to see. Editors voluntarily are making a careful check on the photographs they use.

It must be remembered also that until the Japanese attack on Pearl Harbor last December 7, there were no limitations on the mailing of pictures to foreign countries. It would be futile to ask American editors not to print photographs which could have been taken before that time, for the enemy unquestionably has the information.

MARCH 12

NAVY UNIFIES RULES [25]

Unified rules in naval districts throughout the country in the matter of sinkings of merchant ships and tankers flying the American flag have been developed for dealings with the press as a result of criticisms in recent weeks, representatives of wire services and metropolitan morning newspapers were informed March 12 at a conference with the Public Relations Officer of the Third Naval District, New York. The meeting was called to clear up misunderstandings and irritation at delays in news

[25] By Walter E. Schneider. From "Navy Unifies News Rules on United States Ship Sinkings," newsstory. *Editor & Publisher.* Volume 75:9, March 14, 1942. Reprinted by permission.

clearance after considerable criticism had been voiced in the press, *Editor & Publisher* and elsewhere. . . .

Thursday's conference apparently clarified the atmosphere of navy-newspaper relations in the Third District, providing a better undestanding of each other's problems and even bringing the suggestion of cooperation on "positive" navy news to offset the present predominance of ship sinkings and negative rulings required by reasons of security. Commander Tuthill admitted that the Third District had been "tough" as compared with other districts, but he pointed out that as a result of recent conferences of P.R.O. officers in Washington there would be similar handling of news in every district. Tuthill said that at a recent conference held in Washington he pressed for uniform naval press relations because districts which were "easier" with the press were more favorably considered by newspapermen but the Third District came in for criticism because it was doing its job more efficiently from a navy standpoint.

It was stressed by Commander Tuthill that his office is not one of censorship but "a cooperative agency" on news involving the navy. . . . [He] told of several instances in which newspapers had "jumped the gun" on releases of ship sinkings or picture clearance. He warned that "today is set as the deadline for stopping that" and indicated that Washington would be advised of future violations with the view of indictment of persistent offenders of regulations.

At the suggestion of more "positive" stories of navy activity, Tuthill agreed to assign one of his staff to survey the district for possible feature stories and compile lists of these for the newspapers. . . .

Unless a tip involving naval action or survivors received by a newspaper is confirmed by the Navy Office of Public Relations, at Washington, no details can be furnished until the story is released simultaneously to all services. "It is intended that Commandants (Public Relations Officers) should furnish complete information on the subject in order that an intelligent decision may be made," the Commander said. "No story is going to be cleared as such—only an announcement that 'the American flagship S. S. —— was sunk,' etc."

Upon clearance of news by the Navy Department the local district arranges (as heretofore) a conference call to A.P., U.P., I.N.S., A.P. New York local, Standard News and Transradio, another to C.B.S., N.B.C. and M.B.S., and if pictures are involved, a third call is made to picture services but not to individual papers.

Photos of navy ships now may be obtained from 90 Church Street when the news involved is officially released. Where only one print is available, one of the four picture services is chosen by lot and gives out prints simultaneously to all services.

MARCH 18

PUBLICATIONS LICENSED FOR EXPORT [26]

A licensing system to expedite censorship of publications containing scientific, technical, or professional data for mailing abroad will be put into effect April 1 by the Office of Censorship, with the cooperation of the Board of Economic Warfare.

The procedure calls for advance review of the material by the Technical Data License Division of the Board of Economic Warfare. When the Division finds that the publication contains no information of value to the enemy, the Office of Censorship will grant a license for its export. . . .

The Technical Data License Division will endeavor to review publications within 48 hours. If certain portions are not approved, the material may be rewritten and submitted again.

[26] News release from Office of Censorship, March 18, 1942.

MARCH 23

O.F.F. ISSUES NEWS GUIDE [27]

Policies governing the release of war information by the government, intended as an explanatory statement to the public but serving also as a guidepost to news reporters and commentators of both radio and the press, were made public last Wednesday by the Committee on War Information of the Office of Facts and Figures, which actually is the government's high command so far as war news policy is concerned.

Containing a pledge that the American people will get every bit of war news, bad as well as good, so long as its publication does not give aid and comfort to the enemy, the committee included in its policy statement the long-awaited decision on publication of casualty lists. It ordered that lists of members of the armed forces killed in action will be made public but that press and radio shall not publish nation-wide summaries of casualties, instead confining themselves to those from their own localities.

The O.F.F. committee's statement covers policies for handling news from all of the agencies most actively engaged in the war effort, including army, navy, W.P.B., and Maritime Commission. . . .

It is the policy of this government, [says the C.W.I. policy statement] to make public the maximum of information on military, naval, production, and other matters concerning the war, which can be revealed without giving aid to the enemy. This policy is based upon the firm conviction that the people of a democracy are entitled to know the facts, whether they are good or bad, cheerful or depressing. On the other hand, our people will willingly forego knowledge of those facts whose revelation will help the enemy to harm us.

Where there is conflict between consideration of public information and of military security, every attempt is made to provide such form

[27] From "Official Policy Issued by O.F.F. as Guide to Handling of News," newsstory. *Broadcasting.* 22:22. March 23, 1942. Reprinted by permission.
Full text of specific news policies laid down by the Committee on War Information appears in the Appendix.

of publication as will inform the public while reducing the military risk to a minimum. Under no circumstances does the government publish information which is known to be untrue. Under no circumstances does the government withhold news from publication on the ground that the news is bad or depressing. When news is deliberately withheld, it is withheld for reasons of military security.

MARCH 28

CLARIFICATION OF "TROOPS" CLAUSE [28]

Upon reading the "Troops" and "Ships" clauses of the Code of Wartime Practices for the American Press, you will reach this conclusion:

There should be no identification of soldiers on ships, soldiers on their way to embarkation points, soldiers and sailors in combat areas or coastal defense, or the location of coastal or anti-aircraft forces.

As you may know, the army is furnishing mailing addresses for the various men in combat services, and addresses from this source can be used. The situation is different with respect to the navy, where the linking of a sailor, ship and post office might disclose at least broadly the tactical disposition of the ship. We are informed that the navy would prefer to have lists of sailors' addresses omitted where they include the names of ships.

Names of individuals stationed in combat areas outside the United States may be published after there has been official announcement of the presence of American troops in such areas. No mention should be made of their military units.

Examples of what is and what is not appropriate for publication are as follows:

1. John Doe, recently inducted at Camp Grant, has been sent to Jefferson Barracks, Mo.—That is appropriate for publication.

2. John Doe, recently at Camp Walters, Texas, has been

[28] From a release by the Office of Censorship to editors inquiring for information on identification of servicemen for use in local papers. Reprinted in *Editor & Publisher*. 75:8. March 28, 1942.

transferred to Camp Croft, S.C. His address is Co. B, Inf. 34.—Appropriate for publication.

3. John Doe's parents have rec'd. word that their son would like to receive mail from his friends. His address is Co. C, 14th Infantry, Ft. Knox, Ky.—Appropriate.

4. John Doe, formerly stationed at Baer Field, Ft. Wayne, Ind., has been transferred to Port Angeles, Wash., and writes he expects to leave soon for an unknown destination.—Not appropriate for publication.

5. John Doe, home on furlough from Camp Forrest, has rec'd. a telephone call from Wash., D. C., advising him to be in New York on Feb. 4 to leave for foreign service.—Not appropriate for publication.

6. John Doe's parents have rec'd. word that their son has arrived in Northern Ireland.—Appropriate for publication.

7. John Doe's parents rec'd. word last night that their son is leaving by boat for an unknown destination.—Not appropriate for publication.

8. John Doe is stationed at Clark Field in the Philippines.—Appropriate for publication.

MARCH 31

MAPS REGULATED [29]

Cooperation of map makers, editors, and manufacturers was requested by the Office of Censorship today in making certain that new maps carry no reference to military depots and war production plants.

"No maps should be published or distributed showing military depots of any kind, such as air, quartermaster, or ordnance depots; key war production plants, arsenals, ammunition or explosive plants of any kind," the Office of Censorship an-

[29] A release from the Office of Censorship, March 31, 1942.

nounced.   Omission of military air fields constructed since December 7, 1941, also was requested.

Maps already in existence are not affected by this action. Names and locations of military camps, posts, and stations may be shown, provided that no indication is given of their size or strength.

Byron Price, Director of Censorship, explained that the announcement amplified the reference to maps in the Code of Wartime Practices for the American Press.   The Code asked that no maps disclose the location of munition dumps or other restricted army and naval areas.   Mr. Price pointed out that it is permissible to publish maps showing the general theater of war or large-scale zones of action, because they do not furnish any information to the enemy.

April 15

Tentative Licensing Plan [30]

In Washington late last month the Office of Censorship announced that beginning April 1, export licenses would be required for overseas copies of "publications devoted in whole or in part to technical, professional or scientific matter." *Time* promptly switched all foreign subscribers to the special Air Express Edition it sends Latin American readers.

But last fortnight the Office of Censorship indefinitely postponed the starting date of the new regulations.   As originally conceived, the licensing scheme was to apply only to technical and trade journals and a few special cases like *Time*.   Now the government is thinking about extending the requirement to all magazines.

Theory is that certain war information is fit for the eyes of United States citizens but not for the outside world.   Maga-

[30] From "Export Magazines," newsstory. *Tide*. 16:12. April 15, 1942. Reprinted by permission.

zines leaving the United States (like all outgoing mail) are already subject to censorship by postal authorities. Under the new plan, censoring would be done in advance, and licenses issued, by the Technical Data License Division of the Board of Economic Warfare.

With a special issue for its Latin subscribers already at hand, *Time* had been in an ideal position to avoid submitting its regular domestic edition to censorship. Few if any other general magazines (including *Time's* own running mates *Life* and *Fortune*) could expect to solve the problem so readily.

Many of them have good-sized foreign circulations, particularly in Canada. Samples (as of June 30, 1941): *Collier's* —83,000; *Good Housekeeping*—71,000; *Look*—62,000; *Redbook*—70,000; *Country Gentleman*—94,000; *Mademoiselle*—18,000.

If the licensing proviso should extend over the whole magazine field, publishers with minuscule foreign readership— particularly trade papers—may simply drop their foreign circulation outright to save time and trouble.

But most general magazines will probably adopt the procedure of submitting a copy to Washington at the start of a press run, and printing their foreign copies (with any necessary revisions) at the very last.

Some technical publications do have foreign circulations substantial enough to justify some pains: McGraw-Hill, for example, whose 20-odd books have about 42,000 Canadian and overseas readers (out of 550,000); Chilton, whose *Iron Age* has around 1,200 out of 17,000.

As some others have done, both McGraw-Hill and *Iron Age*, have, incidentally, cut the so-called European neutrals (Sweden, Turkey, et al.) off their lists since Pearl Harbor. When the licensing setup finally goes into effect, it is possible that the censors will discriminate between different countries—being, for instance, more lenient on copies bound for an ally like England, with its own stringent censorship, than it would in the case of some easygoing Latin American nations.

Nobody was making any hard and fast plans, however, until the situation clarified. That was not likely to happen much before next month. The Technical License and Data Division—which had promised to give 48-hour service—originally expected to have one man do the whole job. When the idea of licensing publications outside the trade-paper field arose, it became obvious that a large staff would be required—possibly with regional offices.

Last week the agency was still working on organization details, as well as on the question of how much of the magazine field it should attempt to cover.

April 28

"Loyal" Papers Cleared [31]

Attorney General Francis Biddle has given his assurance that newspapers loyal to the United States, regardless of the language in which they are printed, need fear no interference by the Federal Government. The Department of Justice released Mr. Biddle's reply to Representative Samuel A. Weiss of Pennsylvania, who had wired that "many advertising companies have deemed it advisable to discontinue advertisements" in foreign language publications on the ground that the Department plans indiscriminate suppression. Biddle answered: "Appropriate action against seditious newspapers will be taken regardless of the language in which they are printed, but those loyal to the United States have nothing to fear from the government."

[31] From "Biddle Reassures 'Loyal' Newspapers," newsstory. *Editor & Publisher.* 75:8. May 2, 1942. Reprinted by permission.

JUNE 20

WAR NEWS REVISION [32]

The appointment of Elmer Davis, radio commentator, author and former reporter, as director of government news and propaganda was taken as a concession by the Administration of the need for a better information service and as an expression of its hope that the most glaring faults of the prevailing system can be corrected.

Mr. Davis, briefly, is to absorb into one organization—the Office of War Information—the several "overall" publicity services which have mushroomed into being, with overlapping functions, under direction of squabbling amateurs and professionals. In addition, he is to have full authority to do what he likes with the numerous publicity offices of government departments and agencies, many of which have worked at cross purposes. He is to synchronize and direct foreign propaganda, except in Latin America, as well as to have the final word on domestic information, insofar as this comes from official sources.

There has been widespread criticism of the official information set-up as it has existed to date on two fronts: First, with regard to the type of information made public and withheld; second, with respect to organization and personnel. The two have not been unrelated, most critics agree. To understand the news difficulties, it is advisable to go first into organizational troubles which grew partly from too much machinery and decentralized authorities.

Side by side, there have existed the Office of Facts and Figures, headed by Archibald MacLeish, poet and Librarian of Congress; the Office of Government Reports headed by Lowell Mellett, a former Scripps Howard editor; the division of infor-

[32] By Frank L. Kluckhohn. From "War News System Reshaped." *New York Times.* 91:5E. June 21, 1942. Reprinted by permission.
Full text of Executive Order creating the Office of War Information appears in the Appendix.

mation of the Office of Emergency Management, which, with Robert Horton as its chief, controlled public relations of such vital organizations as the W.P.B., O.P.A. and the War Labor Board. William J. Donovan, with the impressive but misleading title of Coordinator of Information, directed foreign propaganda. The War and Navy Departments built up publicity organizations employing hundreds. And the individual agencies and departments handling war problems beat the publicity drums for their own ideas and projects.

Despite attempts at coordination of this monster, it obviously was inevitable that there should be inter-agency jealousy over prerogatives, widespread duplication and persons back-biting and "politicing" in search for additional power and duties.

Mr. Price, on leave as executive news editor of the Associated Press, has, in the opinion of most observers, shown what a well-trained professional, working with a small but experienced and efficient staff, could accomplish in the face of great obstacles.

The multiplicity of agencies and the spotty nature of their personnel had created chaos in the information field. But the tendency has been to correct mistakes, replace inefficient personnel with superior workers, and, generally, to "shake down" the organization to better shape. Therefore, good ground-work has been laid for the kind of job Mr. Davis is to undertake.

The chief public complaint, which has been voiced widely, is that officials do not seem to trust the public, and that good news has, on all too many occasions, been issued, and bad news minimized, twisted, or long suppressed. This complaint the Administration is understood to be most anxious to eliminate. A second complaint with which several high officials at least agree, is that information is withheld that cannot have military value to the enemy, and a third is that conflicting statements are given out by different officials, thus confusing the public.

Those who get the news to the public through the press, radio and other media of information often have found that one agency of the government was willing, and even anxious, to get out a piece of information, while another has succeeded in getting it suppressed.

The personnel of the army and navy public relations branches, most of those who have dealings with them say, is most anxious to be of all possible aid. But information is withheld from these branches from above, and most of the public relations officers do not even have the opportunity of exercising their judgment.

President Roosevelt conceded at a recent press conference that the time was close when publication of United States war production figures would be more harmful than helpful to the enemy. Public confusion with regard to gasoline and rubber rationing, caused by issuance of insufficient, garbled and contradictory information on conditions caused such an outcry from some parts of the country that it registered at the White House itself. Thus it is hoped, although by no means presumed, that the policy of almost completely bottling up news will be modified.

JUNE 24

RADIO CODE REVISION [33]

Considerably revised and amplified, and incorporating many new provisions based on experience gained since the original wartime censorship codes were promulgated last Jan. 15, the new Code of Wartime Practices for American Broadcasting, bearing a June 15 date, was released in a new format by the Office of Censorship last Friday. It retains the voluntary aspect of the old code, and goes into effect immediately.

Like the Code of Wartime Practices for the American Press, which in part it parallels and a revised edition of which was

[33] From "Revised Radio Code Clears Many Problems," newsstory. *Broadcasting.* 22:7. June 29, 1942. Reprinted by permission.
  Complete texts of the revised press and radio codes are included in the Appendix.

released simultaneously, the new broadcasters' code is designed to clarify many questions arising in the daily handling of news, commentaries, descriptions, quizzes, dramatic programs, commercial continuity and foreign-language programs.

JUNE 28

CHANGE IN NEWS POLICY AHEAD [34]

On Friday President Roosevelt stated that in May the United States produced 4,000 airplanes for war purposes. He said he thought the information would hurt rather than help the enemy. The President's statement represented a change in policy which may or may not have been a reaction to the public feeling that it is not being told enough about what this country is doing in the war. It was only two months ago that irritation was shown in high places in Washington because a member of Congress said in a speech that in the preceding month we had produced 3,000 planes. Now it is the President himself who releases the information.

To a degree this incident raises the issue of war publicity and seems to justify the hope that a way is going to be found to release safely more information about what our army, our navy and our industry are doing toward winning the war. Just as has been the case in other countries, the matter of war information had become immensely involved. It is historical that army and navy leaders are prone to be bearish on the release of facts regarding engagements. That is understandable, of course. Over against the professional fighting man's predilection to the advantages of secrecy has to be put the large question of how much advantage to morale is the greatest degree of frankness which may be safely adopted.

[34] By Edwin L. James. From "Washington Publicity Due for Improvement." *New York Times.* 91:3E. June 28, 1942. Reprinted by permission.

Only a short while ago the matter of the release of information was befogged by the multiplicity of agencies involved. On the one hand there was the censorship, under the able direction of Byron Price, with its set of rules. Censorship is by its very nature a passive and restrictive operation. It could not be otherwise. What has been needed is more information from government quarters.

There was general satisfaction over the appointment of Elmer Davis as head of all government information. On paper, Mr. Davis has enormous powers. He has a big initial job in bringing into working harmony the large number of bureaus, not all working in harmony, over which he has been placed. When that has been accomplished, he will be freer to attack his larger and more important duties. The official statements did not entirely clarify the duties of Mr. Swope for the army and Mr. Bullitt for the navy. But if, as seems logical, these gentlemen have been named to aid Mr. Davis as head of all government publicity, the results ought to be all to the good. Surely, there can be no foundation to the reports that their duties would run concurrently with those of Mr. Davis. That would be merely shoving the situation back to where it seemed to be before Mr. Davis was appointed.

The matter of wartime publicity will never be arranged properly until there is one head who can make policy and who has the power to take his problems directly to the highest authority. That power appeared to be given Mr. Davis in plenitude under the terms of his commission.

Naturally the big problem is to adjust the desirability of keeping the public informed with the desirability of avoiding giving useful information to the enemy. There is the conflict of motives and a good result must represent a nice adjustment of those two desiderata. But a side issue, which has its propaganda importance, relates to explaining to the public why certain information may not be issued. That is something regarding which the public finds itself largely in the dark.

It is true that this angle often explains itself eventually. The Coral Sea business is a case in point. The "Lexington" did not sink until many miles away from the scene of the engagement. It was by no means sure that the Japanese knew the big carrier had sunk. And when it was explained that way when the loss of the "Lexington" was announced every one was satisfied the matter had been correctly handled.

The bombing of Tokyo was another case. For a fortnight the only information the American public had about the air raid on the Japanese capital came from enemy sources, and, it should be borne in mind, there had been many official warnings against believing broadcasts from enemy countries. But when it became plain, as it now has, that Japan does not yet know how the United States planes reached Tokyo, it can be seen that there was a good reason for official quiescence following the raid.

A case which is now worrying the public is that of the Aleutian Islands. The announcement that the Japanese had landed on several of the islands came from Japanese sources. At first Washington denied it; then Washington admitted it. There has been almost no information regarding activity in those regions, except from enemy sources. The statements that bad weather interferes with activity and the obtaining of information is none too impressive when the Japanese make definite statements about what goes on.

But the incident which has caused the most criticism of the lack of information about the Aleutian Islands related to the arrival in Seattle of a ship containing a number of travelers from Dutch Harbor. They gave a graphic description of the Japanese attack on that United States base, estimates of the damage and casualties. The censorship passed this information and it was published. Now the question being asked is why Washington could not have released some such information beforehand, since obviously it was available. Or, turning it around, if it was unwise to make known this information, why did the censorship pass it when the ship reached Seattle? It is

a little too much to ask the public to believe that the arrival
of the ship at Seattle happened to correspond exactly in time
with the moment when it was safe to release the information.
This is not an overwhelmingly important case, but it does serve
well to show why the public feels it is being somewhat short-
changed on war information from Washington.

Another matter which causes public worry relates to the
flood of reports that German U-boats have been landing men
on the United States coasts. Every newspaper gets these reports
all the time. There are rumors of landings of Germans, by twos
and threes, on the Maine Coast, on Long Island, on the Jersey
Coast and on the Virginia and Carolina Coasts. A newspaper
editor got the idea the other day that since many thousands of
Americans are going to the seashore for the Summer, it might
be a good idea if Washington made some announcement regarding the landing of Germans from U-boats or the possibility of
it, for thereby thousands at the seashore might be on the lookout.

The answer was that the navy knew nothing about it, that
if any Germans had landed it was an affair for the F.B.I. and
the F.B.I. until last night would not discuss it.

To put it bluntly, the American public can be depended upon
to take bad news; in fact, the public wants to know what goes
on, bad or good. The public may also be depended upon to be
patient when there is an explanation of why patience is required.
What has the public worried is to be in a sort of mental blackout. It is obviously going to be the job of Mr. Davis to shoot
permissible rays of information through those shadows.

CENSORSHIP IN OPERATION

A SUMMARY OF NEWS RESTRICTION [1]

The people of this country are hearing more and more about censorship of news from Washington and about propaganda agencies set up in Washington. This is raising some question about how much news is being told and how reliable is the information still being issued.

Experience of recent weeks points to these conclusions:

There is absolute restriction upon news of day-to-day fighting. The only information that may be given out is official information. There is much less restriction upon news and analysis not related to specific movement of ships or troops, so long as aid and comfort are not given to the enemy. A growing number of government figures are being suppressed. Weather reports are curtailed. Some outright propaganda is beginning to be manufactured. It is based upon tangible things, however, and there are no agencies writing faked releases in the Nazi manner.

In the field of military and naval information, official communiques give the facts that bear the government's stamp. There is every reason to believe that these communiques are written honestly and are a fair statement of situations, although they are brief and of not much help in appraising the over-all picture. Army and navy officers and officials of the War, Navy and other departments still are permitted to supply writers of proved reliability with background information that is useful in interpreting and analyzing the news. Also, War Secretary Stimson is continuing to be of great help with regular press conferences. Since Pearl Harbor, the navy's press conferences have been few and far between. All in all, the reader continues to have access to important information.

[1] From "Censorship of the News: Effect on Press and Reader," newsstory. *United States News.* 12:17. February 6, 1942. Reprinted by permission.

In the field of general news, President Roosevelt continues to hold his twice-weekly press conferences. He is not as free with comment and news as in the past, but he does submit to questioning and does give information, both on military and on other subjects, that is of great value. Most Cabinet officers have discontinued their regular meetings with newspapermen. They apparently are afraid that, under questioning, they might make a slip that would be giving information that was not supposed to be released.

In the field of statistics . . . the censorship is falling with the heaviest hand. Every figure that the government releases is being subjected to scrutiny to discover if it might in any way give information to the enemy. Detailed reports on exports and imports are discontinued. Publication of figures on army and navy contracts and figures of plant construction now is prohibited. This prohibition may open the way to great abuse, but officials refuse to unbend from their present stand. Treasury Secretary Morgenthau, to date, is successfully resisting pressure to shut off vitally important information on Treasury operations. Censors are even threatening to blue pencil figures on employment of labor and on farm output.

In the field of exported information, censorship . . . is rigid. In other words, information that is sent outside the United States, either in published form or on the air, or otherwise, is carefully scanned by a censor.

Within the United States, no censor sits in the office of a newspaper or magazine and reads, or passes upon, information that is to be published. The censorship is voluntary and self-imposed. Nobody is proposing at this time to bar criticism, or to suppress any information that is outside the field of specific movement of troops or of ships, or which would give aid and comfort to the enemy. In fact, Director of Censorship Byron Price went to bat this past week in support of newspapermen who had learned that Midwestern troops made up the contingent that landed in North Ireland. The army gave up its objection at the censor's urging.

However, there are a few signs that military officials desire to see and to pass upon stories of a military nature before publication. Likewise, it is true that censorship in Britain appears to be less inclusive than here. British officials apparently are more ready to talk than American.

One card is always kept up the sleeve of American reporters. If the present mild censorship should become more drastic than the situation warrants, there always is Congress to fall back upon. Congress can ask questions and receive answers that then are available to reporters.

RESULTS OF THE FIRST SEVEN WEEKS [2]

The Office of Censorship is entering its seventh week of operation.

During the six weeks past, the Radio Division of the Office has turned out about 500 letters, some 80 per cent of them opinions on specific programs presented by radio broadcasters.

These letters were written in response to queries which flowed into the Office following issuance of the Code of Wartime Practices for American Broadcasters.

Most of the requests sought clearance for programs of the man-on-the-street type. Some of them sought the Office's interpretation on specific request programs.

The radio division has not had a difficult job, for most broadcasters realized the necessity for certain controls long before the Office was established and thus were in observance of the code's suggestions before they were written.

This evident alertness of broadcasters and newspapermen to the need for caution justified Byron Price, Director of Censor-

[2] By John Harold Ryan, Assistant Director of Censorship. From "The Test—Can the Enemy Utilize It?" newsstory. *Broadcasting.* 22:15. February 16, 1942. Reprinted by permission.

ship, in his determination to keep the codes of both divisions strictly voluntary in application. Perhaps the most significant statement in the 2,500 words of the Code of Wartime Practices for American Broadcasters is in the second paragraph of the document:

> The broadcasting industry has enlisted with enthusiasm in the endeavor, and the following is intended to be helpful in systematizing cooperation on a *voluntary* basis during the period of the emergency.

The code is a springboard then—a general concept of the industry's problems in time of war. It is the job of the Office of Censorship to see to it insofar as possible, that information of value to the enemy be kept from him. Although the formal staff of the radio division in the Office of Censorship includes only five people, every broadcaster who speaks on the air or supervises the work of those who do perform before microphones is a censor. His conduct during the difficult days ahead should be considered in light of the question, "Will I be helping the fellow who's hurting me?"

The industry's acceptance of suggested restrictions set down in the code has evidenced the broadcaster's thorough understanding of his wartime responsibility. Some there were who didn't picture the quiz program section of the code in the same way that we in Censorship saw it. Certain compromises were suggested for the salvation of the man-in-the-street type of program. But it has been our basis of interpretation in considering these proposals that no informal, catch-as-catch-can interview type of program is free of danger if a given individual can enjoy reasonable guarantee of participation.

The same general interpretation applies in the case of request programs. Any request program which, because of its pattern, lends itself to the machinations of the enemy should be changed or taken off the air. The determinant is, "Can the enemy utilize it?"

It requires little ingenuity to enforce your participation on programs which fall into either of these categories.

The man who operates a small station in some area far from national boundaries might think that such regulation works an unnecessary hardship on him. He must remember that this is an all-out war effort. Although he may not know it, there might be a half-dozen plants in his area manufacturing defense materials. Those plants are potential victims of saboteurs, and such agents as these must have methods of communicating *with each other* as well as with their superiors who may be located miles away. Maybe such a plant manufactures only firing pins for 77 mm. guns. But should the efforts of saboteurs destroy 10,000 of those pins, 10,000 desperately needed artillery pieces would be shelved until new machines could be tooled and new pins turned out.

Remember, too, that you do not know the power of your 250 or 1,000 or 5,000 watts. A manager of a West Coast radio station was in my office the other day. Eight years ago he was a telegrapher on a ship operating in China waters. At nighttime, when standard broadcast channels cleared, he could pick up 287 United States broadcasting stations across those thousands of miles. And his receiver was a one-tube unit. That was eight years ago, and modern transmitters are much more efficient.

The questions put to us in Censorship by broadcasters indicate their awareness to the dangers. We are fearful, nevertheless, that many radio stations are carrying right now programs which unwittingly lend themselves to the aid of the enemy. If we could speak personally to each broadcaster, we would ask him again to read his code, to digest the precautions it outlines and then to re-scrutinize his programs.

Thus far, the Radio Division of Censorship has issued two confidential reports pursuant to that section of the code which provides that certain general communications will be directed to broadcasters as experience dictates the need of deletions or enlargements. There has been evidence that some broadcasters are having difficulty establishing the identity of "appropriate authorities" in observing the news section of the code. The Office of Censorship is bending all efforts toward an early clarification of this problem.

But, in the last analysis, the purpose of Censorship is as much an assignment for the broadcaster as it is for the constituted officers in the censorship division of the government. Only in this nation of all nations, free or enslaved, is the broadcaster a free agent in determining the programs his listeners will hear.

No broadcaster's coverage map describes his audience completely. Within range of his station's signal are thousands and thousands of loyal, liberty-loving Americans; but listening, too— and be certain you believe this—are those who would throttle the institutions and the traditions we believe in. That's what the war's all about. And that's what censorship is all about.

THE CENSOR AT WORK [3]

The office of Censor Byron Price has gone into around-the-clock operation and is clearing an average of 25 stories each day for Washington correspondents and their home offices. . . .

Censor Price maintains overall supervision of both the press and radio codes and is the "court of last appeal" on issues submitted to him by the staff, but direct relations with the press are handled by John H. Sorrels, assistant director.

In the short time the Office of Censorship has been in operation, correspondents have experienced the novelty of immediate and direct contact with the key men, in contrast with the red-tape that must be cut before an interview or telephone conversation may be had with many of the functionaries in federal agencies who bear the title "information specialists."

[3] By James J. Butler. From "Censor's Office Works Smoothly on War News." *Editor & Publisher.* 75:9. February 21, 1942. Reprinted by permission.

The cooperation shown by the press has been "splendid," Mr. Sorrells concedes. And, he added, the general public has been similarly cooperative. Few of the calls received spring from a conflict with public relations officers of the armed services, and only occasionally is there a critical word about censorship as a whole, he finds.

Inquiries from Washington correspondents comprise about 50 per cent of all received, and they come for the most part by telephone. Some long-distance calls are received but the out-of-town business is principally requests for examination of submitted manuscripts.

Surprisingly, the most difficult situation that has arisen since censorship became effective—the "S.S. Lafayette" fire—did not reach the Office of Censor; neither Mr. Price nor any of his assistants was asked to step into the fray caused by Navy Department press relations men in New York City. . . .

The operations of the Office of Censor can, perhaps, be best illustrated by tracing the course of an actual query. A Pennsylvania newspaper telephoned its Washington correspondent to say that an $8,000,000 addition to a munitions plant was being constructed on a site abutting a heavily-traveled highway. While it was common knowledge in the community that the huge foundation work was to support an immense building (even the $8,000,000 figure was generally known), plant officials declined to discuss the subject with reporters for the local newspaper, "on orders from Washington." The newspaper asked its correspondent to inquire whether mention might be made of the project.

The facts were related to the Navy Department bureau of public relations. It was true, the navy replied off-the-record, that an $8,000,000 plant was being constructed in the community named, but the production was to be for lend-lease, and it was suggested that clearance should come either from the lend-lease authorities or the Office of Censor.

The recital was repeated to Mr. Sorrels who quoted the following paragraph from the prohibitions of the newspaper code:

Specific information about the location of, or other information about, sites and factories already in existence, which would aid saboteurs in gaining access to them; information other than that readily gained through observation by the general public, disclosing the location of sites and factories yet to be established of the nature of their production.

Mr. Sorrells inquired whether the newspaper was one of substantially local circulation and was informed that was the case. Applying the section quoted above, he reasoned that much of the information was of a nature "readily gained through observation by the general public." With the admonition that too specific a description must be avoided and none of the material was to be placed on association wires or otherwise disseminated beyond the service area of the newspaper, he cleared the story for publication.

The Pennsylvania city editor had permission to publish his story within 15 minutes after he placed the inquiry at his correspondent's office.

THE CHANGING NEWS PICTURE [4]

The White House is a diminishing source of information in the rapidly changing Washington news picture and is likely to figure even less as the United States expands its military and production lines.

President Roosevelt continues to be No. 1 personage in the dispatches out of the Capital, but the news revolving about him comes from a variety of sources rather than from the Executive Mansion as was the case before Pearl Harbor. . . .

The popular conception that the Office of Censorship is a prolific news source in time of war, is a gross error. That agency issued about half a dozen press releases and these em-

[4] By James J. Butler. From "O.F.F. Instructing Government Services to Issue Propaganda," newsstory. *Editor & Publisher.* 75:5. March 21, 1942. Reprinted by permission.

braced the newspaper and radio codes, and personnel announcements.   Correspondents use the Byron Price office daily, but only
for the purpose of clearing stories for publication.

In World War I, the George Creel office was a productive
source of copy, because it was concerned with both the negative
(censorship) and the positive (propaganda) handling of news.
Censor Price deals only in the negative function. . . .

The war has created several annoyances for Washington
correspondents and censorship rules have interfered with their
copy output.

The War Department has a rule regarding awards of contracts for construction and production which states that Members
of Congress shall be given the information in advance of the
press.   Congressmen frequently wire the facts to friendly newspapers and "call backs" to Washington bureaus result.

The War and Navy Departments are not answerable to the
Price office, but are set up as "appropriate sources" which may,
if their officials desire, release information to the press.   The
navy, particularly, has decentralized its public relations and
material regarding sinkings and other sensational developments
channel through district offices rather than, as in the past, through
the department here.

Defense Plant Corporation which formerly supplied important
items on factory construction financing, no longer makes that
information public; and if D.P.C. did, the code of censorship
would prohibit mentioning the specific location.

Other typical restrictions are:

The navy does not announce its successes at sea, except in
very unusual circumstances.

The Weather Bureau no longer issues information for general
publication.

The War Production Board doesn't release information on
contracts awarded.

Movement of troops between camps within the United States
is "restricted."

Commerce Department statistics on imports and exports are not available.

Crop estimates are withheld by the Department of Agriculture.

Quotas of draft registrants assigned to a state or city may not be published in the newspapers.

THE WASHINGTON CORRESPONDENT [5]

The usual front-page story from Washington today consists of one or two announced facts, amplified by a mass of informed background, and strained through the mesh of the Espionage Act. If it is well done, the reader can almost smell the shoe leather melted into the story in the form of footwork done to develop the background. . . .

From 1920 to 1940, the essentials of my trade were a typewriter, a sheaf of paper and an "authoritative spokesman." The procedure was about the same whether one happened to specialize in White House of Congressional news, in politics generally, in finance or military affairs. These special dispatches, buttressed by the constant flow of spontaneous routine news, kept one pleasantly occupied.

Today's news involves the handling of infinitely more routing, far more work on background, and the absolute minimum of speculation, except in matters of strictly political affairs. Laws and censorship have something to do with that, but the major changes in news-reporting are due to the newspapers themselves.

You may have seen references at times to voluntary censorship by the press. It is a living code, practiced by the great majority of the newspapers. By far the great majority of newspapers are trying to play fair with the country in matters of military intelligence. Likewise, the reporters.

    [5] By Charles Hurd, Washington staff of the *New York Times*. From "Getting the News." *Redbook*. 79:54-6. July, 1942. Reprinted by permission.

In the case of the newspaper in whose bureau I work, the *New York Times,* far more stories containing information of value to the enemy have been edited down voluntarily than the few suppressed because of restrictions in the law. . . .

Except for the rare instance, Washington reporting is no longer a solo performance, but rather a matter of collaboration, sometimes between reporters and officials, but more often between reporters themselves in a pooling of specialized knowledge. . . .

On the night of December 7 there was a grave question as to the future of news-reporting in Washington. Suddenly the same news sources that had been the fountain of reports on the defense program became terribly remote. Since that date there have been mistakes and many foolish actions, but I feel certain we have skirted around the greatest dangers involved in censorship.

But the trend of the news has changed. It has pushed Congress into the background, and made the White House a point of interest even more compelling than President Roosevelt accomplished in the New Deal. It has raised the War and Navy Departments from obscure agencies into the front line of activity. It has submerged many functions of the State Department, as our Ministry of Foreign Affairs, but has brought into prominence little foreign groups which formerly were more a part of the Washington social scene than of its active life.

In the making of news, and control over it, the government has expanded agencies which a year ago were little more than plans, and many of which had not been conceived. There are at least four times as many government officials handling press-releases as there are newspaper correspondents. And on the other side of the same road is the Office of Censorship.

It would seem at first glance that this would simplify the work of the reporters; instead, it complicates it. . . .

Basic sources of spot news in Washington today are the press rooms of the War and Navy Departments. From them have come a flow of communiques on which have been built the glory of MacArthur's forces on Bataan, the day-by-day flashes of victories or losses in Asiatic waters and off the Atlantic Coast, and literally millions of words of seeming speculation on military and naval strategy. . . .

Secretary Henry L. Stimson at the War Department and Secretary Frank Knox, at the Navy, ordinarily hold press conferences once a week, but these are the least of the news sources. Nothing comes from them except material usually prepared and mimeographed in advance. . . .

Each of these press conferences is valuable only as a show-piece. What is important to reporters is the fact that these two secretaries have tried to make proper news available, if a reporter will do a little work to get it.

The Espionage Act and other laws define military secrets. No reporter may, without authorization, describe troop or ship movements, or tell the composition or size of forces, or write any other material which would simplify the task of foreign agents.

On the other hand, when the navy makes announcements of torpedoings by U-boats, it is possible to talk with experts who can explain how and why these things happen, and the problems connected with this phase of warfare. In most cases survivors of lost vessels may be interviewed. We have very little news of fleet operations, but there are obvious reasons for this secrecy.

In the War Department, long-trained officers of the highest rank periodically hold seminars with correspondents to explain by chart and figure what is happening in the various theaters of the war. Sometimes they are mistaken, and yet sometimes we reporters are mistaken. But I have not yet run into a mistake based on a desire to deceive. More often, mistakes are due to partial information.

In the Archives Building, constructed as a monumental repository for state documents, is the new Office of Censorship, over which presides Byron Price, on leave from his routine job as Executive Editor of the Associated Press.

The censorship procedure evolved by Mr. Price probably will improve as the war progresses. Yet, if it only held to the standard already set, there would not be too much cause for complaint.

Censorship in Washington does not mean that the stories we write for American newspapers must be read and blue-penciled by some government officials. This is done by the army and navy on special-feature stories written about special activities, but not regarding spontaneous news. Ordinarily stories go through Mr. Price's office and staff at the request of newspapers and magazines, which wish to be certain that the contents of them are within legal and ethical bounds.

Here is an example of how the system works:

About a week before General MacArthur turned up in Australia, my New York office suggested that we consolidate into a special story the scattered reports in Washington and coming from abroad, indicating plans for early launching of offensive operations in the Far East.

As part of my assignment, I prepared the story—a particularly easy one, since it was based entirely on previously known material, but a ticklish one because of the question whether consolidation of these bits of information into a single story might not overstep the bounds of propriety in printing military news.

Since the story primarily concerned the navy, it was submitted for navy censorship, but that Department passed it on to the Office of Censorship without comment.

The Office of Censorship asked first if the story was based on "competent authority," a question easily answered by citing the data behind it. As the upshot of the affair, the story lost two sentences. One was an incorrect statement regarding the navy; the other named a type of airplane operating in the Southwestern Pacific which at that time was still a military secret.

The result, of course, would be quite different were I to try to obtain approval of a story detailing the number of troops we have in Australia, or to describe the exact disposition of ships in the Atlantic and Pacific Oceans. . . .

EFFECT ON INDUSTRY [6]

Wartime secrecy rules affect—and irk—industry about as much as they do newspaper reporters.

Industry is fast learning that it can't get the statistics and other information which have become customary tools of doing business, can't advertise its plants, products, and customers the way it would like to, and can't "talk shop" as it used to.

Congress turned thumbs down on an "official secrets" bill submitted by the Administration because of a barrage of protests that it would impose criminal penalties for disclosure of anything a smalltime bureaucrat chose to consider a secret—including criticism of himself. But a voluntary code of censorship, supplemented by regulations and policy statements of various government agencies, is operating to shut off public disclosure of much formerly routine business information.

Government agencies are now going over their statistical services and pruning out many figures relating to production, stocks, foreign trade, and domestic distribution. The farther we get into 1942, the more valuable such information becomes to the enemy for comparison with pre-Pearl Harbor conditions. Attempt is being made to keep such restrictions to a minimum and to continue publication of all statistical information of value to business, labor, agriculture, and other elements of the population. But when a government agency stops publishing certain statistics, trade association, business papers, and private organizations must also stop compiling similar data.

[6] From "Censorship Rules Affect Industry." *Modern Industry*. 3:80-1. April 15, 1942. Reprinted by permission.

A statement of governmental wartime information policy, prepared by the interdepartmental committee on war information, contains a section on production information. While this applies primarily to releases by government agencies, the same restrictions are supposed to be applied voluntarily by industry:

General publication of specific information as to contract awards, site locations of war industries, and military installations, estimated supplies of certain strategic and critical materials, specific production schedules and detailed progress reports have been discontinued. General publication of such material can be most helpful to enemy spies and saboteurs. Publication of certain information of this kind is necessary to specific sections of the population, such as subcontractors, suppliers of labor, public utilities and others. Therefore, information of a non-detailed character with regard to plants and installations and the placing of large contracts is released for local publication. Moreover, information regarding the letting of contracts, the construction of factories and cantonments, and the like which are necessary for the proper functioning of suppliers of labor, materials, facilities, and other services, is given directly by appropriate authority.

This same policy should be adopted by industry in its press releases, advertising, and annual reports to stockholders. Where there is any doubt such documents should be submitted in advance to the Office of Censorship. This Office has advised advertisers that:

Manufacturers of material and equipment used by our military forces should guard against specific disclosures of plant locations, either in copy or illustrations. They should not reveal specific details concerning the nature or the type of material or equipment they are producing. They should not reveal production progress in specific figures. They should not reveal their stocks and surpluses of raw materials. They should not describe new designs, or new processes, or even new experiments with new designs and processes.

The War Department has put this policy into a formal regulation, one section of which says:

War Department contractors and subcontractors should—
Refrain from publication of photographs and drawings of army equipment which have not been released by the War Department.

Refrain from referring in advertising, which gives the location of a plant, to specific products being manufactured in that plant.

Refrain from publication of the names of subcontractors or accessory manufacturers to a prime contractor.

Release no production figures indicating total number of employees, backlog of orders, or area of land occupied.

Not permit aerial photographs of plants.

Observe these restrictions in their radio programs, other publicity, including financial statements, and public discussion.

Give no information either verbal or otherwise contrary to this policy.

SCIENCE A WAR SECRET [7]

The National Academy of Sciences, the senate of United States science, called off its annual meeting for 1942. Reason: most of its members are too busy with vital wartime research; and the closely guarded Academy Building, close to the War and Navy Departments in Washington, is overcrowded with military projects.

Not a word about chemistry or physics (mostly war secrets), but a great deal about archeology, was heard at last fortnight's meeting of the American Philosophical Society, most venerable United States scientific body.

Only 50 papers, instead of the usual 150 or more, were read last week at the American Physical Society's Baltimore convention.

Reports on explosives, plastics, rubber technology were omitted at the American Chemical Society's Memphis meeting. The history of chemistry was largely discussed. Attendance was poor.

Even at biological conferences, research reports were vague and evasive. Scientists who wanted more details were told again and again, "Sorry, but I can't answer that question without giving aid and comfort to the enemy."

[7] From "Science Hush-Hushed," newsstory. *Time.* 39:90. May 11, 1942. Reprinted by permission.

Such facts as these add up to the biggest scientific news of 1942: that there is less and less scientific news. Technical journals are thinner by as much as 50 per cent, and they will get more so: much of the research now published was completed a year ago before the conversion of United States science to wartime uses had reached all-out proportions. A year ago one out of four physicists was working on military problems; today, nearly three out of four. And while news from the world's battlefronts is often withheld for days or weeks, today's momentous scientific achievements will not be disclosed until the war's end.

THE CENSOR SAYS "NO" [8]

Holding "there is too much at stake both for the country and for the broadcasting industry to run even the slightest risk", J. Harold Ryan, assistant director of censorship in charge of broadcasting, last Wednesday rejected industry proposals that "open mike" interviews falling in the man-on-the-street category be permitted on a rigidly controlled transcribed basis.

He advised John Shepard 3d, Yankee Network president, as chairman of the N.A.B. National Defense Committees, that the provisions would become effective Feb. 1 as provided in the radio censorship code and remain in effect for the duration.

Mr. Shepard had petitioned for relaxation of the ban under specified conditions prior to the Feb. 1 effective date. It had been estimated that in the neighborhood of $3,000,000 in local commercial business would be affected by enforcement of the ban.

Meanwhile, the Censorship Office has been besieged with requests for interpretations on borderline cases, with several hundred inquiries on hand since the code was issued Jan. 16. In certain instances Mr. Ryan has found it feasible to authorize continuance of particular types of quiz programs and those that appear questionable, it is felt, should be checked with his office.

[8] From "Ryan Denies Shepard's Appeal to Ease Open Mike Decision," newsstory. *Broadcasting.* 22:8. February 2, 1942. Reprinted by permission.

THE CENSOR SAYS "YES" [9]

Adequately safeguarded, certain types of man-on-the-street programs will be permissible under the Wartime Censorship Code—but only after each particular program and its method of presentation have secured the written approval of the radio division of the Office of Censorship under J. Harold Ryan.

This was made known last week after Mr. Ryan's office had given a go-ahead to Hulbert Taft Jr., manager of WKRC, Cincinnati, covering a program in which pre-selected interviewees, chosen by civic and educational organizations, are questioned and the questions and answers pre-written before being broadcast. To guard against deviations from the script, the program keeps two announcers and an engineer on the job at all times.

If this is not sufficient safeguard, it is agreed that the rehearsed program shall be transcribed and that the broadcast will go on only after a time-lag.

Mr. Ryan, in reporting that his office had approved for broadcast this variation of the conventional quiz or man-in-the-street program, upon which the Code otherwise frowns, pointed out that Mr. Taft had "revised the format of his show so as to apply safeguards deemed essential for protection against its possible use for subversive purposes."

He called attention to the fact that the adequacy of the safeguards adopted in this instance was dependent upon the use of more personnel and equipment than ordinarily are available to smaller stations. For this reason, he urged that other station managements consult the Office of Censorship about their specific problems before instituting substitute programs which, in their own opinion, might provide the necessary safeguards.

Virtually every program of this general type varies in some degree from the others [Mr. Ryan said]. For this reason, no blanket approval of substitutes can be given in advance. Broadcasters who feel that they

[9] From "Controlled Remote Interview Allowed," newsstory. *Broadcasting*. 22:14. February 23, 1942. Reprinted by permission.

could make use of such programs and still fulfill their obligations of self-censorship should submit their specific program structures to the Office of Censorship for review and interpretation.

In other words, the approval of the WKRC program is not to be construed as blanket approval for similar programs, each one of which must be acted upon individually. The Office of Censorship is inclined to give station managements the best possible break under the Code, but no chances will be taken that might lead to slip-ups.

Mr. Ryan emphasized that the ruling in the WKRC case was not in any way a deviation from the Code provision which states, "Generally speaking, any quiz program originating remotely, wherein the group is small, and wherein no arrangement exists for investigating the background of participants, should be discontinued." While this section of the Code refers specifically to man-on-the-street interviews, airport interviews, etc., Mr. Ryan asserted that safeguards are provided through the Office of Censorship's rigid requirements that every broadcaster submit his case for individual ruling. There are to be no deviations from the basic purposes of the Code, he asserted.

Conditions to be outlined by station managers in presenting their cases for approval by the Office of Censorship are suggested by the Broadcasters' Victory Council in a letter to all stations last week. The letter suggests:

The broadcaster will maintain complete control over all persons allowed access to the microphone, and the master of ceremonies shall be fully conversant with the Wartime Code.

Participants will be selected in advance from the membership of accredited clubs, civic organizations, or educational institutions.

Precautions will be taken to see that unauthorized persons are excluded from the microphone through the use of an assistant to the master of ceremonies.

Interviewers will be invited far enough in advance of the broadcast to allow presentation of proper credentials to the announcer or master of ceremonies.

The master of ceremonies shall be equipped with a device for instantaneously cutting off the program if necessary.

The program will be transcribed and broadcast at a later time of day so it may be thoroughly checked by the production department before going on the air.

If you write the Office of Censorship on this matter and do secure its permission to proceed on the basis of such safeguards, too much stress cannot be placed on the need for living up to your promised caution. One slip by a single station, and the entire privilege can be revoked, to the detriment—both in reputation and finances—of the entire industry.

BAN ON POLICE-CALL COMMERCIALS [10]

Police-call commercial scripts, because of the possibility of instilling a false alarm spirit in listeners through constant repetition, should be eliminated from station schedules, according to War Department and N.A.B. recommendations. The War Department cited an example in which an announcer, simulating the metallic voice of a police radio announcer, begins: "Calling all men, calling all men—report to Glutz' Bargain Basement. . . ." It was pointed out that during wartime, when all men conceivably may be called for some kind of emergency duty, this type of commercial copy might have the effect of crying "wolf".

SELF-CENSORSHIP DURING CHURCHILL VISIT [11]

Radio was publicly applauded, along with the press, for keeping the faith in regard to the visit of Winston Churchill. Commendation came direct from President Roosevelt, via White House Secretary Stephen T. Early.

Though the impending visit of the British Prime Minister was an open secret for as long as 48 hours before his arrival,

[10] From "Calling All Calls," newsstory. *Broadcasting*. 22:45. January 5, 1942. Reprinted by permission.
[11] From "Voluntary Censorship Working Well, President Expresses Satisfaction," newsstory. *Variety*. 145:30. December 31, 1941. Reprinted by permission.

not a word was breathed outside the trade and official ranks, as far as federal authorities know. Both radio and the press were put on their honor to keep mum, just as they were when Churchill, accompanied by Canadian Prime Minister W. Mackenzie King, left for Ottawa, Sunday (December 28th). By noon of the day Churchill got to town, large proportion of the news and radio legmen were in on the secret and delegations scurried around to cover various possible arrival points. Biggest contingent went to Annapolis, only to be chased by navy officers. The first word that went over the air was the official White House announcement during the dinner hour Monday (22nd) following the British leader's arrival at a local airport and drive to the White House.

Secretary Early said Monday (29th) after Churchill's departure, the conduct of press and radio showed the practicability of voluntary censorship, adding that President Roosevelt several times commented on the sporting way in which the media played along.

CENSORED ANNUAL REPORTS [12]

Even stockholders aren't going to know all about the operations of their companies hereafter, especially if those companies are engaged in war effort of any kind, it becomes evident from the annual report of United States Steel Corporation, issued today.

The attractive 40th annual report carries on its cover the notation, "This report has been reviewed by the army, navy and United States Office of Censorship," and all through the 32-page volume the reader is reminded that too-frank discussion of company operations is out for the duration. For instance, a detailed table of steel ingot and castings production through the years shows 1941 production as "00,000" thousands of tons,

[12] From "United States Steel Issues First 'Censored' Annual Report." news-story. *Advertising Age.* 13:25. March 23, 1942. Reprinted by permission.

while a footnote explains that the actual figure "was omitted at the suggestion of the United States Office of Censorship."

In going through the book one finds scores of excellent photographs of steel operations, but no reference as to their locale, as well as statements like: "In the interest of national security, detailed identification of the various additions, improvements and rearrangements of facilities, completed, in progress and pending, is omitted"; and again: "National security in time of war precludes the detailed indication of specialized activities and the identification of all products manufactured for war and defense purposes."

SELF CENSORSHIP

DISCUSSION

The success of the present censorship program depends largely upon the cooperation exhibited by newspapers and radio stations. If they refuse to cooperate with Mr. Price and the Office of Censorship, even the most stringent regulations would be little more than useless. For if it were necessary to establish a censorship board to watch the columns of each of several thousand newspapers and over eight hundred radio stations in the United States, the job would be impossible. Only through the setting up of an absolute dictatorship, regimentation of every level of society along the lines of a Nazi party, could the government regulate freedom of speech and of the press by force. And that, by its very nature, would be the destruction of democracy and all that the United States is today at war to preserve.

But newspapers and radio stations *have* cooperated to the best of their ability. The majority of the violations of the censorship codes have been through misunderstanding or contradictions among the censors themselves. In a very few cases have violations been intentional, and even some of these were due to lack of clarity of the wording of the codes, a situation which will probably be remedied by the code revisions of June 15, 1942.

How the press and radio have cooperated is best demonstrated by the example of radio broadcasters, which were considered the biggest potential problem of the censor in this war. While the press cooperation has undoubtedly been as extensive and complete, the fact that radio is organized under the National Association of Broadcasters, which in the present emergency has acted as spokesman for the industry, offers more concrete proof of self-censorship activity. Through the N.A.B. all stations were notified of suggested censorship activities the moment war was declared. The N.A.B. also was instrumental in framing the code of wartime practices for radio, for it had already issued its own code two weeks after Pearl Harbor.

Less organized, the press was forced to depend primarily upon the discretion of individual editors and await government instructions in specific instances. Some important clarification of the meaning and application of government censorship regulations was carried in the trade publications as it applied to advertisers, manufacturers, promotion and publicity men throughout the country. But the American Newspaper Publishers Association and the American Society of Newspaper Editors, leading spokesmen for the press, lacked the unified organization which radio possessed in the N.A.B. As a result, the press wasn't as quickly informed or in operation under any planned self-censorship prior to the organization of the Office of Censorship January 15, 1942. Of course, both media are cooperating fully today, both in carrying out the provisions of the censorship codes and in helping solve the news problems which face Mr. Price's office as censorship continues.

N.A.B.'S PLEDGE [1]

Following up the admonition voiced by President Roosevelt in his address to the nation last Tuesday night, N.A.B. President Neville Miller immediately after the nationwide broadcast sent telegrams to all United States radio stations urging them to "exercise unusually careful editorial judgment in selecting news."

In his wire Mr. Miller declared it was "equally important that announcers and newscasters report war news calmly, slowly and deliberately, so as to avoid horror, suspense and undue excitement", agreeing also with a War Department recommen-

[1] From "Care in News Broadcasts and Measures to Safeguard Nation Advised by N.A.B.," newsstory. *Broadcasting*. 21:51. December 15, 1942. Reprinted by permission.

dation that definite broadcast periods be established to handle war news. He pointed out that the program policy already had been adopted voluntarily by a large share of the industry.

Early last week the N.A.B. mailed the first of its special bulletins, including in the four-page folder cautions against program practices that might afford unintentional aid to the enemy. It was pointed out that every type of program must be carefully considered and watched, even such features as man-on-street interviews and quiz programs, which conceivably could bare important military or defense information.

Last Thursday Mr. Miller . . . reemphasized the radio industry's intention and desire to cooperate fully in the war effort, in letters to both President Roosevelt and F.C.C. Chairman James Lawrence Fly.

I know I speak for the entire broadcasting industry when I say we appreciate the grave responsibility we bear to the nation now and for the duration of the war regarding the handling of the news of the war [he reassured the President]. May I again take this opportunity to pledge to you the whole-hearted cooperation of the broadcasting industry and to assure you that we shall at all times be conscious of our responsibility and endeavor in every way to fulfill our obligation to our country. I hope you will call upon us if we can be of any assistance to you in discharging the arduous duties of your high office.

In a letter to Chairman Fly Mr. Miller declared:

I want you to know that the N.A.B. wishes to cooperate with you and all divisions of the F.C.C. in every way to help solve the many problems which are arising due to the present emergency. I and various other members of the N.A.B. staff have the honor to serve on several committees of D.C.B. and have been in constant touch with many members of the F.C.C. staff. However, new problems are arising every day, and if any of us can be of help to you in any way, we shall be very pleased to have you call upon us.

Mr. Miller's telegram to all United States stations follows [in part.]:

In this war period, it is extremely important that broadcasters exercise unusually careful editorial judgment in selecting and broadcasting news so that the public will have a well-rounded report on verified developments; and, it is equally important that announcers and newscasters report war news calmly, slowly and deliberately, so as to avoid horror, suspense and undue excitement. We are in agreement with the War Department recommendation that for the handling of the war news definite periods of time be established, rather than the constant interruption of program service; except for news of transcendent importance.

CREATING A NEW CODE [2]

Recognizing war censorship as its No. 1 problem, the broadcasting industry is pitching in with the recently created Office of Censorship toward evolution of a full-scale voluntary code which will change the complexion of many programming practices, not restricted to the pure news field.

Working with Director of Censorship Byron Price and his assistant director in charge of radio, J. Harold Ryan, industry representatives last week set in motion machinery designed to produce a new wartime code, which would be invoked at the earliest possible time.

Ideas of government agencies identified with war operations, as well as those of industry leaders, will be submitted to Mr. Ryan with a view toward placing in immediate effect standards to govern operations of stations domestically and probably internationally. The alternative would be a mandatory set of rules and regulations drafted by the Office of Censorship.

While high praise already has been voiced by government officials for the voluntary cooperation of the industry in steps to prevent use of broadcasting facilities for subversive purposes, it nevertheless is recognized that additional restraints must be imposed. By the same token, it is realized that imposition of extreme restraints might tend to hamper the usefulness of radio and affect public morale.

[2] From "Industry Cooperates in Censorship Plan," newsstory. *Broadcasting.* 22:10, January 5, 1942. Reprinted by permission.

Mr. Ryan . . . was delegated by Mr. Price to cover all preliminary ground on evolution of a new code. Mr. Ryan's plan, it is understood, is to confer with all government agencies identified with the war operations and obtain their ideas. The N.A.B. and other groups likewise will solicit the industry on similar factors and the results will be pooled.

The N.A.B. wartime code, [3] produced a fortnight ago, will be used as the base, though it is felt that the document, thrown together quickly, is not sufficiently comprehensive.

Some of the knotty problems that confront the industry, totally aside from handling of news broadcasts and commentaries, involve coverage of stations along the borders and use of request numbers on networks and outlets having more than local or regional range. Use of request programs as vehicles for transmission of intelligence outside the country is regarded as a distinct danger.

Some confusion has developed over issuance of orders regarding censorship. One incident last week was due to an order from a West Coast Interceptor Command that network programs carrying request numbers and testimonials be not fed to the coast.

This Monday (Jan. 5) representatives of the news departments of the three major networks were to meet with Mr. Ryan to discuss problems that have developed since the war. This session is to be followed by other meetings with industry representatives, all geared toward the production of the revised and enlarged code.

The intention of Mr. Price's organization, it has been clearly indicated, is to accomplish as much on a voluntary basis as possible. Censorship at the source of all military information already is in full effect. Little difficulty has been experienced in the handling of news broadcasts despite one or two untoward instances. The most difficult problems appear to be encompassed

---

[3] Text of the N.A.B. Wartime Guide appears in Appendix.

in non-news programs and in the coverage of stations along the borders. Every effort is being made, obviously, to plug all possible leakage of espionage.

In evolving the new code, emphasis is expected to be placed upon self-policing operations. Stations along the borders will be called upon, it is expected, to eliminate all types of requests, open microphone (man-on-the-street, etc.) programs and other features where intelligence might be conveyed by subterfuge.

QUIZ PROGRAMS [4]

New York ad agencies with quiz programs received the audience participation provisions of the government's censorship code with little dismay after they had gone into a thorough analysis of the situation with network executives. Quiz shows, as far as network outlets are concerned, are conducted before audiences of more than 50 persons and the agencies feel that if any modifications are necessary in the selection of contestants they will be able to take them in stride and also adopt all precautions necessary without causing any diminuation of entertainment value to the program. It is believed that the only thing that would bring about the actual elimination of quiz programs would be the promulgation by the government of a rule barring attendance at broadcasts.

N.B.C. had the following comment to make on the censorship code:

We do not anticipate that the censorship code will cancel any of the quiz programs now on N.B.C. Instructions have been issued to producers, announcers, and masters of ceremonies on these shows to veer away from all subjects which the government regards as tabooed. For some time these shows have been monitored with extra care in Radio City and at other division points. This practice will continue so that if, during any of these so-called ad lib shows, objectionable state-

[4] From "Quiz Programs Can Easily Meet Government Wartime Precautions and Retain Values, Admen Think," newsstory. *Variety.* 145:24. January 21, 1942. Reprinted by permission.

ments are indicated by audience participants, which are in violation of the censorship code a cut will be immediately made.

We do not anticipate any difficulty, but nevertheless we shall not relax our vigilance. We should reiterate that ever since the war the National Broadcasting Company has had a self-imposed censorship in effect so that the promulgation of the code finds us already meeting its terms. . . .

Mutual's statement on the same subject was as follows:

The Mutual Broadcasting System is confident that our affiliates and member stations will recognize the practicability and the soundness of the newly issued government radio censorship instructions and will comply with them in all their programs which are transmitted to the network. Since the outbreak of the war the network and its stations have imposed many voluntary regulations applying to program operations, particularly those concerning news, musical requests and audience participation broadcasts. The latter type are produced before large studio audiences and are carefully supervised.

None of the quiz or audience participation programs transmitted to Mutual by the stations originate from remote locations such as airports, railroad terminal or similar public gathering points. These regulations, we believe, will help radio exercise its part in the great national war effort.

THE PROMOTION MAN [5]

It goes without saying, of course, that the code issued by the Office of Censorship for the guidance during this war period applies equally to promotion managers.

The single purpose of the code is to prevent information being published that conceivably might be of some help to the enemy. All the information issued by a newspaper does not appear in its news columns. Much of it appears in the form of advertising and promotion. Your editor will keep watch over the news columns. But you would better keep your own watch over your promotion.

[5] By T. S. Irvin. From "Promotion Men Must Obey Censorship Code." *Editor & Publisher*. 75:36. January 24, 1942. Reprinted by permission.

The nub of the code, as we read it, is in asking yourself this question, "Is this information I would like to have if I were the enemy?" Having answered it, act accordingly.

Right at the start, a whole bunch of promotional material that has been issuing thick and fast from newspapers all over the country will be ruled out. We refer particularly to market promotion. Ever since the defense program got under way, newspapers everywhere have been bellowing about how much their markets have got in the way of defense contracts, what defense building is under way, how many workers have been added to employment rolls, how many men are stationed at Camp This and Fort That in their territory, etc. From now on, we don't even whisper about these things.

This may come as a blow to some newspapers whose only promotional activity in the past year has been to disseminate market information, showing how fat their markets are growing because of the defense program. Some of them may even try to get around the code in some way, looking for loopholes here and there through which they might squeeze this sort of stuff.

Our own advise is not to try it. It woud be too bad for newspapers to come through this period with a clean and honorable record of performance so far as the news columns are concerned only to fall into the bad graces of the government—and the people—because of some ill-advised promotional activity. It would be too bad for promotion.

It's far better in a situation like this to lean over backward. And for the alert and enterprising promotion department, the censorship code does not pose an impossible problem. If your market is prospering from the war effort, there is no ban on telling advertisers about it. The ban is on publishing specific information about the war effort that you, if you were the enemy, might like to have. The enemy won't care that your market is doing well. He will care, though, that your market is doing well because Camp Soandso, just completed, is now housing so many men of such and such a division, who, on this date, are scheduled to move to such and such a place, etc.

WAR SERVICE BULLETINS [6]

Immediately after the outbreak of the war, the National Association of Broadcasters started sending to every station in the industry War Service Bulletins designed to guide stations on wartime operation. Included in these bulletins were numerous suggestions as to various types of programs, especially news programs. The effect of news upon the national morale is so great that the industry realized its ordinary peacetime practices in news broadcasting would have to be changed in some respects. News broadcasts likewise could be used to divulge vital information to the enemy if not carefully guarded. This latter situation has now been taken care of by the Broadcasters War Time Code issued by the Office of Censorship, prepared with the cooperation of the industry.

ADOPTION OF N.A.B. NEWS PLAN [7]

Consistent with the industry war policy of self-regulation, the N.A.B. Code Compliance Committee, at an all-day session last Friday approved a series of suggestions to control broadcasting of war news to insure maximum good taste in the handling of war news.

Basic suggestions advanced by John Shepard 3d, Yankee Network president and chairman of the newly created Broadcasters' Victory Council, were adopted. Additional suggestions, relating to middle commercials and banning of sponsorship of individual and sporadic news bulletins, were adopted by the committee with the sanction of Mr. Shepard. . . .

[6] From "Commercial News Programs." *War Service Bulletin.* No. 7. February 6, 1942. Released by the National Association of Broadcasters.
Excerpts from the first N.A.B. Service Bulletin entitled "War Service" are included in the Appendix.
[7] From "N.A.B. Code Group Votes News Control Plan," newsstory. *Broadcasting.* 22:10. February 9, 1942. Reprinted by permission.

Some criticism of handling of commercials in news programs, in the light of the war, had been voiced. The suggestions adopted, it was felt, can be observed without any substantial loss of revenue for any station, while at the same time resulting in more efficient handling of news.

THE   ADVERTISERS [8]

Advertisers probably do not need to be reminded that they are affected by the same rules of censorship that have been set up for media. The restrictions which apply to circulating information which may be of value to the enemy relate not only to editorial material or radio comment, but also to anything which appears over the signature or with sponsorship of an advertiser.

We believe that those who have been charged with the enforcement of the censorship program realize that they are faced with an unpleasant but necessary task. In wartime many of the freedoms which we are accustomed to enjoy are dispensed with for the duration, and editors and advertisers are cooperating with good spirit not only with the letter but the intent of the letter. Nevertheless, human nature being what it is, and differences of judgment being what they are, it is certain that there will be controversial situations in which either censors will be regarded as having exercised poor judgment, or editors and advertisers will be accused of having overstepped the bounds.

As a nationally famous editor said recently, in addressing a group of advertising executives, no one is intimidated by the threat of fine or imprisonment because of running counter to the rules and regulations laid down in the administration of the censorship program, but no one wants to be labeled an enemy of his country. Yet editors, and to a lesser degree advertisers, have a responsibility for circulating information

[8] From "What About Censorship?" editorial. *Advertising Age.* 13:12. February 2, 1942. Reprinted by permission.

which will aid public morale, assist in the war effort and provide constructive criticism when this is necessary.

We have heard of instances in which publications have been questioned regarding editorial content which contained not factual information, but merely expressions of opinion—certainly a field in which censorship should not attempt to operate; and there are also cases where advertisers have been advised that copy dealing with certain types of war production or similar activity is not proper material for publication. In each case it was necessary to determine whether the judgment of the editor or advertiser, or that of the censor, was correct.

We do not believe that the censorship situation will become more difficult, provided good faith is constantly in evidence on both sides. The objectives of censorship are important; the only question relates to its enforcement. We have reason to expect good feeling and cooperation on both sides.

ADVERTISING COPY [9]

E. L. Shaner, president of the Penton Publishing Company, Cleveland, and editorial director of *Steel*, told members of the Chicago Business Papers Association, Dotted Line Club and Chicago Industrial Advertisers Association at a luncheon meeting here yesterday that questionable business paper editorial and advertising copy should be cleared through army and navy public relations officers.

In counseling use of the armed service branches, Mr. Shaner reported that replies to censorship questions were quick and reliable, and that in general the army and navy offices were inclined to be lenient in what they permitted to be published. Aerial photographs particularly, he said, should be placed before these officials before publication, since such pictures are apt to

[9] From "Clear Ads Through Army and Navy, Shaner Counsels," newsstory. *Advertising Age*. 13:16. February 16, 1942. Reprinted by permission.

give many distinguishing identification marks which could be of use to the enemy.

Mr. Shaner also asserted that every industrial advertising man and business paper editor should ask himself, "Is this information I would like to have if I were the enemy?"—even though, in some cases, the article or picture in question might have been passed by a government censor.

In a question session that followed his speech, Mr. Shaner reported that no "drying up" of advertising because of censorship was likely, that "slight changes in copy have satisfied the censor," and that "some copy has been made more effective with the elimination of questionable items."

C.B.S. CONTROL OF NEWSCASTS [10]

New wartime standards for commercial news broadcasts have been put into effect by C.B.S. reducing the amount of time allowed for commercials by 20 per cent, prohibiting lengthy opening commercials, ensuring that commercials be duly distinguished from the news content of the programs and surrounding the entire news broadcasts with appropriate decorum.

The new rules limit opening commercials to 40 seconds on 10-and 15-minute news programs and to 25 seconds on 5-minute broadcasts. Opening commercials must not lead the listener to believe he is hearing news instead of a commercial.

Opening with sponsor identification, reading a few headlines and then going into a commercial is to be avoided as it "confuses the listener and compels him to listen to a commercial before he really finds out what the news is all about."

Jingles and other devices of giving the commercials "undue gaiety, humor or excitement" are barred for all commercials on news broadcasts. Middle commercials are permitted only in

[10] From "Commercials Cut on News by C.B.S.," newsstory. *Broadcasting.* 22: 20. February 23, 1942. Reprinted by permission.

newscasts of 10 minutes or more and then only at the option of C.B.S. Middle commercials must be preceded by a minimum of three minutes of news and are not allowed to interrupt a continuing description of a single situation.

All commercials except obvious opening ones must be set apart from the news content either by use of a different voice, which C.B.S. says is preferable, or by the announcer invariably separating them "not solely by a pause but by some such appropriate phrase, such as—now a few words from our sponsor . . . now let me tell you something about our product, and so forth."

The sponsor's message may not resemble a news item, so such introductions for commercials as "flash" and "bulletin" or "now news about Blank's product" are barred. There is no ban, however, of such phrases as "now here is something new and interesting about the product." Commercials must be "temperate and restrained" and rapid-fire delivery or over-emphatic selling is not permitted on newscasts. C.B.S. also reserves the right to make further conditions if time and circumstances make them advisable.

CENSORSHIP CONTROVERSIES

SUPPRESSION OF PUBLICATIONS

"TOWNSEND WEEKLY" CASE [1]

Somebody slipped badly when an order was issued withholding from the mails an entire issue of the *Townsend National Weekly*, pending an examination of an editorial by the Solicitor of the Post Office Department. It is to be hoped that that mistake will not be repeated. Press and people alike have accepted a censorship of news that might be of value to our enemies; they have not abdicated an iota of the free press right to criticize government policies or their execution.

While the Townsend old-age pension plan has always looked to us like economic insanity, there isn't the shadow of a doubt that Dr. Townsend and his followers have the right to advocate and fight for it, so long as they violate no laws. And *Editor & Publisher* will fight for the maintenance of that right, regardless of our disbelief in the cult's credo. . . . Fortunately, the Post Office Solicitor found no ground for action. It must be the sincere wish of every American that he will find no ground in future, where the expression of opinion concerns public matters and does not transgress laws against sedition or decency.

"SOCIAL JUSTICE" BARRED FROM MAILS [2]

Social Justice, sounding board for Rev. Charles Coughlin's political and social views, has been barred from second class mailing privileges on order of Postmaster General Frank C. Walker.

[1] From "No Curb on Opinion," editorial. *Editor & Publisher.* 75:26. January 24, 1942. Reprinted by permission.
[2] From "Social Justice Barred From Mails for War Criticism," newsstory. *Editor & Publisher.* 75:37. April 18, 1942. Reprinted by permission.

Walker acted on advice of Attorney General Francis Biddle who found that the magazine "has made a substantial contribution to a systematic and unscrupulous attack upon the war effort of our nation, both civilian and military." . . .

The Postmaster General . . . said two grounds will be stated: 1. That *Social Justice* is not a newspaper or other periodical publication within the meaning of the law governing second class mailing; 2. That the magazine has continuously violated the Espionage Act of 1917. . . .

The Espionage Act provides a penalty for violation with maximum fine of $10,000 or imprisonment for not more than 20 years, or both.

The Attorney General reported an examination of editions since Dec. 1, 1941, shows that 10 major themes broadcast by enemy nations have been closely followed in *Social Justice* writings. Instanced was the issue of the magazine which carried whole portions of a speech made by Joseph Goebbels with no crediting or other identification of the source.

Some of the themes emphasized both by the magazine and in enemy propaganda, said Mr. Biddle, are pride in the achievements of the Axis powers and sympathy with their aims; disparagement of the intentions and motives of Great Britain and of the United States; blame for the war on international bankers and their control of or influence in the present national administration and in the governments of the Allies; creation of racial hatreds and distrust; constant and frequent attacks upon the war policies of the present government; and doubt as to the ability of the United Nations to win the war.

THREE PUBLICATIONS SUPPRESSED [3]

Social Justice, vitriolic medium for expression of the political and economic views of Rev. Charles E. Coughlin today gave up

[3] From "Three Publications Denied 2nd Class Mail Privileges," newsstory. *Editor & Publisher*. 75:6. May 9, 1942. Reprinted by permission.

the fight against revocation of its second-class mailing privileges and okayed suspension of publication. The "Radio Priest's" promised contest failed to materialize when the hour was reached for hearing on an order to show cause why the mailing privilege should not be permanently withdrawn.

Meanwhile Postmaster General Frank C. Walker cited the Philadelphia *Herold* to show cause why its second-class mailing privilege should not be revoked for violation of the Espionage Act of 1917. A newspaper published in part in German at Philadelphia, the Herold has reprinted articles from *Social Justice* and has roundly criticized entry of the United States into the war. . . .

Also cited to show cause why its second-class mailing privileges should not be revoked was *The X-Ray*, a weekly published at Muncie, Ind., and edited by Court Asher. . . . The Department of Justice accused the publisher of emphasizing, jointly with Axis publications, disparagement of the intentions and motives of Great Britain; creation of racial hatreds and distrusts; and uniform and frequent attacks upon the war policies of the United States.

Third publication to come within the Attorney General's interdict was *Publicity*, a weekly published at Wichita, Kan., against which a federal grand jury has returned an indictment on eleven counts charging Elmer J., and James F. Garner with obstructing the war effort through their publication.

SUPPRESSION OF PROGRAMS

VARIED STATION INTERPRETATIONS [4]

New radio censorship regulations found several Connecticut Valley radio stations right on the ball, while among others there was little uniformity in the interpretation of the rules. Most stations immediately cancelled "man-on-the-street" pickups,

---

[4] From "Censorship Strikes Hard at Types of Program Dear to Local Stations," newsstory. *Variety*. 145:24. January 21, 1942. Reprinted by permission.

though ban does not go into effect until Feb. 1, and restricted recorded request number programs and foreign language broadcasts. WBZ-WBZA clamped down hardest.

All foreign language artists, even on special broadcasts, will be required to show birth certificates, according to Program Director R. J. Stafford. Two quiz shows will go on.

WMAS, according to manager Albert W. Marlin, has already put most rules into effect. All foreign language programs will be more carefully directed and edited, though still in the original tongue.

Program Director Wayne Henry Latham has instructed spielers at WSPR to stagger requests for specific titles, holding them for later programs. Translations of foreign language programs are kept on file. Sidewalk shows are out.

Hardest hit is WHYN at Holyoke with no network affiliation and many recorded programs. Walcott Wyllie, program director, ordered end to Saturday and Sunday request programs, especially popular with men from nearby Westover field. Station has had direct wire into studio. "Holyoke Speaks" program is among fatalities. Polish programs will henceforth be given in English and well edited.

Chicago Program Ban [5]

New Office of Censorship code has ruled off WJJD [Chicago] "What's Your Opinion?" which was broadcast daily from the Telenews theater.

Also out was the use of telegraphic requests for special songs and recordings on WIND "Night Watch" program.

"Mail Bag" Show Dropped [6]

"Mail Bag" programs, long a feature of General Electric's shortwave WGEO and WGEA, Schenectady, and KGEI, San

[5] From " 'What's Your Opinion?' Obliterated by War," newsstory. *Variety.* 145:24. January 21, 1942. Reprinted by permission.
[6] From "Drop 'Mail Bag' Programs; WGEO, Schenectady, Got Peabody Award in 1941," newsstory. *Variety.* 145:24. January 21, 1942. Reprinted by permission.

Francisco, have been dropped, to avert the possibility of broad-casting a letter for an Axis agent writing home. The Schenec-tady short-wavers originated the "Mail Bag" idea at the time of Admiral Byrd's Antarctic expedition. In 1941, WGEO received a George Foster Peabody citation for its "post office" work on the second Byrd trip to little America.

PROGRAM RESTRICTIONS IN NASHVILLE [7]

Restrictions placed on remote and quiz programs by the Bureau of Censorship caused WLAC [Nashville] most worry locally. Station carried "Curbstone College," "Air Traveler," and "Man on Street."

"Curbstone College" will continue on air with show originat-ing in station's studios with talent selected from reputable groups with no pro-Axis sentiments.

"Air Traveler" show is off due to special request of Censor-ship Bureau.

WSIX, with "Man on Street," and "Watkins Forum" as its open-mike shows, was less affected by the order. No regularly scheduled man-on-street or open-forum shows are aired by WSM.

SUPPRESSION OF NEWS

FLORIDA CENSORSHIP [8]

THUMBNAIL EDITORIAL

If it's anything WE can't print,
YOU shouldn't be talking about it.

We picked that up the other day in . . . the *Palm Beach Post*, of West Palm Beach. It looked like a story, and it was. The *Post*, and its opposite number, the *Times*, were sitting on a

[7] From "WLAC, Nashville, Loses Several Programs Under New Censorship Code," newsstory. *Variety*. 145:24. January 21, 1942. Reprinted by permission.
[8] By Arthur Robb, editor of *Editor & Publisher*. From "Shop Talk at Thirty," column. *Editor & Publisher*. 75:36. March 7, 1942. Reprinted by permission.

story that the navy wouldn't release, and everybody along the Florida coast was talking about it wherever two or more folks gathered together.

It was news, in the sense that it was a topic of animated discussion, probably based on totally wrong assumptions of facts as such discussions generally are without the aid of print. The American mind has no difficulty whatever in guessing at or inventing details.

Over the Washington Birthday week-end, we learn from Don Morris, editor of the *Post* and *Times,* people in the vicinity of Palm Beach heard several heavy explosions and saw flames at sea. Obviously an enemy submarine was at work, with deadly effect. The first sinking took place at 10:40 P.M. on February 21, and the survivors were brought ashore a few hours later. Reporters for the *Post* and *Times* talked to them and got the story. The papers didn't print the news in the Sunday edition. They didn't print it, in fact, until Tuesday. The only reference to the suppressed news appeared in the above quoted front-page editorial, which did not stop a flood of telephone inquiries as to why the papers were holding out news that was familiar to everyone within its circulation area.

Despite the terse admonition of the editor, people just wouldn't stop talking. Two other ships had met the fate of the first one between dark and dawn on Saturday night, but the navy maintained strict silence until Tuesday afternoon. The afternoon paper then was permitted to print the news of the first sinking. The first and the second were combined in a story released for Wednesday morning. The third did not become news until Friday night, and was published in the Saturday morning paper.

Meanwhile, Mr. Morris who shares the general editorial idea that news ought to be printed while it is fresh, started asking questions of the Office of Censorship. His first telegram read:

For some 60 hours we have been sitting on the lid of a story which every bootblack and streetwalker for 100 miles knows and repeats to all within hearing. Tourists drive a few miles to see the upturned hulks of ships, which, for all we can print, must be products of the imagination. Although Santa Barbara can immediately announce its shelling, the fact that our 'incidents' were two or three miles offshore puts our story in a different category, apparently, despite the fact that a German communique this morning announces eight ship sinkings in the Atlantic, five of them tankers. Unable to print news to stop a flood of rumors much worse than the actual facts, we look to our readers like fools and ourselves feel like it. We are hard put to think of a better way to damage confidence in the press. Respectfully, we ask that the Office of Censorship provide us with an explanation that we can give to our readers at the time the story is released of the reasons for the extraordinary delay. . . .

The reply, signed by Nathaniel R. Howard, editor of the *Cleveland News*, who is now on duty in the Office of Censorship, advised Mr. Morris to be guided by the releases of the Navy Bureau of Public Relations. That raised another question. The local public relations officers were, apparently, willing to release the story but were held down by their Washington superiors, for no reason that the local men could tell the newspaper people.

Further inquiry elicited this reply from Censorship:

Think you will concur Navy and Maritime Commission must be final professional authority at what point no further risk of information to enemy. Dissemination of a ship sinking story very different thing from local observation. Navy was guided in "Republic" case up to moment of release by circumstances you would appreciate. Story was not held up for any capricious reason. In these times other considerations must be placed before news value of any such story.

Supplementing that telegram, Mr. Howard added in a letter to Mr. Morris this advice:

You doubtless know that enemy submarines off the Atlantic Coast are without good communication. You will understand also that they are not ordinarily in a position to remain for several days in any small area of the ocean. The Navy and the Maritime Commission undoubtedly know what they are talking about when they say that to withhold actual extent of damage and its effect in the United States, as long as is feasible, will keep the question marks in the mind of the attacking submarine commander, which will have much to do with the submarine's next activity.

There is a further consideration of the effect of announcing a sinking of an American ship some days after it happens. The public—which means all over the United States—does not, it can be observed, react quite as violently to the piece of bad news as if it had been immediately announced. This is an important consideration in these days of many submarine attacks. . . .

In the final analysis, we must all depend on the judgment of the navy to protect us against the enemy, and that judgment must include protection of information helpful to the enemy. This office is in close touch with the Navy Bureau of Public Relations on the ship stories, and gives you its assurance that the navy is neither halting nor indifferent to the flow of public information in its handling of these important news items. . . .

Mr. Morris replied, agreeing (as we do), with Mr. Howard's views on the authority of the navy and Maritime Commission and his statement that the delay in the story's release was not capricious. Mr. Morris, however, also pointed out that while his newspapers and the Associated Press withheld certain obvious details of one ship's fate, in order not to give the enemy important information, the facts that they suppressed were carried in another news service's report and also broadcast over a country-wide chain. And he asked Mr. Howard if a feature story could not be written for general publication in newspapers, explaining the censorship operations and their relationships with other departments, particularly the army and navy. He noted that to date, there has not been the coordination of effort that was expected after the creation of the Office of Censorship.

To which Mr. Howard replied that the Office of Censorship neither creates nor gives out news. It does attempt to tell an agency which has news to give out how its facts square with the press code.

The army and navy, [Mr. Howard continued] do create and release news. It is in connection with the news they have to release that they exact stipulations as to its publication. However, any newspaper which has facts of its own independent knowledge and submits them to this office will be told whether it can publish, irrespective of the exact army or navy desires in a similar case where the newspaper must depend on either department. . . .

We are still a new and untried bureau. We make mistakes daily. We need your patience; we need your understanding that "news value" is no longer the sole consideration of publication, nor enterprise in gathering news; and so we need most of all a certain tolerance from you.

Frankly, we have had misgivings about publishing portions of this correspondence, even with the permission of one of the parties.

All of the people involved are personal friends and have been for many years and there can be no doubt of the professional competence and complete integrity of any of them as newspaper operators. And as Nat Howard points out, the Office of Censorship is a new and untried bureau, operated by men who never in their lives have thought of news as something that shouldn't be printed. Undoubtedly Byron Price, John Sorrells and Nat Howard beat a tattoo on the floor and bite their tongues whenever they have to hold up a story on the advice of technical authorities. Undoubtedly, also, they are bit by bit making the newspaperman's views felt in the public relations branches of the armed services. And, granted the undoubted good will toward the press which exists in both the army and navy public relations bureaus, there has not been universally an understanding either of the philosophy of news or the technicalities of newspaper work.

Our own counsel would repeat that of Mr. Howard—patience and understanding on the part of newspaper people, in the hope that some of the obvious errors of past policy can be corrected.

We don't go along with him at all in deprecating the present value of "news" or "enterprise." Regardless of what the Office of Censorship or the army and the navy think, the public looks to newspapers both for enterprise in uncovering and integrity in its presentation. The public can't be expected to understand why its newspapers don't mention the fact that a ship has been torpedoed when its poor torn hulk can be seen a few hundred yards offshore. They don't understand the thinking that forbids a newspaper to mention a snowstorm and slippery streets in a city where these conditions are unusual, and which makes newspapers report traffic delays and accidents resulting from those conditions without a word about the extraordinary weather. Such rules, for all their admirable purpose, seem to us to serve no useful purpose. The Japanese are not relying on the papers, say in Seattle, to learn of weather conditions there on a certain day. They have meteorologists who can plot storm conditions anywhere in the world with the same skill as our own—provided they can get regular telegraphic information. If they can get that today, they are getting it from people who see the weather with their own eyes and not through newspaper reports. And if Tokyo cannot get telegraphic reports from United States sources, which we assume to be the case, why put newspapers under such ridiculous restrictions. . . .

We can't see much point in holding up for several days the news of sinkings whether they are offshore near a large population or far at sea. The submarine's communications may be feeble, as Mr. Howard says, but a U-boat commander certainly knows whether his torpedoes missed or hit. He is one guy who isn't in doubt as to immediate results, and, ordinarily, he doesn't get around to regular reading of American newspapers.

Certainly, news of such importance as the sinking of a ship, with possible loss of life, is not to be handled casually. There should be as much delay as is needed for verification of all major facts, including casualties, and notification of the owners of the ship, the families of the survivors, and the insurance underwriters before publication. We have no quarrel whatever with that. What we do protest is the holding up of news for days after all of these conditions have been met, for the sake of policy—for minimization of bad news or emphasis on good news. We can't agree with Mr. Howard that delay in the release of a ship's loss by several days at all lessens the shock with which it hits the public.

Then there was the story of the air victory over Japan somewhere in the far Pacific. The navy communique gives neither the time nor the approximate area of the fight, nor any but the vaguest indication of the number or character of ships involved, but the *New York Herald Tribune* believes that the story released on March 3 referred to the battle announced by the Japanese on February 23, with claims to have damaged the "U. S. S. Yorktown." This enemy claim is neither acknowledged nor specifically denied by the navy—probably for reasons which would stand up firmly if they could be explained. Psychologically, however, we think it is bad that our enemies get their stories and their claims out first, and in fairly specific terms, while our own, tagging along three, four or ten days behind the event are often less circumstantial.

The big task that the Office of Censorship has is the maintenance of the public's faith in the integrity of its operations, and beyond those, of the news in newspapers and on the air. Our war effort will be badly tangled if the people get the notion that the news they are getting is manufactured or manipulated from day to day according to the needs of a government department. Once that distrust is created toward a part of the news, there is grave danger that it will spread to all news and to all announcements of the government.

The Case of the "Coimbra" [9]

The grim necessity for firm censorship of news at a time when deadly submarine warfare is raging off our coastline is apparent to all newspapermen. We are equally certain that the

[9] From "Censorship, but Not Strangulation," editorial. *Editor & Publisher.* 75:22. January 31, 1942. Reprinted by permission.

wartime censorship could and should permit publication of the full stories of these ship sinkings without unnecessary delay and without strangulation of press initiative when news sources are authentic and official.

This week several disturbing incidents of apparently pointless censorship came to our attention. Woven into the growing mosaic of conflict and confusion over confirmation and release of war news, they strengthen our belief that the United States censorship can be made to work smoothly, if common sense and understanding are mutual aims of press and government.

Dispatches on Wednesday from San Juan, Puerto Rico, told of the arrival there of survivors of a sea disaster in which 250 lives were lost, including many Americans. Washington released the story with the torpedoed ship described as "an Allied steamer," although Canadian accounts immediately identified her as the Canadian liner "Lady Hawkins." Alarmed relatives of passengers on American vessels flooded newspaper offices with anguished calls for the name of the ship and news of their kinfolk. If Canada could identify the torpedoed liner at first why not the United States?

The same day Rear Admiral Adolphus Andrews cancelled his weekly press conference and announced its discontinuance. Unofficially it was stated that the Admiral felt his work was too important and of too secret a nature to be discussed with the press. Officially, no explanation was given.

Admiral Andrews not only is Commandant of the Third Naval District in New York but of the North Atlantic Coastal Frontier, extending from Cape Hatteras to Halifax. His responsibilities are great, but we believe he should remember that his Commander-in-Chief, with greater responsibilities, still finds time to keep the public informed through the press. These are times for censorship, but not news blackouts, and much news of importance to America is occurring daily in the Admiral's domain.

Admiral Andrews previously refused to see the press on Jan. 14, when the British tanker "Coimbra" became the second U-boat victim off Long Island. One press association sought confirmation of the story in Washington from 9 A.M. until after 3 P.M. that day, but the Navy Department said it had no knowledge of the disaster. This was true, because it was learned unofficially that Admiral Andrews had not yet reported it to Washington. Finally this service sent out its story and stood on a Coast Guard source as official as well as authentic.

The confusion and delay of 20 hours in confirming the "Coimbra" sinking led to issuance of a Navy Department order which, unless rescinded, places all newspapers and press associations on equal footing on such news for the duration. Simultaneous release of coastal sinkings through a central releasing authority in Washington means no more scoops in this phase of the war, no matter how correct the information in hand might be. Even eye-witness accounts of an off-shore disaster are forbidden.

Admiral Andrews' attitude toward the press in New York, most important center of all shipping news sources, is in direct contrast to the navy cooperation with newspapermen elsewhere in their difficult war liaison work with the public. In Norfolk, for instance, the navy's press relations work has included taking newspapermen out to meet survivors of torpedoed vessels.

In this war the press doesn't want to be pampered by the navy. As we size up the situation, it wants only to tell the facts quickly, without giving aid to the enemy, so the public will be fully and promptly informed. And in the performance of this service we feel that the newspapers, which live by competition, should be permitted now and then an authentic scoop. Press initiative that won't harm the war effort should not be throttled and become a censorship casualty.

Navy Apology in "Coimbra" Case [10]

The Navy Department, Jan. 17, over the signature of Lt. Com. Paul C. Smith, editor of the *San Francisco Chronicle* on leave as Navy press relations officer, issued an unprecedented explanation and apology to the editors of the country for confusion surrounding Jan. 15 wire service reports on the sinking of the "Coimbra" east of New York. The navy assumes primary responsibility for the confusion.

The navy statement also revealed steps taken to correct the situation and the concentration of "releasing authority" in the Navy Office of Public Relations, Washington, where information on sinkings will be issued simultaneously to all services. No reports on ships sunk or damaged can be printed until cleared by this office.

Editor & Publisher has received special permission from the navy to print the "not for publication" Jan. 17 release titled "memo to the press for the information of all editors." The complete text follows:

This is a note to editors for the purpose of explaining—and apologizing for—the confusion which surrounded Jan. 15 wire service reports of the sinking of the "Coimbra" east of New York.

The primary responsibility for the confusion was the navy's. Through a mix-up, the Navy Department in Washington had no information on the reported sinking. The Navy Department was without authentic information until Friday afternoon. It was, therefore, impossible to confirm any of the reports relayed to us by the press itself.

The result was a state of confusion under which some agencies carried the story, others killed the story, while the Navy Department could do nothing to straighten out the situation because of a complete lack of official information.

We appreciate the problems of the news services under such conditions. We are trying to clear up our end of the general confusion prevailing in the whole field of press relations under present war conditions.

[10] From "Navy Apologizes for Confusion on 'Coimbra' Sinking," newsstory. *Editor & Publisher.* 75:7. January 31, 1942. Reprinted by permission.

As an initial step toward such correction, the navy has now concentrated releasing authority in the Office of Public Relations, Navy Department, Washington, and all District Commandmants have been so notified. There are officers on duty here in the Press Section 24 hours a day.

The result of concentrating the release authority here is as follows:

1. No newspaper or news service should publish any report or information of ships sunk or damaged by enemy action until such information has been cleared for release by this office. This rule applies even though the incident may be within the view of shore observers, and even if the information has been given by local officials, naval or otherwise.

2. This office will endeavor to release such information as will not give aid and comfort to the enemy at the earliest possible moment, and to all services simultaneously. There should be no attempts to scoop information which may be vital to any phase of naval security.

3. Once the story has been released by this office, the story may be carried by the press within the limits of the authority granted here and without regard for the views of local officials, naval or otherwise.

4. This office, as soon as releasing such official information, will instruct local authorities to make such facilities as may be necessary for more complete coverage available to the press at the source of the story. This office will instruct local naval authorities to cooperate with the press within the limits defined by us in the individual case.

We appreciate here the cooperation of the press, which has been extremely patriotic and patient. We hope the press will understand that we are making every effort to clean out the bugs in the whole censorship and news problem of the hour.

By working together we'll lick the problem. Your suggestions and advice are always welcome.—Paul C. Smith, Lieutenant Commander, U.S.N.R., Press Relations Officer.

Explanation of "Coimbra" Confusion [11]

We come to the matter . . . regarding the sinking of the British tanker "Coimbra" off the Long Island coast on Jan. 14, 1942. Up to that date no directive regarding these matters had been received by me regarding the dissemination of news

[11] By Adolphus Andrews, Rear Admiral, U. S. Navy, Commandant of the Third Naval District. From "Admiral Andrews Tells His Part in Navy News," a letter mailed to *Editor & Publisher* in answer to an editorial printed January 31, 1942. *Editor & Publisher*. 75:32. February 7, 1942. Reprinted by permission.

of this type. I am sure that any intelligent newspaperman can understand that an officer in my position is concerned first with his primary mission, which is to sink or capture the enemy submarine, if possible. To do this, or to make the attempt to do it, is not a matter of wishful thinking or the pressing of a button. It is a matter that requires split second decisions, a great deal of telephoning, conferences with certain staff officers and others, the sending out of ships or bombing planes, or both, and a multitude of other details too numerous to mention. It means hours of fast, concentrated work on the part of all hands concerned.

This was the situation that I found myself in on Jan. 14 when the first tip came to my attention that the "Coimbra" had been torpedoed. We were unable to give out any information about this ship until such time as we had first verified the facts; secondly, make an attempt to locate the enemy submarine; and thirdly, to hold off the news until such time as we were convinced that the enemy ship had escaped. Lastly, we had to clear the information that we had with the office of the Director of Public Relations, Navy Department, Washington, D. C.

Due to the delay in disseminating the news, I then directed my Public Relations Officer, Lieutenant Commander Tuthill, to confer with the Public Relations Office in the Navy Department in the matter of a directive which would coordinate the efforts of the main office in Washington with this district office so that in the case of future enemy attacks there would be as little delay as possible in serving the press. This was done immediately and within a few days a directive was written and approved and sent out to the various district Public Relations Officers by the Navy Department. Since then, matters of this kind have functioned as smoothly and efficiently as we believe it possible for them to function until some other incident arises that may need further smoothing out.

FIRST CENSORSHIP IN FORTUNE [12]

This month *Fortune* comes out five days behind schedule, two days late because of Pearl Harbor and the necessity for a quick turn-around on stories; three more days because of wartime censorship, specifically a story on the American Locomotive Company, its war boom (making tanks and gun carriages) and its prospects for a post-war economy. Submitted to the War Department in Washington for approval, the first draft of the American Locomotive story came back four days before closing time with whole pages marked for indiscriminate deletion. *Fortune* then sent its representative to the War Department to protest; but, right up to closing day it got nowhere. With no time to rewrite or to argue further, *Fortune* was then obliged to accept the censorship, and to re-print the front-of-book pages which had already gone to press (hence the three days lateness) with this foreword:

The article that follows represents *Fortune's* first experience with wartime censorship in the United States. Because it dealt with military matters, the manuscript was submitted to the War Department, which returned it with profuse deletions ordered. As the reader will perceive, much of the information deleted is available in any corporation reference service such as *Standard Statistics*. Much of the rest has appeared in the daily press or authoritative periodicals like the *Infantry Journal*, a publication that the enemy presumably follows with some attention. Nevertheless, the War Department was adamant on grounds of either "military secrecy" (viz., location of American Locomotive's plants), or of "morale" (viz., criticism of United States tank design).

The story itself begins thus:

At *Censored* on the shores of Lake Erie in western New York stood an abandoned foundry. Its great steel rafters were gabled by six inches of dust; its floor was pocked with gaping holes where the core ovens once stood.... That was eighteen months ago.... Today that same foundry, swept, painted, and whole of body, throbs with the clangor of industrial creation. Within, 550 workmen with hammers

[12] From *F. Y. I.* (For Your Information), Time, Inc., house organ, release on *Fortune* censorship, January 26, 1942. Reprinted by permission.

and honers, wrenches and reamers, make the steel framework on which giant field guns will roll into battle. It is the *Censored* arsenal of American Locomotive. . . .

What happened to the *Censored* foundry is roughly symbolic of what has happened to the entire locomotive industry in two years of wartime expansion. . . .

With the blessing of a *Censored* priority, America is building twenty-five locomotives for the Yunnan-Burma Railroad, which will run from *Censored*, China, to below the Burma frontier. . . .

THE "NORMANDIE" CASE [13]

Protests by editors in New York against censorship delays and prohibitions encountered in handling the "Normandie" fire story mounted this week and brought official action both in Washington and New York to clear up the muddled situation.

Simultaneous release of news of the disaster an hour after the smoke began billowing across Manhattan, to be seen by millions, was a highlight of the censorship. Another phase which evoked editorial criticism in the *New York Daily News* was an order prohibiting press photographers from taking pictures of the "Normandie" turning over in the early hours of Tuesday, although many photos were made before and after this happened.

In Washington Captain Leland P. Lovette, assistant director of public relations for the Navy Department, told *Editor & Publisher* Feb. 11 that navy press relations in the New York City area have been responsible for many protests and the subject was being thoroughly explored.

Lieutenant Commander John T. Tuthill, Jr., Third Naval District public relations officer in New York, already has been in Washington, at the instruction of headquarters there, to discuss the operations of his office. The complaints also have been investigated to some extent "on the grounds," Capt. Lovette

[13] By Walter E. Schneider. From "Editors Decry 'Normandie' Censorship; Navy Acts," newsstory. *Editor & Publisher*. 75:9. February 14, 1942. Reprinted by permission.

said. Because the inquiry has not been completed, Lovette explained, no conclusions have been reached.

In New York, a navy spokesman of the Third District summoned representatives of press associations, newspapers and *Editor & Publisher* to a press conference Wednesday afternoon, Feb. 11, to discuss some of the criticisms of naval censorship which have been made. Last week Rear Admiral Adolphus Andrews, Third District Commandant, replied to an *Editor & Publisher* editorial which directed attention to some phases of the naval censorship in New York.

Replying to criticism on the handling of the release to the press of the "Normandie" story a spokesman for the Third Naval District, New York, told reporters Wednesday that the 45-minute delay came about because the Navy Department in Washington had to censor the story first.

He said the first report to the Third Naval District was called in at 3 P. M. the day of the fire. Five minutes later it had been confirmed with the city fire department, and 10 minutes after the first report the story had been transmitted to Washington.

At 3:33 the spokesman said, Washington informed the Third Naval District that it could release the story and the Press Relations Section there set 3:45 as the automatic release time so that all services and newspapers would be covered simultaneously.

The spokesman stressed the fact that no story dealing with navy vessels could be released for publication without authorization first from the Navy Department in Washington.

SATURDAY EVENING POST VS. COLLIER'S [14]

Two recent issues of national magazines add another clause to the indictment of censorship. The *Saturday Evening Post* of February 14 carried a tintblock relating that an article on defense

---

[14] By Arthur Robb. From "Shop Talk at Thirty," column. *Editor & Publisher.* 75:40. February 21, 1942. Reprinted by permission.

of our Western frontiers by Richard Neuberger had been deleted by request of the Office of Censorship. The material had been gathered before the Office of Censorship was established, and it had been approved by the appropriate government departments. Voluntarily, the *Post* and the author decided to submit the story to Byron Price's office, after the issue was ready for the presses. The run had actually started when the Office of Censorship decided that publication was against public policy. Even though our enemies had some knowledge of the facts disclosed, the grouping of these facts in an integrated whole might give them a perspective which would not be apparent by looking at separate parts. The *Post* agreed and replaced the article. The Office of Censorship voluntarily absolved both the paper and the author from any charge of revealing military secrets, and, in fact, permitted the publication the following week of several pictures with deletions from the underlines that made the whole performance farcical.

In *Collier's*, which appeared the same week as the *Post* dated Feb. 14. there was an article on Western defense by Jim Marshall. It was an interesting piece, as Mr. Neuberger's undoubtedly was, and so far as our civilian eye could see, it provided no aiming points for Jap guns or planes. Whether or not *Collier's* saw fit to submit this material to censorship after its original approval (through source material and photographs) we don't know. In any case, one magazine was able to print a story that was forbidden to one of its principal competitors—with good faith equally balanced on all sides.

Heaven knows, we're not trying to tell Byron Price or John Sorrells how to run that censorship office. They have more advice now than they'll be able to use if the war goes on for another five years—a lot of it selfish and a lot more plain cockeyed. They have to learn a completely new job by experience as they go along, but we do suggest that they apply, as universally as is possible, the principle that the public is entitled to know everything that cannot be turned to advantage by enemy

nations.   There doesn't seem to be much sense in concealing
the fact of a snowstorm in Seattle, or the existence of an airplane or tank plant which sprawls over a mile or so of prairie. . . .

Several minor notes have been sounded by newspapers on
the navy releases of the story of the raid on the Marshall Islands.
As the *Chicago Tribune* points out, the navy issued a terse
summary of the fight on February 1, the day after it happened.
Detailed stories were not released until almost two weeks later,
although, according to the *Tribune*, correspondents' reports were
in this country two days before their publication was permitted.
The *Tribune* hints that the delay was caused by a "desire to
have some good news to present to the public to blanket the
expected bad news from Singapore." . . .

We speak for all newspapermen, we think, when we protest even the possibility of holding up good news to blanket
a possible unfavorable break.   That's the kind of stuff that
newspapermen have been damning for years.   It is of the essence
of press agentry, and it has no place in the relations between
a democratic government and the people of a democracy.   As
a device, it can be worked once, twice, maybe three times.   After
that, the mechanism becomes self-evident—and whatever government department is responsible is stamped as a propagandist.
Let us not have that now.

The Case of the L. A. Times [15]

Disclosure that Los Angeles newspapers destined for subscribers in other countries are being opened by an army censor
at the post office and material deemed as likely to give aid or
comfort to the enemy freely cut out was made to *Editor & Publisher* today by L. D. Hotchkiss, managing editor of the *Times*.
In one case 5,000 copies of the *Times'* midwinter number were
held up for days and the newspaper finally had to bring them

[15] From "Censors Clip L. A. *Times* at Post Office," newsstory.   *Editor &
Publisher*.   75:6.   February 21, 1942.   Reprinted by permission.

back to the office and remove one entire section and rewrap them before they could be released. While the army requested all Los Angeles papers for lists of their out-of-country subscribers which were furnished, it was not learned how they were being censored until recently when subscribers in Canada and Mexico began complaining and in some cases returning their copies.

The army itself gives the publishers no statement as to what has been eliminated. According to Hotchkiss the papers are laid flat on a table and the questionable articles cut out with a razor blade resulting in not only the elimination of one story but cutting through pages underneath. One subscriber in Chihuahua, Mexico, reported that while his *Los Angeles Times* came to him censored he receive the Texas paper untouched with presumably the same A.P. and U.P. material in it that was cut out of the coast paper, indicating that different rules prevail in different sections of the country.

Among the stories cut from the *Times* was one of the change in Allied command in the Pacific and one about the funeral of Carole Lombard.

The midwinter section which had to be eliminated was devoted to army activities in California and was prepared from material the army had supplied including a map showing location of air bases. That was before Pearl Harbor, however, but while the midwinter number was published Jan. 2 it was not until Jan. 16 that the *Times* was informed it was being held up and it was several days later before release was okayed.

The "Langley" Case [16]

On Feb. 27, the aircraft tender "Langley" was sunk off Java. On March 1, the naval tanker "Pecos" was torpedoed. Seven

[16] By Palmer Hoyt, publisher of the *Portland Oregonian* and national president of Sigma Delta Chi, journalistic fraternity. From a statement in a founder's day message to the fraternity, as reported by *Editor & Publisher*. 75:86. April 25, 1942. Reprinted by permission.

hundred American lives and much valuable equipment was lost. It was a major disaster and yet the news of this debacle was not released until April 3. Why?

It couldn't have been because of "aid and comfort" to the enemy for the reason that these ships were sunk by dive bombers who had hunted down their prey for days. The Japs knew what they had done.

It must have been rather a reflection of the general American attitude of distaste for bad news and the very particular distaste of the United States Navy for the same commodity.

Naturally bad news is unpleasant for all of us to take—particularly in view of our long held belief in the invulnerability of our navy, but if ill events befall, we must know about them. Bad news, when it is there, becomes a vital dosage. We cannot survive unless we know the truth.

More than a month elapsed between the sinking of the "Langley" and the public's awareness of that disaster. That month represented a loss of time in the further national recognition of our serious plight. Who knows what added impetus might have been given the sale of defense bonds or the solution of labor problems by an earlier acknowledgment.

I doubt if there is a general and real understanding of the importance of news—and newspapers—in the present crisis—even among newspaper men themselves.

We have an excellent laboratory study of the effectiveness of telling the truth no matter how it hurts. I refer to England. After a stumbling start in the Ministry of Information, the realistic British decided it was good business to tell the truth—all the time—particularly about naval losses.

Has it been effective? It has kept England in business. It has kept the rumor mongers on the back streets. It has restored faith in the British press and government.

One of the greatest disasters in naval history and certainly the most severe debacle on the seas as far as Britain is concerned was the sinking of the "Prince of Wales" and the "Repulse."

But England faced this as she had faced other body blows, with the result that the Empire knew of it within a few hours.

One of the sound war procedures that we could learn from the British is this business of giving out bad news as well as good. Because we have to learn to take it just as the British have.

Of late, I have been very much interested in the sayings and pronouncements of the critics of criticism—particularly those critics who have suggested that this would be a good time to suspend freedom of the press insofar as criticism of the operations of government are concerned.

It occurs to me that at this point all of us should have clearly in our minds the difference between proper and improper criticism.

Proper criticism is that type of comment directed at our obvious failures to properly implement our war effort, extravagance in government, playing politics with American lives and the general boon-doggling of peacetime politics.

Improper criticism concerns itself with the fact of war; such as denials of its propriety; a return to pre-war isolationism; deliberate attempts to drive the wedges of popular feeling between ourselves and our Allies, and all other evidences of twilight thinking.

Fortunately, most newspapers are sound enough in their concepts and if they are guilty of giving aid and comfort to the enemy, it is only because of careless and competitive practices which have been the outgrowth of doubtful procedures in peacetime.

With most critics of the press I have scant sympathy, but of the fact that the press needs criticism as well as government, there can be scant doubt, and that criticism should come primarily from within the press itself. I refer specifically to loose policies of editing and headline writing.

It is unfortunately true that government releases have too often played up good news and minimized bad news.

But in an overall picture, with as much blame as possible attached to failure of the army and navy properly to release the news, still newspapers in a general way have failed properly to evaluate and to balance headlines against the facts. . . .

Let us all remember, whether we be of the government or of the press, that this is the people's war. That our big job is to keep them informed.

One of the things that is going to win this war for America and the United Nations is a rising consciousness among the people that we might lose it. As a result, one of the mightiest ground swells in this history of the world is now afoot. In this ground swell, the voice of the people rises to a mighty roar . . . a roar of disapproval of anything that holds us back from victory. The people want to know why we are still playing politics when our very lives are at stake; they want to know why deeper cuts have not been made in non-essential spending. They want to know all about the rubber situation. They want to know why a ceiling has not already been set on wages, profits and prices.

In such a manifestation as the foregoing, the press plays an important part. But the press should remember that just as it has the proper role of fostering and forwarding proper criticism of government in times of crisis, so should the press actively defend the government in such periods against all improper and subversive criticism.

Censorship Secrecy [17]

United States censorship may or may not be keeping information from the enemy, and it is strikingly successful in keeping important news out of print in the United States. Just how far the United States Government is fighting World War II without taking its own people into its confidence was indicated by four incidents last week:

[17] From "What Sense Censorship?" newsstory. *Time.* 39:58-60. June 22, 1942. Reprinted by permission.

Five weeks after the battle of the Coral Sea the navy admitted the sinking of the aircraft carrier "Lexington." This delay was an excellent example of justifiable military censorship —withholding news that might be of value to the enemy. For a new Japanese attack was expected, and although the Japanese announced the sinking of a carrier of the "Saratoga" class, presumably they had not known for sure that the "Lexington" was done for.

After the news that Dutch Harbor had been bombed, nine days passed before the navy admitted that the Japanese had made a landing on remote islands in the Aleutians (blaming the delay on bad weather, which prevented air reconnaissance). This week first results of United States air attacks on enemy naval units were disclosed, but the United States public still knew little about what was happening in Alaska. For months censorship has almost stricken the word Alaska from print. Since Pearl Harbor, no outside reporter or photographer has been allowed a peek inside Alaska. As one correspondent in Alaska put it: "You people back in the 'old country' just plumb don't know the meaning of the word censorship." The Office of Censorship has even made a "special request" that the press services submit all stories about Alaskan military operations or installations for censorship *before* publication.

National censorship has been clamped on the information contained in a story which detailed certain dispositions not of United Nations' but of enemy forces. There was apparently good reason why the information should never have been made public. Nevertheless it was published by papers in several parts of the United States. Outraged, the government cracked down, forbidding not only mention of its crackdown but any reprinting of the information, which had already had a circulation of some 5,000,000 copies and was therefore hardly a secret, by any definition.

Censor Byron Price congratulated the press on its "magnificent" performance in keeping mum about the six-day Washington visit of Soviet Foreign Commissar Molotov—"news of very high importance . . . known to hundreds of newspapermen and broadcasters." (Only paper that talked was the tabloid Philadelphia *News*, which gossiped: "The talk in official Russian circles here is that Premier V. M. Molotov of Soviet Russia is in this country on a secret mission of vast importance.") Actually, while photographers waited at the White House to catch the Duke and Duchess of Windsor, Molotov strolled slowly past them and not a camera clicked.

It was debatable whether the press silence on Molotov was something to be proud or ashamed of. The silence may have given the Russian politician some protection from Nazi interference as he flew around in his big, lumbering Soviet plane. But no such protection has been deemed necessary for other important Allied figures (e.g., British Production Tsar Oliver Lyttelton, Harry Hopkins, General Brehon Somervell) *after* they had safely reached Washington or London.

Since the censorship on Molotov's whereabouts was clamped down at Russian request, it looked as if a Russian muzzle had been put on the United States press in order to please Stalin. And since the effect of the censorship was to keep secret from the public the fact that an agreement between the United States and Russia was pending, the inference was that here was a case of political, not military, censorship.

N.A.M. CENSOR CONFLICT [18]

A group of crack Washington correspondents last week practically blew the roof on censorship. They had just finished a 24-day tour of leading war plants as guests of the National Association of Manufacturers. Their wrath was aimed not at

[18] From "Censorship Fantasia," newsstory. *Time*. 39:64. June 8, 1942. Reprinted by permission.

N.A.M. but at the six army officers who accompanied them as censors (of the one navy censor who went along they thought better).

Said the Chicago *Sun's* W. A. S. Douglas at the N.A.M.'s farewell dinner in Buffalo: "Our office has wasted its money and we have wasted our time on this trip, because of the censorship. I have been reduced to a practice for which I have little talent, namely that of writing trivia."

Said the St. Louis *Post-Dispatch's* Richard L. Stokes: "I have seen things on this trip that would inspire and electrify the country, but everything inspirational that I have written was cut out by the censors."

Words, sentences and paragraphs, said the correspondents, were altered or deleted at will by the censors, with frequently bad-tempered admonitions that military orders were not to be questioned. Conflicts between the traveling censors and the local public-relations officers at ordnance plants were frequent.

Typical censorship ineptitudes that haunted reporters:

In Dayton correspondents were allowed to describe in detail a .50-caliber machine gun. Two days later, at an ordnance plant, no mention was allowed of the caliber of cartridges for these same guns. In two other plants mention of the guns' caliber became taboo.

At one plant no objection was raised to saying that the Bell Airacobra was driven by Allison liquid-cooled motors; but at Bell Aircraft itself the engine could not be named.

Told that one plant was so secret they could not even say they had seen it, let alone its product, correspondents a few days later beheld the selfsame product, in color, peering out of a full-page ad in the *Satevepost*.

They found that local newspapers, repeatedly carried full stories that were forbidden nationally.

In Akron, where the biggest tangle came between censors and correspondents, complete censorship was imposed on statements by rubber experts that Washington had given deceptive estimates of future synthetic rubber production.

A Philadelphia Story [19]

The fact that New York's two 50,000 watters, WJZ and WOR, are heard widely in the Philly area threw the Philadelphia police department and the F.B.I. in a dither Sunday night (28th).

It all started when the coppers found five bombs in the Harbor Police headquarters Sunday afternoon. The newspapers got wind of the find and were all set to spring with the story in the bulldog edition when the Director of Public Safety requested that the yarn be held out until midnight in order to give police a chance to find the culprit who planted the explosives.

The United Press, however, sent the story out to several of the local stations it services. The police director then hurriedly called the radio coordinator of the Defense Council, Horace Feyhl, to keep the story off the air.

Feyhl succeeded in stopping the yarn from being aired over the local stations but forgot the two Gotham outlets. At 6 P. M. the bomb story was flashed by WJZ, with WOR on the air soon afterward.

The newspapers who had been forced to "sit on the story" all day, were wild, but police authorities begged that the yarn still be held back, on the chance that the would-be saboteur hadn't heard of the New York newscasts. But at 9 P. M., Walter Winchell announced the bomb discovery over his "Jurgens Journal"—and still the Philly police demanded that the Philly papers hold the story.

At midnight, almost ten hours after the story broke, the two local morning papers, finally were given the okay to print the yarn.

[19] From "New York Stations Break Story While Philly Newspapers Bite Fingernails in Local Police Censorship Mix-Up," newsstory. *Variety.* 145:30. December 31, 1941. Reprinted by permission.

"Town Hall" Self-Censorship [20]

To clarify the question period of the Blue Network "America's Town Meeting of the Air" program in light of the censorship rules announced by the Office of Censorship, Town Hall, New York, has announced its ten-point program for "Freedom of Speech in Wartime," as prepared by George V. Denny Jr., president of Town Hall.

Since shortly after war was declared, all questions have passed through the hands of an editorial board composed of members of the Town Meeting staff, before they reach the air, according to the statement. Anyone may ask a relevant question following the prepared addresses, but rather than have Mr. Denny, the moderator, reject improper questions on the air, a member of the staff reviews them before they are asked.

Vagaries of Censorship [21]

Two incidents of the past week illustrate to newspapermen how difficult, and at the same time how utterly simple, it is to operate effectively under the strict censorship now in effect in the United States.

From the *New York Daily News* we learned how it and other newspapers and photo agencies had importuned military authorities for more than two weeks for permission to photograph and publish scenes of anti-aircraft defenses of New York. The *News* and others persisted, without avail. All trail-blazing efforts wound up at a stone wall—the Army Information Service, 90 Church Street, New York. This branch refused permission to all.

Monday afternoon, Dec. 29, Acme Newspictures came through with a full set of pictures of New York's anti-aircraft defenses. Captions, of course, were discreetly vague as to loca-

---

[20] From " 'Town Hall' Adopts Rule To Abide by Censorship," newsstory. *Broadcasting*. 22:14. February 23, 1942. Reprinted by permission.
[21] From "Vagaries of Censorship," editorial. *Editor & Publisher*. 75:22. January 3, 1942. Reprinted by permission.

tions of the batteries. Acme had obtained permission to make the shots simply by approaching directly the New York anti-aircraft command. Permission to publish, once the pictures were made, was granted readily by the army censorship, provided that information of value to the enemy was not divulged.

On Christmas eve, Free French forces executed a *coup* in occupying the islands of Miquelon and St. Pierre, near Newfoundland. Various picture services immediately besieged official sources, all the way from the United States State Department to the De Gaulle headquarters in London, for photos depicting the occupation and the plebiscites which followed. It developed that an A.P. request directed to Vice-Admiral Emile Muselier, commander of the Free French forces which occupied the islands, brought quick response and delivered the goods.

Both incidents carry for newspapermen the lesson that censorship red tape can be severed effectively if an appeal is made to the proper official at the proper time, all previous unavailing efforts to the contrary notwithstanding. No matter how simple the request, direct action seems to be the answer to problems facing the press under present censorship conditions—at least until order is brought out of the current chaos.

RACE RIOT BAN [22]

On the ground that the news value was not sufficient to compensate for the resultant harm, the Office of Censorship continued the radio "no publicity ban" on the race riot at Fort Dix, N. J., April 3, according to J. Harold Ryan, assistant director of censorship in charge of radio.

The Army Radio Branch first advised "no publicity" on the story, after a call had been received early Friday morning on the brawl which resulted in three fatalities and several woundings. After the facts became known, the ban was lifted but Mr. Ryan ordered it "continued and sustained." It was pointed out at the Censorship Office that there was precedent for such action, a

[22] From "Censorship Bans News of Race Riot," newsstory. *Broadcasting.* 22:48. April 13, 1942. Reprinted by permission.

similar black-and-white incident having developed several months ago in a Louisiana camp. Axis propaganda, it was pointed out, has tended to emphasize purported racial difficulties in this country.

Ed Kirby, chief of the Radio Branch of the Army, declared that from time to time a news situation arises in which, until full facts are known, it appears wise for the War Department to request "no publicity." He explained the Fort Dix story was brought to the attention of the Radio Branch about 3 A. M. Friday.

Later in the day, when details of the incident were available, Mr. Kirby said, the Department lifted the previous restrictions on broadcast. "From then on it became a matter for decision by the Office of Censorship," he said.

N.B.C.'s Agronsky Case [23]

Navy Department officials discussed with network officials yesterday the need for closer coordination with Washington authorities in handling the broadcasts of the webs' foreign staff correspondents. The networks were asked to bear in mind that while the correspondents might get clearance from censors at the originating points the contents of the broadcast might at the same time be contrary to the requirements of the United States censor.

What instigated the meeting was a recent broadcast by Martin Agronsky, N.B.C. staff man now in Australia. During the broadcast Agronsky quoted a United States Navy officer as belittling some anti-aircraft ammunition.

Uneven Censorship [24]

Control of the flow of news affecting military and naval operations is a job that calls for experience, cool judgment, and

[23] From "NBC's Agronsky Draws Blast from Navy," newsstory. *Variety.* 145:28. March 4, 1942. Reprinted by permission.
[24] From "Uneven Censorship," editorial. *Editor & Publisher.* 75:26. January 24, 1942. Reprinted by permission.

tact on the part of the censors, and it is not surprising that these qualities have shown up with wide variation in the opening days of the war.

Last week, for instance, the coast guard reported the sinking of a ship off Long Island, adding that one of its planes had dropped food and whiskey to a boatload of the crew survivors. But the navy, of which the coast guard is a part, denied all knowledge of the incident for a whole day, and a week later had given the press little beyond confirmation of the sinking.

On the West Coast, the army public relations officers incurred newspaper displeasure by conduct which seems, at a charitable rating, stupid. A balloon broke loose over Seattle and its dragging cable cut municipal and private power lines, paralyzing street car traffic, tying up elevators, etc. The fact of the blackout was evident to all, but the afternoon papers were forbidden by the local censor to mention the cause. Later in the evening, the censor allowed the facts to be disclosed in a radio broadcast and then released them for morning paper publication, leaving the evening paper editors with very red faces.

We suggest that the censors be guided by one major consideration—will publication help the enemy? Unless that question can be clearly answered in the affirmative, there is no reason for forbidding publication.

SNOWFALL CENSORED [25]

Thousands of New York newspaper readers must have gotten a chuckle or two from the editor's note in the *Times* last Monday. There was a front page story, with a picture of the Capitol, telling of Washington's heaviest snowfall in 20 years.

That was certainly news, and after letting people in on the secret, the editor added:

[25] From an editorial in *Editor & Publisher*. 75:18. April 4, 1942. Reprinted by permission.

"Because of censorship restrictions which allow mention of storms in only one area of the country in any one issue of a newspaper, the *New York Times* does not print this morning a report of weather conditions which obtained in New York yesterday afternoon and last night."

Certainly every man, woman, and child within the city circulation area knew that the metropolis had been swept by one of the most curious Spring snow storms in many a year, with wet snow, rain, hail, sleet, thunder and lightening contributing to the spectacle. Ordinarily, the story might have been worth a column or two in the next morning's papers—but not now.

With the policy of concealing broad weather news from the enemy, we are entirely in sympathy. There is good reason for omitting widespread reports and forecasts, but we can see no reason for suppressing news of weather conditions that have already passed. If that information is useful to the enemy, he already has it without regard to the press, and so long as he cannot get it out of the country, we see little reason to worry about it. If a close watch is kept on the cables and the radio and mails which cross our borders, we see no reason whatever for keeping such obvious news as an unseasonable snow storm out of the newspapers.

A "SECRET" TORNADO [26]

Last week's tragic mid-south tornado, with a death toll of 125 and scattered over the three states adjacent to Memphis, blew local radio stations into an embarrassing censorship dither. Wartime regulations on broadcasting weather news had the four stations in an uproar for most of Monday night (16th). No two handled the problem alike.

[26] From "Tornado a Radio Secret for Hours Until Wartime Clearance Is Given," newsstory. *Variety.* 145:25. March 25, 1942. Reprinted by permission.

Storm broke in the late afternoon. WMC and WMPS decided quickly to stick to the radio code, wired Washington for permission to make news reports on a weather subject. This was not forthcoming until 10:55 P. M. Meantime, as early as 6:57 P. M., WREC and WHBQ had both issued appeals for Memphis doctors and nurses to report for duty in the stricken area, but had kept information on the actual locale and damage of the gale to a minimum.

That brought a flood of calls to all stations. WMPS stuck it out until final word came through from Washington. But at 9:30, WMC revealed that a storm had struck and that doctors and nurses had already been sent. At 10 P. M. WMC's news announcer, Aubrey Guy, explained for the first time that no details could be given because of censorship. By this time, WREC was backing away, its 10:30 newscast studiously avoiding mention of either the storm or the rescue work from Memphis.

Meanwhile, however, WHBQ, using International News Service reports, gave details of the disaster at 9 o'clock, even revealing the extent of damage suffered at Western State Hospital for the Insane at Bolivar, Tenn.

Official censorship clearance came through just before 11 o'clock and all stations immediately smacked the ether with full reports. The *Commercial Appeal's* early editions, with considerable coverage, had been on the streets of Memphis since 9:30.

Situation soon provoked storm of discussion as to who did right and who did wrong under circumstances. One station executive contended that his opposition's "violation of the code is an open invitation for Washington to cancel all news services to all radio stations, except probably a government news service." He said the regulation on weather broadcasts of any sort is clear and "forbids any mention of a weather story without specific release is granted by the censors."

Another manager contended that they had observed the spirit of the ruling by withholding information regarding actual location of the storm's fury and that the issuance of appeals for doctors and nurses was a public service in an emergency rather than a means of circumventing the restrictions.

MORE "CENSORED" WEATHER [27]

Minnesota tornadoes, which caused loss of lives and did considerable damage to several sections of the state, also blew up considerable radio turmoil the repercussions of which now are reaching Washington and which are expected to bring out of the capital a clearer cut policy relative to weather news broadcasting.

KSTP and WLOL are perturbed because, in tabooing warnings of the series of tornadoes, they adhered to the federal "no weather reports" censorship rules, while other stations, including WCCO, WTCN, and WMIN, carried the storm stories over the ether waves. KSTP and WLOL didn't relish the idea of being "scooped."

When KSTP and WLOL sought permission from the local general weather bureau head to broadcast a storm program it was refused and the stations were referred to the Chicago regional headquarters, which also said "nothing doing."

However, it appears that Al Sheehan of WCCO contacted somebody in Chicago, who told him to go ahead. KSTP and WLOL even appealed to Office of Censorship in Washington without approval. He stated that news of the tornadoes was permissible only for publication in the newspapers, not over the radio.

But with KSTP and WLOL laying off, WMIN relayed a newspaper description of the tornadoes. After the newspapers were on the street WTCN also carried reports regarding the storms. Then Cedric Adams, WCCO newscaster, during his night broadcast, went into details and even had an eye witness on his program describing what he saw.

[27] From "Tornado Remains Radio Secret," newsstory. *Variety.* 146:37. May 20, 1942. Reprinted by permission.

THE PROBLEMS OF CENSORSHIP

DISCUSSION

In the words of a popular song of the last World War period, the chief problem of wartime censorship today is "Where do we go from here?"

It's much too early to criticize the efforts of Byron Price and the Office of Censorship on the basis of past accomplishments. But what is important to every American is the question of how far can we permit censorship to go?

As a people we have learned that in this era of total war, no single action of an individual can be wholly free. News, for the first time, takes its place on the battle front as a major weapon for defense, for morale-building. And on the other hand, censorship or suppression of news is even more important.

Few people realized until the Office of Censorship was established just how complete and how extensive any system of censorship must be in order to stay clear of that double-edged threat of "aid and comfort to the enemy." But, progressively, censorship moved into the field of war news, military movements, production, construction, weather, draftee lists, ship sailings, vital statistics and countless other fields. Even now the trend hasn't ended. With each new advance by the Office of Censorship, new problems appear to complicate the situation. And it is in the magnitude of these problems that the real limitation of censorship is found.

One of the oldest and most important problems of censorship is the possibility of its extension into the field of suppression of opinion. Already there has been some indication that many persons in authority would prefer to have all criticism of the government, of the war and production efforts, and of our military strategy the object of strict censorship. The implications of such a development are obvious.

A second problem and one which has been very nearly solved by the pressure of public opinion is that of the anti-British press. Although officially the government must permit freedom of speech, the public is easily aroused against newspapers which attack the British, our plan of cooperation, or the combined war effort of the United Nations. The anti-British press, at present a very insignificant minority opinion, is sufficiently unpopular with the overwhelming majority of the public that it really presents almost no problem, except from that of arousing antagonism among our Allies.

Hand in hand with the problem of anti-British opinions is that of the need for coordination of Allied news. Much of the ill feeling among press correspondents since the beginning of official censorship in the United States has been due to the fact that while news has been censored or withheld in this country, full details have appeared almost instantly in the press of England, Canada, Australia or Mexico. One outstanding complaint of United States newsmen is that our Allies are better informed than is the American public, in spite of our extensive and well-developed system of news coverage. Not only that, but we know far more, and more quickly, of the battle for Libya than we have yet been able to discover of the last days of Bataan and Corrigador.

Among other problems which censorship has imposed upon its directors and upon the American public is what to do with the foreign language press in the United States. And as the operations of censorship become more firmly established, there is always the widening gap of discrimination between censorship of the press and of the radio.

THE THREAT TO FREEDOM OF CRITICISM [1]

More difficult than protecting freedom of the press is the problem of preserving freedom over the radio—an instrument that did not exist in the First World War, but is now even more powerful than the press. Certainly there must be enough censorship to prevent military information from falling into the hands of the enemy. The real question is how to keep the radio open as a source of unbiased news and a forum of free and democratic discussion of issues. . . . Excellent as the work of broadcasting stations has been, there is a growing tendency, by no means universal, to rule out speeches or comment suspected of being criticism of the Administration from a leftist angle. . . .

This unofficial but effective censorship by private companies appears to arise in part out of fear of what the government might do, and in part out of a mistaken conception of certain managers of what patriotism in a democracy requires.

I have merely this to suggest: Let the Administration continually make it clear that it will not take over radio corporations in order to set up a government monopoly, and that it will not play a dictatorial role in censoring opinion. Let the responsible officials of broadcasting stations remember, as many of them do, that one of their great services is to provide the people with authentic information, and another to keep clear the channels of discussion.

If this is done, the hope that America in war and peace can escape a totalitarian fate will be greatly increased. Unquestionably to a Hitler, a Mussolini, or a Stalin, absolute control of the radio has been a more important instrument of power than secret police or concentration camps.

Let us be warned in time.

[1] By Norman Thomas, Socialist candidate for President. From a speech over WQXR, New York, January 11, 1942.

THE NECESSITY OF FRANK DISCUSSION [2]

Broadcasting stations, unlike newspapers, cannot do business without a government license. If the Federal Communications Commission suggests the possibility that a station's license will be revoked unless it stops spreading Mr. X's denunciations of high officials, Mr. X is pretty sure to change his tune. Even without any action by the Commission, the broadcasting stations and the networks may very likely exercise considerable private censorship of such commentators in response to resentment against their opinions. Another cause of radio trouble is likely to be adverse criticism of governmental decisions after they have been made. I am told that radio speakers are to be free to say in advance what they think the government ought or ought not to do, but that, once a decision is made, they must refrain from questioning it. This distinction is plausible, but is it wise? . . . Certainly it is arguable that when the government has decided to do something very unwise, then the sooner the decision is revoked the better. If this be so, then frank discussion after the decision is necessary in order to canvass its wisdom.

For example, President Wilson's decision to send American soldiers to Murmansk and Vladivostok was made unexpectedly so that there was no opportunity for previous discussion. Hence it might have been very desirable to subject the wisdom of his action to widespread subsequent examination. If there had been able outspoken objections to our invasion of Russia before the troops actually arrived there, conceivably they might have been recalled and we should have avoided one of our worst blunders during the last war. At any rate, whatever the nature of limitations on the radio ought to be, the problem of such limitations seems almost as important as censorship of newspapers. Furthermore, any suppression of newspapers is pretty sure to be widely

[2] By Zechariah Chafee, Jr., Harvard University. From "The Limits of Censorship, A Symposium." *Public Opinion Quarterly.* 6:19-20. Spring, 1942, Reprinted by permission.

known at once so that mistakes can be quickly corrected, while control over the radio is anonymous and works so quietly that the public will probably be unaware of its extent and so unable to express disapproval.

THE ANTI-BRITISH PRESS [3]

On December 8, the day after the attack on Pearl Harbor, the Hearst chain of newspapers, which stretches from New York to California, printed prominently the following declaration of editorial policy:

Our main concern now is about England. This attack by Japan upon us is largely to create diversion. We must not be diverted any more than is necessary for our own protection. The war is our war now—not only in Asia but in Europe.

On January 2, however, the same newspapers printed with similar prominence these words:

Mr. Churchill's address was most eloquent, and it may truthfully be said in praise of democracies that they do unerringly select their best talkers for the conduct of their wars. However, it might interest Mr. Churchill to know that the average American . . . does not think it makes a lot of difference in the eventual issue of this war who owns the sand dunes of the Libyan desert. . . . Is it not about time that the United States thought less of the Atlantic Ocean and the Mediterranean and more of the Pacific Ocean . . . and even more about the United States of America?

And on January 28 they followed with this:

England has systematically sacrificed her Allies to her own safety and her own immediate objectives. She sacrificed Norway—withdrew from the battle front without informing the Norwegian forces, with which she was in physical contact, what she was doing and why. She sacrificed Belgium in identically the same manner. . . . England abandoned France at Dunkirk and executed a masterly retreat to England. The French term it as "masterly" desertion of the Allied cause. . . .

[3] From "The Rake's Progress," editorial. *The Nation.* 154:180-2. February 14, 1942. Reprinted by permission.

England's plain policy seems to be to have Allies, but not to be an ally. A nation can render any aid or service to England it pleases, but it must not expect any aid or service in return.

Articles of similar purport, with many letters to the editor emphasizing the same points, are continually appearing in the *New York Daily News,* the *Washington Times-Herald,* and other papers. The *Washington Times-Herald* recently referred to the string of Atlantic bases acquired in the destroyer deal as "a lot of time bombs which will one day blow up in our faces," because they were only leased (for ninety-nine years) and not permanently annexed. And all the same points are daily emphasized by the German radio in its efforts to prevent support of the Allied cause by the people of France, Norway, Belgium, and Holland, and to sow distrust in the minds of the people of Australia, New Zealand, South Africa, and all the colonial territories. Similar expressions of American opinion are quoted in the German broadcasts to Britain in order to foster anti-American feeling in that country. . . .

We know now by the experience of other countries—which also believed that their national unity, in wartime at least, would stand up against all assaults—that the enemy strategy counts enormously upon the divisive and disruptive elements in popular feeling; upon nationalist hostilities, racial prejudices, historical animosities, economic rivalries. Such ferments, working actively enough in France before the war to destroy the alliance with Russia, continued after the declaration of war to such degree as to undermine the ties with Britain and prepare the way for a separate peace. They did this by creating first of all that "Maginot mind" which goes with a nationalism that has become hostile to cooperation with foreigners and is compelled therefore to fall back upon purely "defensive" strategy.

But there are two points in France's tragic story which should concern us now. The first is that the divisive forces by which Hitler profited did not come to full fruition until *after* war had begun. While anti-Semitism, anti-Sovietist, Anglophobia did exist before the war, they were regarded as relatively harmless. Plenty of persons in France were ready enough to pass on the slogan "Britain will fight to the last Frenchman" (the German radio now sends out daily the slogan, "Britain will fight to the last American"), but had you suggested to one of those Frenchmen that he was preparing the way for a government of surrender that would one day allow France to be used for the German conquest of Britain, he would have been not merely completely incredulous but profoundly shocked.

The second point we should recall is that the decision to carry on the war from Africa with a government in Algeria supported by the French Navy was defeated only by a margin of three votes in the French Cabinet. A slightly better morale among the leaders, a little less defeatism and Anglophobia, and today the whole of Africa would be unquestionably an Allied bastion, and Anglo-French fleet would command the Mediterranean, Dakar would be an American outpost, Indo-China would never have been handed over to Japan by a Vichy government, immense forces would have been liberated for dealing with Japan, and the lives of tens of thousands of Americans who must die this year or next would have been saved.

The military authorities tell us that wars are won by a final margin of military power which may perhaps be quite small. It is clear that that is true of morale as well. Let us face the facts. . . . In these last few years there has probably been more dislike and fear of Russia in this country than there was in France. The fear of Communism has been more hysterical. Distrust of "Europe"—which usually means Britain—goes deeper here than Anglophobia went in France. How could it be otherwise? For years the view has been hammered into the minds of Americans that this country was swindled into participation in the last war; that our participation was achieved mainly by the cunning, lying propaganda of the British and of cynical financial interests; that the character of the peace proved America's costly intervention to have been completely futile. Add to this an aversion to war which found support about equally in materialist cynicism and Christian idealism, and you get some idea of the strength of the feelings to which the American isolationist—and the German propagandist—could appeal.

And to those feelings both are still appealing with undiminished vigor. For the American isolationist the honeymoon of national unity which is supposed to have begun at four o'clock on the Sunday afternoon of December 7 at Pearl Harbor, is over.

The average American liberal will accept that statement with considerable skepticism. This is partly because it is not his habit to read the isolationist press, which consists mainly of newspapers owned by William Randolph Hearst, Joseph M. Patterson, and Robert R. McCormick, whose publishing enterprises stretch across the entire continent. Their papers have a combined circulation larger than that of any other newspaper group in the United States, and they are able to present to tens of millions of readers the same idea, voice the same prejudice, make the same attack, at the same moment from one end of the country to the other. Do we really assume that such an instrument, used in such a way and appealing to forces like those just described, in a Congressional election year, has no bearing at all on the war effort?

CENSORSHIP DUE TO FEAR [4]

On the whole I admire the way radio in this country has kept open the channels of information. . . . They have done even better than the British, and in all other countries radio is entirely the creature of the government.

[4] By Norman Thomas, Socialist candidate for President. From a newsstory entitled "Fears Censorship by 'Fright' of Owners and Personnel of Stations." *Variety.* 145:28. February 11, 1942. Reprinted by permission.

But there is a tendency in the United States to set up an unofficial censorship, largely on the part of the people who are afraid of what the government might do rather than on what has been done.

There are, however, many stations which have taken a broad attitude and it is important that this should continue since all our future depends on an informed democracy. . . . Outside the military-information field there's a terrible lot of territory to consider in questions of censorship. It's possible that the present rules could be interpreted to protect the government against the consequences of incompetence.

NEED FOR ALLIED NEWS COORDINATION [5]

Official confirmation is lacking but reports persist in Washington that the plan for newspaper censorship will not be publicly unfolded for several weeks.

This delay is said to be occasioned by a decision to withhold announcement until a method is developed for coordinating censorship within the United States with the systems of other countries embraced in the United Nations.

There is evidence of need for coordination in the repeated instances where United States newspapers have been asked to withhold information only to find the facts openly published in newspapers abroad, notably in Great Britain, it has been pointed out.

Dutch communiques have revealed operations in the Pacific theater of war which not only have been deleted from War and Navy Department announcements but also are in the categories of "restricted" information.

The departure of Winston Churchill from London for Washington was publicized in England but, at the request of the

[5] From "Coordination of Censorship with Allies Is Seen," newsstory. *Editor & Publisher.* 75:27. January 10, 1942. Reprinted by permission.

White House, was not referred to here until the Prime Minister reached the White House; likewise Mr. Churchill's trip to Canada was covered in detail by Dominion papers but, again on order of the White House, was treated only in broad outline in the United States.

THE PROBLEM OF SELF-CENSORSHIP [6]

Biggest single American propaganda event of the war—landing of the A.E.F. in Ireland last week—was muffed completely for 24 hours by three and perhaps more of the most important shortwave outlets in the United States. Failure to get the big news on the air to Europe resulted from uncertainty as to the application of the censorship code to the international stations.

Trio of transmitters which are definitely known to have refused to broadcast the landing are N.B.C.'s WNBI and WRCA, and Westinghouse's WBOS, which is permanently hitched to and programmed by N.B.C. Although announcement of the A.E.F. came from the White House and was carried by the news services, N.B.C. didn't air it because it was under the impression that censorial code prohibited mentioning troop movements unless it was given specific permission.

This permission would ordinarily be contained in one of the half-dozen to a dozen "directives" the shortwavers are fed each day by the Coordinator of Information and the Coordinator of Inter-American Affairs. These "directives" instruct the stations in what they can mention, what they can't mention, what should be played up and what should be played down.

Inasmuch as it got no "directive", N.B.C. remained mum. Offices of the two coordinators apparently never thought to send on, figuring that inasmuch as it was a White House announce-

[6] From "NBC Strictly Conforms to Censorship, Doesn't Report Irish Incident on Shortwave Until Direct Okay Is Given," newsstory. *Variety*. 145:26. February 4, 1942. Reprinted by permission.

ment and so widely carried by the wire services, stations would naturally pick it up. Staff member of one of the government agencies suddenly discovered in amazement the next day that N.B.C. hadn't aired the landing. Point was immediately cleared up and the stations then put it on the ether.

Meantime, C.B.S. had waited for no instructions and had the A.E.F. story on the air in German less than 15 minutes after the White House announcement was made. It came at 1 P.M., just at the start of a 15-minute news broadcast to Germany, and before the end of the program it had been bulletinned in. It was pounded in various languages all through the day and night.

C.B.S. beat B.B.C. to the air with the story by an hour. B.B.C. recognizing the full propaganda value of the move, sent it out in a continuous barrage to Europe, Africa and Asia in 24 languages.

THE JAPANESE PRESS IN AMERICA [7]

A newspaper man who knows his Japan very well writes *Editor & Publisher* in protest against the continued publication of Japanese language newspapers in the United States. He cites one paper, published in a prohibited zone on the West Coast, which claims that its circulation, at $1 a month, has increased 3,000 since Pearl Harbor.

Discounting the official reasoning that these papers should be permitted to publish because the government can get its messages through them to Japanese who do not read English, our correspondent holds that Japanese in America who don't "read Yankee" should not be at large. He points out the danger of secret communications through the 30,000 characters of the Japanese language, and adds that the great Feb. 26, 1936, revolt in Tokyo was started by a signal in the classified columns of the *Tokyo Asahi*.

[7] From "A Present Danger," editorial. *Editor & Publisher*. 75:20. May 16, 1942. Reprinted by permission.

One Pacific Coast newspaper, he declares, carried a straight report of Gen. MacArthur's arrival in Australia in its English-language section, while its Japanese news conveyed through the use of ideographs that the general had deserted his troops and fled to Australia "escaping from the jaws of death."

As we recently pointed out, the Japanese newspaper problem is different from that presented by the German or Italian news-papers. Many loyal Americans, whether or not descended from those Axis stocks, can read these languages fluently. The num-ber who can read Japanese is limited, indeed, and the problem of watching Japanese press utterances in native characters is difficult, if not impossible. If by shenanigans in one or more of the Japanese-American newspapers, we let ourselves in for another Pearl Harbor disaster, the people will have little patience with tolerance. The matter looks like one for immediate atten-tion from the Department of Justice.

THE FOREIGN LANGUAGE PRESS [8]

What to do about the more than 1,600 foreign language publications printed in this country is a problem perplexing the officials of two branches of the government. Both the Justice and War Departments have been studying various suggestions for restricting the foreign language press for several weeks but no agreement has been reached to date.

Army officials are reported to favor suspension of publications in German, Italian and Japanese tongues, and licensing of papers printed in any other foreign language. Justice, on the other hand, prefers some system of general licensing which would make it possible to weed out undesirable periodicals without forcing all papers in languages of our enemies to shut down.

There is no question that ample authority exists to impose any type of control. In addition to emergency legislation enacted

[8] From "What To Do with Foreign Press Puzzles Officials," newsstory. *Advertising Age.* 13:25. April 20, 1942. Reprinted by permission.

since this war began, the 1917 Trading with the Enemy Act is still on the statute books.

Military chiefs favor a blanket suspension of German, Italian and Japanese periodicals because the tremendous task of translating and checking could be avoided, and the problem of codes completely eliminated. The Attorney General's office points out, however, that such publications which are not un-American are extremely useful in bridging the gap between the government and unnaturalized residents. Justice's experiences in alien registration, enemy alien identification and surrender of contraband has proved this point.

It is also felt that elimination of the foreign language press, or a large part of it, might lead to unrest in certain areas. In addition, many aliens who are loyal to America but who do not read or speak English would lose all contact with policies of their adopted land, and the government would be deprived of a useful medium for gauging sentiment in regions populated largely by aliens.

DISCRIMINATION BETWEEN PRESS AND RADIO [9]

How it can be done admittedly is a problem nobody yet has solved, but really serious study is being given drastic additional censorship control over broadcasting. The federal supervisors actually would like some means of chopping off signals from domestic transmitters at the Mexican and Canadian borders and the ocean shorelines.

In response to yelps of newspaper publishers whose sheets have been recently scissored before going out of the country, suggestions have come from federal authorities that a way will be found to keep radio stations from spraying into foreign territory the same information that is deleted from the public press.

In view of the undeniable technical impossibility of fencing

[9] From " 'Requests' Anent Radio Have Force of a U. S. Order," newsstory. *Variety.* 145:1+. March 4, 1942. Reprinted by permission.

in all signals, there is growing alarm that the federal authorities will resort to far more stingent censorship at the source. Even that the present power limits may be cut in various instances, no matter how much the F.C.C. objected to reduction of service. Conceivably, stations using maximum wattage along the coasts and borders could be made to return volume and install additional directional antennas to fan their signals back over the mainland, but obviously this will not solve the puzzle.

That means there is even stronger liklihood of more discrimination between radio and the press. Already federal censors are drawing lines of this sort, as well as treating different classes of newspapers differently (such as allowing only "local publication" of stories about new war industry plants, forbidding sheets with state-wide circulation to use items approved for rags that sell only in a small area).

In the ten weeks since Pearl Harbor, several instances have occurred where communiques and statements were given out with a blunt order that they be kept off the air. More of this is threatened, while some sporadic talk has been heard about stationing blue-pencilers in each transmitter and network point of origin to monitor the copy.

Censorship has gone farther already than many who were called calamity howlers forecast. Between the Office of Censorship, the Army-Navy-Maritime Commission, and the Office of Facts and Figures, broadcasters are hemmed in by "requests" and sets of "approved practices."

One bright ray gleamed last week, however, when J. H. Ryan, assistant censorship director who handles radio matters, decided that man-in-the-street pickups don't have to be abandoned entirely. Though the code said these should be ended for the duration, Ryan gave one station permission to put on such a show with added safeguards against fifth-columnists or agitators. Ryan explained that other broadcasters may get consent to resume such features if they take precautions which receive official approval.

"Virtually every program of this general type varies in some degree from the others. For this reason, no blanket approval of substitutes can be given in advance," Ryan commented. "Broadcasters who feel they could make use of such programs and still fulfill obligations of self-censorship should submit their specific program structures to the Office of Censorship for review and interpretation."

Meanwhile, the army has laid down more rigid controls, interpreting the provisions in the approved practice code dealing with withholding of information having military value. Six-page circular goes into great detail in telling what can and cannot be said regarding industrial production, new factories and defense installations, contract awards, and related phases of the war program.

EDITORIAL COMMENT

THE PRESS VIEW

DAVID LAWRENCE FOR THE U.S. NEWS [1]

The Administration is keeping the war production effort from attaining maximum efficiency, because it is not permitting the people to keep a check on production itself. The stimulus that can come from an aroused nation is being quietly anaesthetized.

Under the policy of suppression, it is improper for any newspaper, for example, to tell the production figures by months because that presumably would be "aiding the enemy." Actually the production may be bad, we may be suffering defeats at home but nobody must know of it. Abstractly the enemy can get aid or comfort out of anything, to be sure, but the truth is the words "aid and comfort" relate to actual military help. The phrase is being given an exaggerated meaning to hide incompetence.

There can be no military help to the enemy in stating our production figures promptly by months. It is not necessary to tell the kind of planes made or where they are made. But some standard of efficiency and overall checking must be set up. This is the people's war—not the bureaucrats' experiment in sociology.

We know, for instance, when the enemy lands troops and occupies a strategic port or island. But we do not know when General Complacency or General Selfishness or General Labor Privilege lands on a given plant or situation and administers a defeat at home. These mistakes and obstructions are concealed from the American people by a convenient censorship, and nobody in Congress evidently has the temerity to come out and

[1] By David Lawrence. From "Defeat at Home," editorial. *United States News.* 12:22-3. March 13, 1942. Reprinted by permission.

tell the American people what is delaying production. As a constructive force in helping to win the war, the Congress and its committees, with a few exceptions, have thus far proved a tragic disappointment. . . .

What Washington has done to cloak its incompetence by means of a broadly operating system of suppression at the source has already cost our war effort plenty. This will continue to hurt us, because the correctives of public opinion cannot set in when the facts about our mistakes are officially withheld.

We have not, moreover, been given the casualty lists. These, it seems, are not to be published nationally, but only locally, and as yet no overall figures have been given out. When the names of those we know come out on those lists, when the totals are published, when the flower of American youth has begun to suffer numerically large losses, will Washington then wake up to the fact that this is a war?

TIME, LIFE AND FORTUNE [2]

Ever since the United States geared itself for wartime censorship this department has been curious about the mechanics of it in relation to our magazines. Here's a glimmering of how we've been functioning since actual operating regulations got underway.

There are many kinds of censorship, but two principally concern us: First, voluntary self-censorship which covers dissemination of information within the borders of the United States and is based on the official policies that have come from United States Director of Censorship Byron Price; second, peripheral censorship, which requires that all editorial material of a "scientific, technical or professional nature" for mailing abroad must be reviewed by the Technical Data License Division, Office of Export Control, Board of Economic Warfare, and licensed before it can be released.

[2] From a discussion of *Time's* relations with censorship in *FYI* (For Your Information), Time, Inc. house-organ, May 18, 1942. Reprinted by permission.

Peripheral censorship takes quite a bit of doing as it calls for getting stories passed, obtaining a license number, getting the license number stamped on the wrappings of all export copies—and getting it done on time. Fortunately, this is the only license-imprinting we have to go through in all of our censorship dealings. To simplify matters, first drastic step taken here was to lump automatically all export copies of *Time* into the TAE flyweight edition, thereby unifying the production and distribution problems and, at the same time, leaving *Time's* United States edition with plenty of editorial latitude. Next step was to see that the editorial material got passed and licensed in time to meet *Time & Life's* very tight printing schedules. Working that out has been a major task for our chief censor Eric Hodgins and Walter Belknap and Philadelphia Production Head Kenneth McKean. Although at first Hodgins had quite a time explaining to functionaries that we couldn't submit advance galley proofs because most of the time our news goes via teletypesetter and there just isn't such a thing as a galley proof before we go to press. Mondays Hodgins confers with *Life* Editor John Billings, Thursdays with *Time* Editor Tom Matthews, makes sure that the Board of Economic Warfare has a look-see. If B.E.W. approves, the license (a new one every week) follows. License numbers, incidentally, are imprinted by the good old-fashioned rubber stamp method right at the plant and any employee directly concerned with the license-imprinting or wrapping of export copies must have had an affidavit filed in Washington attesting to the fact that he's trustworthy and not connected with any subversive activities. *Fortune,* because it is a monthly, doesn't create as many time-pressing problems but because it contains more technical information might be liable to increasingly stricter censorship. Since April 20—when peripheral censorship actually started to function—we've had no trouble; all our magazines have been cleared and licenses issued. The only request for modification concerned the story of the treatment of dysentery by a sulfa drug. On the grounds that it would "give aid and comfort to the enemy" it was eliminated from the export copies of *Time's* May 4 issue.

All stories filed by our correspondents from overseas and in the battle areas are automatically censored at the point of origin by the authorities on the spot. Ordinarily therefore this material does not go through the censorship mill again in this country but is cleared direct to our offices. Occasionally the Office of Censorship will inquire the sources of a story. This is not for check-up purposes on any individual correspondent or editor, but merely so the Censorship office will know what field censor's office of what nationality released the story to the cables.

The operations of Byron Price's Office of Censorship, which is charged with policing the Voluntary Code, is becoming more and more ramified but the relationship between this office and Time Inc. continues cordial and cooperative. The basic objective of the Voluntary Code is obviously to prevent publication of any information that could be of aid to the enemy or his agents in this country, at the same time to provide as much latitude as possible for the free publication of news in this country.

Of Time Inc's three major magazines, *Life* with its long pre-war experience in dealing with governmental agencies tangles with censorship least, works most frequently by pre-arrangement with the armed services and therefore has army or navy clearances all along the line; *Time* running on its fast news schedule submits almost nothing to the Office of Censorship or the armed services in advance, has been questioned on news publication only a very few times; *Fortune* with its elaborate and heavily documented stories feels most the burdens of restrictions. But even these restrictions so far are not unduly onerous. Rates of production and delivery of war materials, performance rates, over-exact locations of war plants, too much specification as to floor areas, payrolls or other information that can shed light to the enemy on the extent of the war effort—these are the standard things which call forth objections from censorship and the armed services, and such statistics our magazines have largely eliminated without serious loss.

On several occasions we have carried adverse review opinions of junior officers in the armed services either to their superiors or to the Office of Censorship and in no case have we failed to be satisfied with the results of appeal.

As for those who make wry faces at the Office of Censorship on the alleged grounds that it is withholding information or using its power to cover up government incompetence, there is no evidence as far as Censor Eric Hodgins can see from his experience in representing Time Inc. publications in Washington on this front.

ERNEST K. LINDLEY OF NEWSWEEK [3]

How to inform the public without disclosing facts of military value to the enemy is one of the most difficult problems in a democracy at war. That the press and radio are under censorship is common knowledge. An exact understanding of the censorship rules is almost as important to an intelligent reader as to an editor. This understanding is almost impossible to achieve for the simple reason that the authorities in Washington are still at odds.

The chief facts which the press refrains from publishing without official authorization are about movements of troops, ships and planes, fortifications, and production. There are limitations on information about the weather, the use of maps and photographs, casualties, the movement of high-ranking officials, munitions, etc. Some facts are made available to the press "for background" to aid writers and editors in forming opinions. The conclusions expressed in well-informed publications may

[3] By Ernest K. Lindley. From "Washington Tides: A Report on the Growing Pains of Censorship." *Newsweek.* 19:29. February 16, 1942. Reprinted by permission.

therefore be based on detailed information which cannot be passed on to the reader.

As to the need for censorship there is no dispute. But some of the rules seem unnecessarily strict and some downright senseless, especially as they are interpreted by certain officials. The conflict within the government itself is indicated by the fact that while Byron Price, Director of the Office of Censorship, insists that censorship is entirely voluntary, the army has threatened to invoke the 1917 Espionage Act against anyone publishing information against an army injunction.

The most serious difficulties are arising from the censorship of facts about war production. This clause in the press code prohibits:

> Specific information about war contracts, such as the exact type of production, production schedules, dates of delivery, or progress of production . . . or nationwide 'roundups' of locally published procurement data except when such composite information is officially approved for publication.
>
> Specific information about the location of, or other information about, sites and factories already in existence, which would aid saboteurs in gaining access to them; information other than that readily gained through observation by the general public, disclosing the location of sites and factories yet to be established, or the nature of their production.

Washington decides to put a new aircraft plant in a large southern city. This cannot long be kept a secret from the citizens of that community. The local paper publishes the story, with details and pictures of the site. But newspapers and magazines elsewhere are prohibited from publishing it. Yet that local paper can be bought in most of the metropolitan out-of-town newsstands in the United States, and probably in Latin America.

Last week the Army Procurement Division refused permission to publish the locations and builder-operators of several new aircraft and other plants. By this ruling, about all that could be reported was this: "The War Department has awarded a contract for (censored) dollars to the (censored) corporation for

the construction of a plant at (censored) to make (censored)."
From another official, *Newsweek* obtained permission to publish
the central facts.

The censorship was made ludicrous by the publication last
week in the January-February issue of a leading service journal
of many details about war production which the press had been
prohibited from mentioning. This is a publication to which
anyone can subscribe and which is watched most closely by foreign agents. Other technical publications have come out recently
with details far more useful to a spy than are less technical facts
barred to the general press.

Price said most of this matter was on the forms before his
office began functioning and that there would be no more such
infringements. But the real solution is to inject more common
sense into the censorship. Behind the scenes, Price, various other
civilian officials, and the press are trying to do this. A little
headway has been made. Meanwhile, what may be a perplexity
for the discerning reader is a headache to the press, and especially to its representatives in Washington.

Arthur Robb—Editor and Publisher [4]

Never before in our history, unless you except the blowing
up of the Maine in 1898, has the United States begun a war
with the problem of what to do about casualty lists—before a
ship or soldier had moved on a hostile mission. As this is written, there seems to be some uncertainty in Washington on what
to do with reports of men killed or wounded in the service of
their country. There seems to be the underlying fear that publication of lengthy lists of casualties might (1) give information
to our enemies that they do not already have; (2) dishearten
the people and inhibit voluntary enlistments in the armed services.

[4] By Arthur Robb, editor of *Editor & Publisher*. From "Shop Talk at Thirty,"
editorial. *Editor & Publisher*. 74:36. December 20, 1941. Reprinted by permission.

All we can advance in opposition to the present (and not very definite) ideas that have been published is the experience we have had during a long quarter century as an ordinary human being, a newspaperman, and a soldier. As a human being, we'll declare that we're ready along with many other millions who live under the flag to take the news as it comes, the bad with the good. As a newspaperman, we'll say that bad news can't be kept from the knowledge of the people for long, and that rumor emphasizes and exaggerates the import of bad news. No better example of that can be found than the rumors which flew through the halls of Congress last week in the absence of definite news from Pearl Harbor.

If members of Congress and newspaper readers had been disposed to panic, all the necessary seeds for it were sown last week—and the facts, bad as they were, fell far short of the disaster indicated by the legislative gossips. As a soldier, we'll say that one of the first lessons war teaches is that you can't fight without hurting somebody, and the somebody is as likely to be yourself as it is one of the other fellows. War calls for fortitude, and we think the American people, in and out of the fighting forces, have plenty of that. They've shown plenty of it during the economic distresses of the past ten years— far more than has often been credited to them by some of their leaders.

We are happy to comment that neither newspapers nor radio stations contributed to the public confusion by speculation without facts. They had to report, as news, what was said in Washington, but they were careful not to give the rumors the weight of authority. Even with that precaution, people could have been found in many a town to give credence to half-read or half-heard reports of what Senator Whatsis was said to have said. We'll always have them with us, and the only means of combatting their idiocy is to supply the sensible majority with credibly complete facts.

The whole question of censorship is now wide open. Presumably the army and navy have drawn their plans for wartime censorship, and also presumably, have them ready for submission to Byron Price, who will have to administer whatever censorship we have. We doubt very much that any scheme "half mandatory, half voluntary" as the first stories described the plan, will work to anyone's satisfaction. The task of imposing even a "half-mandatory" system on press and radio seems to imply placing a censor in at least every large city, with powers of immediate action in the case of a violation of the rules. That, at this writing, seems both impossible and unnecessary.

We surmise, and we hope we're right, that the plan contemplates the publication of basic rules for the guidance of editors and public relations officers of the services, with close monitoring of radio programs, especially in foreign languages, and a less immediate supervision of the press. Ninety-nine per cent of the war news will come over news service wires, and all of the services have bent over backward to comply with the rules laid down by Washington since last January. Since the bulk of radio war news also comes through these channels, clearing from Washington or New York, it should not be difficult to check the release of any unauthorized information. Newspapers and broadcasters alike, during the first two weeks of the war, have set a record for conservatism in their reports, in the face of one of the most dramatic situations that has ever confronted them. If their purpose had been to demonstrate that no direct censorship is necessary, they could not have submitted more cogent proof than their behavior during the past fortnight. That can't be emphasized too often.

Our policy, then, would be to have the minimum of censorship at the point of publication. Make it plain what may and what should not be printed, in the opinion of the men who are guarding our destinies. Permit some argument before the rules are made final, and also permit their amendment whenever they don't work in practice. Consider carefully every statement that is issued from the White House, the War or Navy Departments, or any of their regional headquarters, so that newspapers and broadcasters can consider anything of such origin official and free for publication. Obtain, as quickly as possible, uniformity in the application of censorship rules in all parts of the country—something which has not yet been arrived at.

Common sense is the great solvent of these problems, and neither censors, soldiers, nor editors will have a monopoly of that quality.

Mr. Roosevelt is correct, we believe, in suggesting that newspapers and news services refrain from compiling mass lists of casualties, which would give alert enemy intelligence a key to information which might have been withheld for good reasons. Along the same line is the idea that names of units or ships ought not to be given to newspapers by the next-of-kin of casualties. We doubt that the latter suggestion will stand up in practice, especially in small cities and towns. Editors will not see the point of concealing a detail that will be gossiped in every bar and cigar store, as it certainly will be.

As we learned while working in the last war, we'll learn again that secrecy often serves no purpose beyond enhancing the vanity of the censor.

ARTHUR KROCK ON CENSORSHIP [5]

The censorship which has been set up in Washington . . . has repeated "the errors of our earlier performance," though not all of them. It is divided and conflicting. It is part "voluntary," which is an unfair and inefficient method. Its numerous administrators differ every hour on what "constitutes information of value to the enemy." It shuts out news which would and should warn the public of our danger. Its attempts to suppress news are at times unsuccessful, the lack of success arising from the

    [5] By Arthur Krock, *New York Times* columnist. From "The Limits of Censorship, A Symposium." *Public Opinion Quarterly.* 6:24-6. Spring, 1942. Reprinted by permission.

fact that what one official has authorized another seeks to delete
—after publication. . . .

There is censorship at only the federal official and trans-
oceanic sources, and these are separately administered. . . . We
have several censorship authorities, all final, all in disagreement
on particular items. These are from time to time addressed
by an interdepartmental group, most of them without practical
experience in such matters, who seek to formulate a publications
policy and have no power to enforce it. . . .

The Office of Censorship controls incoming and outgoing
communications; helps to solve the perplexities imposed by
"voluntary censorship" to the extent it can; attempts to educate
the military and coordinate the practices of the army and navy,
and to fit these into a pattern with the units of armament production. It is ably and intelligently administered.

But in the areas of defense and of combat the armed services
themselves control the communications. And in Washington
they exercise their own disparate judgments of what should be
given out and what concealed.

THE NEW YORK TIMES [6]

Washington officials frequently declare that the country does
not recognize the real seriousness of the situation, or that it is
complacent; yet these same officials are constantly giving out
rosy or one-sided statements calculated to hide this very seriousness and to promote complacency. Our defeats or losses are
seldom stated in their full extent, even when it is virtually certain
that the enemy knows that extent or that the knowledge could
no longer make any material difference.

Let us grant, for example, that there may still be good reason
for withholding a full account of the damage done by the Japanese to our ships at Pearl Harbor. What possible reason can

[6] From "Knowledge and Morale," editorial. *New York Times.* 91:14 L,
May 25, 1942. Reprinted by permission.

there still be, however, for withholding the figure on the number of airplanes we lost there? The Japanese must have a pretty good idea of how much damage they did in this respect. In any case, the number of planes turned out since Pearl Harbor must be many times the number lost there, and the lost planes must have been long since replaced. There seems even less reason for withholding the story of how Japan acquired command so quickly of the air over the Philippines; or of telling how many planes we had there originally, and how many were destroyed on the ground. In this case the American people are being denied knowledge of some things that the Japanese must now know exactly. This policy has extended in other directions. Our government, for example, has been less frank and prompt than the British in revealing our ship losses in naval engagements.

If there is one direction above all others in which Americans must be brought to recognize the seriousness of the situation it is with regard to merchant shipping. Rear Admiral Greenslade pointed out in a recent speech to shipyard workers on the West Coast that already "war goods are piling up at the docks of both coasts and are backing up at some inland war plants." The blunt truth is that in spite of the huge American building program, ships are being sunk faster than they are being built. As long as this continues, the situation is deteriorating. Even if launchings just keep pace with sinkings, the situation is deteriorating for we are not adding to total tonnage, but we are losing precious cargoes and far more precious crews. Yet Secretary of the Navy Knox prevents the people from recognizing the full gravity of the present situation when he makes optimistic statements. The President can only blunt that recognition still more by declaring that the problem "is being solved."

The American people are not subject to meaningless waves of pessimism or optimism, nor will they be cheerful or grave simply in response to advice from Washington that they should be so. Their mood will respond, as that of the Washington officials themselves does, to the facts as they know them. They will acquire the necessary mood when they are told the necessary facts. They can be treated like grown-ups. When they are given the proper knowledge, they can be depended on to make the proper response.

NICHOLAS ROOSEVELT OF NEW YORK HERALD TRIBUNE [7]

Freedom of the press is, as a matter of fact, separable from freedom of speech and freedom of the air. When a government takes over control of what may be said in print or over the air, this control is not limited to what the publishers and broadcasters themselves may say. Government censors will hold these men responsible for what they print or allow to be broadcast—which means that they will be held responsible for what other people say, as well as for what they say themselves.

Not only will they not be permitted to air views of their own which the censor does not like, but they will be forbidden to circulate the views of anyone else which rile the censors. In this manner government will easily assume control over everything which anyone may write or say. It is but a step from such censorship to the punishment, not only of publishers, editors, writers, and broadcasters, but also of any individual who persists in expressing his own views or in circulating articles, pamphlets, books or broadsides which express his views.

PRESS MISCELLANY [8]

Navy censorship of news about counter measures against the submarines is accepted unquestioningly by the press. However, the Philadelphia (Pa.) *Inquirer* (Ind.) suggests: "We'll

[7] By Nicholas Roosevelt, editor of the *New York Herald Tribune*. From an address during a pilgrimage to Gunston Hall, Washington, D.C., printed in "Free Press, Air Viewed as Vital," newsstory. *Broadcasting*. 21:20. October 20, 1941. Reprinted by permission.

[8] From "U-Boat Attacks: Press View," newsstory. *United States News*. 12:12. February 13, 1942. Reprinted by permission.

all feel better when the navy can tell us how many of these marauders have been sunk—for they will be sunk." The Boston (Mass.) *Herald* declares that though the navy has "not chosen to let us know what success our protective cordon has had against this menace, information that a few of them have been sunk— if they have—would be comforting to the people and probably would be of no value at all to the enemy in the absence of identifying data regarding time and place."

On the other hand, the Austin (Tex.) *American* (Dem.) declares: "It is sound policy to withhold details. While we would like to have more details, we aren't nearly so anxious for them as the Nazis are."

THE RADIO VIEW

The Networks [9]

Officials of the three major networks expressed confidence . . that the new radio censorship code released Friday by the Office of Censorship would cause little difficulty in their operations. Digest of the comment follows:

C.B.S.—"After study of the radio censorship code announced today by Byron Price, executives of C.B.S. replied that they regard the rules as both reasonable and intelligent."

N.B.C.—Clarence L. Menser, N.B.C. program manager, said: "We do not anticipate that the censorship code will cancel any of the quiz programs now on N.B.C. Instructions have been issued to producers, announcers, and masters of ceremonies on these shows to veer away from all subjects which the government regards as taboo."

M.B.S.—Fred Weber, general manager of M.B.S., stated: "M.B.S. is confident that our affiliated and member radio stations will recognize the practicability and soundness of the newly is-

[9] From "Censorship Rules Bring Net Praise," newsstory. *Broadcasting.* 22:55. January 19, 1942. Reprinted by permission.

sued government radio censorship instructions and will comply
with them in all their programs which are transmitted to the network. None of the quiz or audience participation programs
transmitted to Mutual by the stations originate from remote
locations."

BROADCASTING: DECEMBER [10]

War—grim, swift, terrible—has struck home. In a twinkling
the "defense" program has become a "victory" drive. Radio, for
the first time in its meteoric development, goes to war. It faces
the supreme test, as does the nation itself.

The shock of the Jap attack threw things off balance momentarily. Mistakes were made; confusion was provoked; there was
hysteria. Radio was not entirely faultless in the spread of "unconfirmed" rumor, fed through customary news channels. But,
all in all, radio has acquitted itself well.

Let's not delude ourselves about censorship! Military censorship is on and will remain on until victory is won. The almighty
"scoop" must be forgotten, until it is checked for fact and has
passed government scrutiny as matter that will not give aid and
comfort to the enemy. That edict comes from the President of
the United States, the commander-in-chief of the armed forces.

Every broadcaster, every man who faces the microphone
should read and re-read the words of the President in his address
to the nation last Tuesday. Every newspaper and every broadcast
station, Mr. Roosevelt said, has a most grave responsibility now
and for the duration. And in his words, neither has the "right
in the ethics of patriotism to deal out unconfirmed reports." That
is the solemn warning. It must serve as the guide-post for journalism, whether printed or aural.

In material things, radio is going to be affected, particularly
in the earlier stages. Shutting down of stations on the coasts
during imminent air attack or during black-outs, means com-

[10] From "Radio Goes to War," editorial. *Broadcasting*. 21:38. December
15, 1941. Reprinted by permission.

mercial cancellations and rebates. Release of time for war communiques, for government informational broadcasts, and for morale purposes, also may cut in on normal schedules.

These may be only temporary dislocations. After the period of trial and error, readjustments will come. There is no disposition to disturb normal operations beyond absolute necessity. . . .

To predict the future would be sheer fantasy. The military establishment is calling the moves: the F.C.C. insofar as broadcasting is concerned, executes them. The safe, sane policy is for radio to follow orders, avoid controversy, be on the alert, and use its head.

Stations must avoid use of microphones by unknown persons. The "man-on-the-street" type of broadcast should be rigidly controlled and supervised lest some crack-pot, or even subversive influence, gain access to an audience and spread rumor that might result in panic. Transmitters should be guarded, particularly those outside city limits. Radio is a military objective. It must be guarded against sabotage. The function belongs to state or municipal police, not the army.

BROADCASTING: JANUARY [11]

The wartime censorship code is a bitter pill, particularly for rank-and-file stations. A substantial amount of income is derived from "open-microphone" features falling within the rigidly banned renditions. There are other provisions that appear onerous and stringent.

But it could be worse!

Censor Byron Price and his radio assistant, J. Harold Ryan, a practical broadcaster, feel that the open mike presents too easy access for enemy exploitation. To the 250-watter in Peeweeville, a thousand miles from any border, this appears ludicrous. It is!

[11] From "It Could Be Worse," editorial. *Broadcasting.* 22:24. January 26, 1942. Reprinted by permission.

But the stakes are too great at this stage to howl calamity. The code is flexible. It can be altered, and probably will be as the industry makes its case.

To us, for example, it seems entirely feasible to transcribe man-on-the-street, at-the-airport, or other quiz programs, edit them before rendition for deletion of even remotely suspicious material, and then present them on a staggered basis, so that no possible timing element would be involved. But even that is collateral.

Certainly broadcasters have proved themselves sufficiently versatile to supplant the banned types with other programs. Accounts won't be lost simply because a station is acceding to a government mandate in the war effort. And what a beautiful opportunity for the sponsor to tell his audience that he has switched from a banned-type program to something else in the interest of the national welfare!

We don't contend that the industry should take every government edict lying down. It has taken too many that way already from other agencies during peacetime. But this is war. And war can't be molded to suit the convenience of any industry or group—not even labor which has been administration spoon-fed till now. Radio must orient itself. By logic and some patience it can remedy injustices.

BROADCASTING: FEBRUARY [12]

A month has elapsed since the broadcasting industry began operating under the Wartime Censorship Code. The result has brought no wild acclaim from Washington officialdom, the public or the industry. It really hasn't meant material change, save for the loss of some business by some stations which can ill afford it, and perhaps the sloughing off of listener interest in some early-morning or late-night requests. The shock has not been too severe.

[12] From "Censorship Loopholes," editorial. *Broadcasting*. 22:30. February 16, 1942. Reprinted by permission.

But there are other aspects of the censorship picture that do cause concern, raising the question whether the Office of Censorship is running the show or whether the military goes its own way and the Office of Facts and Figures yet another way.

The Office of Censorship, under the able direction of Byron Price and J. Harold Ryan, his radio lieutenant, has not been unreasonable, though complaints may be heard in isolated instances. The rub has come in orders from the military, usually from a subordinate in the field whose edicts must be honored but who nevertheless may not have the authority to establish policy. That, in any event, has been the experience thus far.

There was the case, immediately following Pearl Harbor, of the army major on the Pacific Coast who banned all testimonials and all request programs as possible purveyors of aid and comfort to the enemy. His orders were countermanded by Washington afterward, and he was "relieved" of his assignment.

There is the instance of a Midwestern station advised by a local public relations officer to cease a popular commercial dealing with war industry, under threatened pain of violation of the espionage laws punishable in the extreme by death! Then last week there was the case of WMCA, New York, relating to a commentator's observation that the "Normandie" fire might be the work of a Vichy-minded saboteur, which brought a rebuke from the Naval Commandant and a court-martial demand by a New York newspaper.

All these may be ascribed to inexperience, lack of coordination and possibly hysteria. They certainly don't help morale.

Yet another incident, which causes some wonder as to whether newspapers are being favored over radio, is reported from St. Louis. There a live-wire station executive and commentator learned that a St. Louis boy who was at Pearl Harbor during the attack was back home on leave. The local naval public relations officer authorized an interview, with the script to be checked. But before clearance came for the air, the same story broke in a St. Louis newspaper—the result of an interview evidently arranged by Naval Intelligence. The whole episode, we are told, was "shot through with preferential treatment for the press".

This is only one of a number of instances of suppression by radio of material cleared for newspapers. Several radio people have commented that radio is being played for a sucker, while the harder-boiled press is being treated with deference.

Then there is what appears to be the futility of the censorship code because of the border station situation. Neither Mexico nor Canada has a code of the scope and magnitude of ours, though several of the Canadian border stations voluntarily are observing our restrictions. The big loophole is Mexico, which has a half-dozen superpower border stations booming into the Southwest and Midwest, all still operating without restraint as to requests, program content, etc. They are catering to the American rather than the Mexican audience.

All these instances are cited, not because we have despaired of equitable treatment under wartime censorship, but in the hope that remedies can be found. Radio is anxious and willing to help to the utmost in the war effort. It realizes, however, that the effort may be futile unless there is effective centralization of control, and unless the border situation is adjusted.

PHILOSOPHY OF CENSORSHIP

DISCUSSION

Most of the discussion of censorship in wartime thus far has dealt with actual events and the problems of censorship today. But there is a little more to the censorship picture than actual happenings. Behind the control of news in wartime is an entire philosophy. This philosophy is a vital part of the overall philosophy of total war and the effect of total war upon a democracy.

Not only that but the theories which underlie censorship today are every bit as varied as the conflicting opinions of the authorities on the subject regarding the meaning of censorship and its value to the war effort. Philosophy certainly has its place in any discussion of censorship. On it is based the major adjustments in news control as the war situation changes.

It was to reconcile one phase of the philosophy of censorship that the government revamped the news picture, permitting more news of production facts and figures. This is in line with the theory that information is more important at times than secrecy, even if that information conveys aid and comfort to the enemy.

But generally speaking, the philosophy of censorship refers to the pattern which is adopted prior to the application of censorship, or to the theory which forms a basis for certain changes or modifications in an already formulated censorship policy.

In the following pages are a number of theories, which combined form the philosophy of wartime censorship of radio and the press in the United States in World War II.

PRE-WAR VIEW OF CENSORSHIP [1]

We have received the "reassurance" of President Roosevelt who stated in his letter to Mr. Wallace that "free speech and a

[1] By Carl W. Ackerman, Dean, School of Journalism, Columbia University. From "How Free Is the American Press?" *Vital Speeches.* 7:541-3. June 15, 1941. Reprinted by permission.

free press are still in the possession of the people of the United States." The President's personal statement constitutes one of the very few victories for a free press in the recent history of journalism. Such a pronouncement, at this time, should prove to newspaper editors that eternal vigilance is a better form of security than editorial complacency. If this letter is a victory for the press, there is reason for us to continue our vigilance because the tempo of world events, the "chain of crises" abroad, the emotional nature of public sentiment under the impact of war and the critical attitude of mind of certain high government officials toward newspaper publishers and the reporting and interpretation of Washington news, may change the status quo, overnight.

Whatever our individual views may be in regard to foreign affairs, we are face to face with the inescapable fact that the President and the government of the United States are in the war even though this country is not actually at war. Therefore, the question of keeping American news lines open must be considered realistically, dispassionately and constructively because there is a difference between the assurance that we still possess our constitutional rights and that, *ipso facto,* news channels will remain free and open.

Before recommending a course of action . . . may I ask: "How free is the American press today and how wide open are American news channels?"

Press dispatches from London last week brought to our attention one outstanding fact confronting newspapers and press associations since the passage of the Lend-Lease bill.

A more vigorous self-censorship must be imposed in the United States . . . to stop leakage of information on which secrecy is considered essential to Britain's war effort. The final decision whether a voluntary restraint will suffice or some kind of government censorship will be necessary must rest with the United States. . . .

Since H. R. 1776 was added to the statute books of the United States, American journalists are no longer free agents insofar as certain war news is concerned. Our future course of action, under the law, must be adjusted to the commitments of our government to those foreign powers we are obliged to aid under the Lend-Lease Act.

The bulk of live news today is about foreign affairs including national defense. All news dispatches, photographs, radio broadcasts and other forms of communications from Europe, Africa, and Asia are censored. Therefore the American press today is not free to obtain or distribute any information from abroad which is not controlled or approved by the respective belligerents.

Under the circumstances of control, restraint, intimation, criticism, expulsion fears and threats, bombing of offices and separated families, American correspondents abroad have been performing their tasks heroically as men and admirably as journalists. Nevertheless their news sources are not open and their lines of communication are controlled [and] even if they are free agents of a free press their news lines are open only because of the vigilance as well as the resourcefulnss of the correspondents. . . .

Similarly Washington correspondents are not as free to obtain information and report it as they were in time of peace. News in Washington is supervised by news releases and "off the record" conferences. . . .

Insofar as foreign affairs and national defense are concerned American news lines from Washington are not completely open and news lines from abroad are completely controlled. Furthermore, the trend is toward more drastic control even in light of assurances that the American press is free, at this time. . . .

Furthermore during the past two months the President of the United States has publicly questioned the ethics, morals and patriotism of the press and an official agency of the government has described the A.N.P.A. as an enemy of the government. A survey of the government's position reveals a united and coordinated front under the leadership of President Roosevelt.

Repeated attacks upon newspaper publishers have profoundly influenced the public attitude toward many daily newspapers and placed all newspaper owners who disagree with or criticize the President or his administration on the gridiron of public opinion. . . .

Today, as we consider how to keep American news lines open, we are confronted by the President's power and authority as well as by his prestige. Under the Espionage and Trading-with-the-Enemy Acts of 1917 and 1918 the President has the authority to establish a censorship "when the United States is at war." Under Sections 3 and 4 of the Act, which is still on the statute books, the Postmaster General "upon evidence satisfactory to him" may declare offending newspapers non-mailable. Under the Lend-Lease Act of 1941 the President has the authority to establish censorship of military, naval and national defense news whenever he deems it to be necessary or desirable to our national safety and security. At the time of the "Malaya" incident Secretary Knox proved that my interpretation was correct when he issued a public statement basing his request to "all press, radio and photographic agencies to refrain from reporting in any form, the movements or presence of British men-of-war in this country for any purpose whatsoever," upon the authority of the government under the Lend-Lease Act. Even though the people still possess the freedom of the press this does not mean that news is to be freely accessible to the press.

In addition to these statutes there is the bill H. R. 3368 authorizing expenditures for the Office of Government Reports, which was passed by the House by a vote of 201 to 144. When this bill becomes a law, the President will have an official agency of government to implement his authority if the war emergencies should require a change of policy overnight and he decides that it is desirable or necessary to exercise his power and authority over news. . . .

If we intend to meet our obligations to society, to the government and to our profession as representatives of a free press this is the time for us to be realistic. We cannot escape the fact that under the Espionage and Trading-with-the-Enemy Acts of 1917 and 1918, and under the Lend-Lease Act of 1941, the government of the United States has the legal power and authority to take such action to control American news channels, as the President may deem desirable or necessary in the defense of the United States. That the government has this great potential power and authority over the press may be in part due to the fact that for decades too many editors and publishers have considered editorial pronouncements as having the effect of law, because of their influence on public opinion, while the government has included in its strategy the field of law. Today the free press is actually encircled by laws, regulations and requests.

If it is our intention to be realistic we will recognize that we cannot keep American news lines open by fighting the United States government in time of war. During this "chain of crises" we cannot change the laws or claim immunity, exemptions, or privileges. The government has the power, the authority and the prestige to establish a censorship in time of war, to control newsprint supplies and to influence or determine the amount of national advertising under defense contracts. Freedom of the press today is nine-tenths vigilance and one-tenth law.

Furthermore, national unity in time of a sequence of international crises cannot be achieved if high officials of the government continue to condemn the press by sniping at incidents or individuals. If reader faith in the publications which distribute news is destroyed, government censorship and control of every newspaper, all press associations and every broadcaster will not suffice to persuade or regiment the American public opinion. Even if freedom of the press today is nine-tenths vigilance and one-tenth law the government cannot consume this final tenth of liberty without destroying the whole structure of our democratic institutions. The primary obligation of the press in peace and in war is to serve as an instrumentality of the public, not as an agency of government. The fulfillment of that obligation is the greatest of all the domestic ways and means of insuring the security of our form of government and of keeping news lines open.

FORTUNE'S CENSORSHIP POLICY [2]

Prime points of a censorship policy that *Fortune* believes to be in the best interest of the nation in this emergency:

(1) Unequivocal opposition to press censorship in any form, with this exception:
> Press cooperation in maintaining secrecy of a limited list of truly vital technical secrets and of troop, ship, and plane movements and other information of strictly military value so long as they are secret in fact.

(2) The most effective way of keeping valuable information from the enemy is:
(a) Secrecy at source
(b) Peripheral censorship (outgoing communications), which may, if necessary, include a limited censorship of radio.

(3) The army and navy have the undisputed right to control correspondents and photographers in military areas and to censor their news and pictures. Such censorship, however, should be limited to vital military and naval information and not extend to the vague fields of politics and public morale.

(4) The greatest service the press can render a democracy in wartime is to remain aggressively free, critical, and informative.

THE PRESS IN ALL-OUT WAR [3]

In this all-out effort to win the war, every element in American life is being called on to do its full part. One of the most

[2] From "Censorship." *Fortune*. 23:153. June, 1941. Reprinted by permission.

[3] By Don Belding, president of the Pacific Advertising Association and member of the Committee on Public Information of the State Council of Defense. From a statement released through the California State Council of Defense, May 11, 1942. Reprinted by permission.

important of these elements is the American press, which is the watchdog of our Bill of Rights. Unlike the press of the Axis countries, and more than any other country of the world, we have a free press—a press not controlled by any group.

This press today, under a voluntary censorship, is giving the American people the news—quickly, fairly, and freely. The fact that all editorial and news comment is not exactly the same is proof in itself that there is no arbitrary control of news. The people are not just given one side of it—they get all sides and can thus draw a fair conclusion.

Under the guise of assumed war necessity, there are those who would like to control the press so that only one side is presented. Some of these people represent subversive forces who would like to do away with our democratic way of life and put in its place a controlled system. . . .

America has seen by cruel example what happened to France, where a large part of the press was controlled by subversive forces, who told the people only what they wanted them to know. America wants no part of that kind of control.

The function of a newspaper is to inform—whether it be through the news columns or in the advertising pages—where the public, including business, labor, and organizations of every kind and creed, at all times has the right to express its opinion, providing that opinion will not give aid and comfort to the enemy.

Let us continue to have a free and sound press. After all, that is one of the freedoms we are fighting for.

THE "WISDOM" OF TOO MUCH CENSORSHIP [4]

I think it should be apparent that there will be opposing views as to whether the "workings of the censorship" should be a closed book to the lay citizen.

[4] By Ralph D. Casey, director of the school of journalism, University of Minnesota. From "The Limits of Censorship, A Symposium." *Public Opinion Quarterly.* 6:21-4. Spring, 1942. Reprinted by permission.

Secrecy in censorship operations will hardly prove helpful to public morale, nor will it be acceptable to editors and radio station operators. For instance, Secretary Knox almost a year before the outbreak of war acted unwisely when he sent a notice marked *confidential* to newspaper editors urging them to withhold from the public four major categories of news concerning naval operations, the first of which was the movements of vessels or aircraft of the fleets. His action prevented editors from explaining that the government wanted this type of cooperation or from indicating *why* a high official thought publication of this type of information was dangerous. In order to protect their standing with readers, some editors boxed notices in their newspapers after the Secretary's notice reached their desks, explaining what types of news would not be published. Surely it would have been better had Knox made an open request. The public would have supported it.

This illustration is cited only to make the point that the public should be taken into the government's confidence. This was done, of course, when the Office of Censorship was set up. In his address of December 9, President Roosevelt reassuringly said that war facts would be released as soon as two conditions had been fulfilled; first, that the information had been definitely and officially confirmed; and, second, that the information did not convey vital information to the enemy, "directly or indirectly." Soon Byron Price issued his Code of Wartime Practices for the American Press. Voluntary censorship was in effect.

Alterations and changes in the Code as they occur should be made known to the public just as have been the original regulations. While few persons would argue that the public should be informed of the frequent suggestions by Mr. Price's office as to whether an editor should print this or that specific item in the day's run of news, it would be unfortunate if secrecy were invoked in the broader working of the censorship. . . .

At no time did the censorship plan contemplate the funneling of all government wartime or defense news through Price's office. At the outset it was assumed that various departments were to make themselves accessible to reporters as they had in the past. Each department was not to constitute itself an independent censor, unrelated to Price's department. In fact, when the Interdepartmental Committee on War Information was set up, the subservience of individual departments on matters of censorship to Price's office seemed to be implied in the statement of the Committee's purpose released on January 17 by its chairman, Archibald MacLeish. . . .

That the relation between the Office of Censorship and government departments is a developing one is indicated by the number of recent requests made to newspapers in relation to newsstories that have come from the Navy Department rather than from Price's own office.

The request made by Stephen Early, presidential secretary that speeches of cabinet members, under secretaries and federal administrators be submitted in advance to the Office of Facts and Figures for approval, was intended to make certain that the central governmental policy is understood before cabinet members and others go off half-cocked. It is to be hoped that minor and major officials will not conclude they must also submit major items of information for scrutiny to the O.F.F. before their release. This would establish a second office of censorship and would have some of the effects also of an Official Secrets Act which, in the case of Great Britain a year or two before the war, dried up the sources of important official news. . . .

Happily, this country divorced censorship from those agencies that have propaganda responsibilities. We can only hope that the censors will avoid the mistakes of European censors in World War I and of the British censors in the early part of this war. They conceived it to be their duty . . . to build morale as well as to withhold vital military news from the enemy.

Whenever a censor suppresses news which is of non-military value to the enemy, or times the release of news so that a favorable item may follow quickly on the heels of unfavorable information of our combat forces, or seeks to cover up blunders or stupidities of either military or governmental leaders, then he departs from the function wisely assigned to him by President Roosevelt following the Pearl Harbor attack.

What are the results when the censor attempts to organize opinion and attitudes by making use of the blue pencil? When the legitimate news he has suppressed does leak out, confidence in the government is impaired. The press and radio suffer loss in prestige, and those elements in society which wish, deliberately or otherwise, to create distrust of the communications agencies have their innings. The public, which must live on news, is torn from its mooring. Finally, national unity is endangered and the support of the war effort will suffer.

THE NEED FOR CRITICISM [5]

We are in this war and the only road out of it is victory. There will be no personal liberty anywhere if we lose the war.

Inside America we are vibrating between two poles. We are fighting to preserve personal liberty and representative government in the world. Yet we must suspend part of them at home, in order to win. And suspension creates grave dangers because liberty rapidly atrophies from disuse. . . . It would be a vain thing to fight the war and lose our own liberties. If we would have them return we must hold furiously to these ideals. We must challenge every departure from them. There are just two tests: "Is this departure necessary to win the war?" "How are we going to restore these freedoms after the war?"

And the exploration of these questions calls for a calm and philosophical disposition. . . . That there must be restraints upon speech and the press needs no discussion. But there is left ample room to free speech and free press through pep-oratory and criticism of the conduct of the war.

[5] From an address before the Conference Board by Herbert Hoover, May 20, 1942.

And criticism of the conduct of the war is necessary if we are to win the war. We want the war conducted right. The margins between victory and defeat in our foreign campaigns are so narrow that if pressure groups are to take advantage of war to advance their interests, or if we make blunders, or keep incompetent men in office, or allow corruption, bad organization and bad strategy, they can bring about defeat. Democracy can correct mistakes only through public exposure and opposition to them. . . .

The enemy may get mental comfort by reading these exposures and criticism. But he will not get comfort from the remedy.

Criticism of the conduct of the war may rightly lead to criticism of public officials. In a democracy even the President is not immune from rightful criticism. . . . No public servant can be free of criticism if democracy is to continue to live. But the first rule of criticism is that it must not take the form of personal detraction and abuse. The moral limitations on the liberty to smear should be increased drastically as a war measure. . . .

From a philosophical viewpoint, I would like to see the sixth columnists given a little more liberty. They are defined as the ones who discuss the war or speculate or even criticize in private conversation.

To a person who is reminiscent of American life it would seem that particular restraint is too drastic. The American people have always been a debating society. They get immense satisfaction out of gossip. They always have views. They always speculate about events. They are profoundly anxious over the fate of their loved ones and the welfare of their country. And all this cannot be stamped out of them by a hob-nailed heel. . . . United is not to be confused with uniformity. When uniformity comes we will have ceased to be free men.

THE CHANGED PICTURE [6]

The philosophy of censorship hasn't advanced greatly since it was first applied on a major scale in the Franco-Prussian war of 1870. The belligerents then had learned many lessons from our recent Civil War, in which censorship was applied at haphazard, and the newspapers of both sides printed as routine news advance information of their own armies' plans. From that foolish extreme, we went to the other, equally foolish, among an intelligent and literate people—complete suppression of military information. By the time of the next major war—between Japan and Russia in 1904, censorship was in full bloom, with the imitative Japs as its most expert exponents. By 1914 the British and French had progressed so far that it was many weeks before correspondents were permitted to approach either headquarters, and the French never did learn to distinguish between news and fiction from the front.

Between 1918 and 1940, however, a new element of communications had become available. The radio made instantaneous transmission of the spoken word possible around the globe. The reporter of 1914-1918 could not even hint to his office, usually, what the censor would not permit him to write. He could not even hint that there were things of which he could not write. He was shackled and helpless before many a big story. The public knew little of his plight. Today, with the air buzzing every minute with broadcasts, many from the scene of action, normal censorship is always apparent and not especially resented; unusual censorship is given away by the broadcaster's intonation, his peculiar choice of words, or a break in his speech at a moment which seems to be leading to something important.

The very fact that the censor is making extraordinary efforts to keep information off the air immediately stirs ominous thoughts

[6] By Arthur Robb, editor of *Editor & Publisher*. From "Shop Talks at Thirty," editorial. 75:32. January 17, 1942. Reprinted by permission.

and resentment in the public mind. And the radio reporter, like his colleague of the printed newspaper, stirs his mind constantly for expedients to beat an unjust censorship and get the news out. Sooner or later, he usually does.

PHILOSOPHY OF CENSORSHIP [7]

Anyone who has examined in detail America's censorship activities in World War I will understand why there must be limits to censorship in a democracy, even in wartime. In this field during that earlier struggle there appeared, among other shortcomings, a noticeable lack of any preconceived plan of operation, continuous duplications of effort, agencies working at cross purposes with one another, and a hastily selected and occasionally unqualified personnel. With proper curbs clearly defined, there is no reason for us to repeat the errors of our earlier performance. In the following discussion the attempt has been made to make the criticism of the limits of censorship constructive and positive in its approach.

Long before actual hostilities have begun, the ways and means of censorship need the careful, intelligent, cooperative study by and of all agencies concerned with the creation and transmission of information. Those agencies include the Departments of State, of War, of the Navy, of Justice, the Post Office, the Federal Communications Commission, the broadcasting companies, the motion picture producers, the telegraph, telephone, and cable companies, and the various press and publishing associations.

From the deliberations of this group should come the recommendations for the nation's only censorship—a censorship by federal authorities created first by executive order, and as soon as possible thereafter authorized by law. This statute

[7] By James R. Mock, author of "Censorship—1917." From "The Limits of Censorship, A Symposium." *Public Opinion Quarterly.* 6:3-9. Spring, 1942. Reprinted by permission.

should define the kind of information and the channels to be censored, and the duties of the personnel. Finally, it must provide an appropriation to defray the expenses of censorship. This last point is especially important. Failure to make such provision for our first censorship board—in 1917—was one of the chief reasons for its lack of success. If it is to function unhampered, the censorship agency must be a separate and a distinct body in the Federal Government.

In defining the nature of the information to be censored, the framers of the law have the power to make censorship a specific, efficient instrument or a nightmare. Granting that censorship will apply only to information of value to the enemy, the censors must be told just what constitutes "information of value to the enemy"; and only the above-mentioned deliberations can have determined that. Briefly, such information relates only to the military, naval, and related combat plans and intentions of our government. Revelation of these items is of no lasting benefit to the public, since the plans and intentions are subject to repeated changes to meet unforeseen situations as they arise.

Great Britain supplies evidence of the results of this failure to define such limits of censorship. In the last war this failure allowed censorship to broaden and broaden, until it became a means not only of injustice but even of absolute folly. The censors suppressed not alone information that would have been of benefit to the enemy and of injury to Great Britain—which was their duty—but they, at the same time, shut out news that would have warned the British public of the danger in which it stood. And since the present struggle began, the Ministry of Information has been reorganized three times, largely because it cannot agree upon what constitutes information purely of value to the enemy.

Careful delineation of the censor's powers will eliminate the recurrence of an evil we had during World War I. There will be no place and no necessity for voluntary censorship. In

1917 and 1918 the government made an arrangement with the press whereby the latter undertook to exclude from print certain kinds of information. While approximately 99 per cent of the papers and periodicals lived up to this agreement, violations by the non-conforming one per cent helped to make the agreement a farce.

With all censoring recognized as belonging solely to the Federal Government, the amateur censors need not come into existence during this war. In the earlier struggle, the work of the Department of Justice was hindered and many innocent persons throughout the country were more than plagued by the censoring activities of well-meaning but over-officious private— or at best semi-official—individuals and organizations.

Before actual censoring begins, and during the entire existence of the activity, secrecy must be invoked. Here, too, there are limits to be observed. The actual operation of the censorship must be kept as secret as possible if it is to function effectively. If possible, its workings should not become public knowledge. At the same time, however, if it is not possible to keep information concerning censorship from the public, it should not be attempted. It is a wise rule for any censor not to try to keep any information secret unless he can do so successfully.

This necessity for secrecy is greatly reduced in scope if censorship is applied only at the source. And there it should relate to military or naval affairs directly concerned or connected with operations in the combat zone. Even in that area, as has been stated previously, information suppressed should concern only impending or contemplated military and naval movements, not what has occurred already. The people have a right to know what has happened, whether the news is good or bad.

Censorship at the source is sufficient if it is coupled with a control of all means of rapid communication of information. With radio, cables, telegraph, telephone, and mail channels under the scrutiny of able censors—the first channel at the broadcasting station, and the others where they cross our boundaries—the enemy agent in this country or with our forces would face almost insurmountable obstacles in getting valuable information to his superiors while it still had some immediate military significance. . . .

If men are carefully selected for the actual task of censoring, and are not skimmed from some hastily-prepared or unrelated civil service register, one of the chief weaknesses of a rapidly organized censorship will be overcome. Even with the mistakes of World War I before it, and although repeatedly warned of the shortcomings of an untrained personnel, our government has not heeded these warnings. Long before April 1917, it had received from its agents in London information to the effect that all the censorship difficulties the British encountered were readily chargeable to one thing—lack of preparation. According to the informants, there were not available at the outbreak of the war any officials of the government who had any idea of their duties as censors. As a result, the British censorship was said to stand out as one of the worst examples of mismanagement and unpreparedness that the war produced in England. With this in mind, representatives of our government urged their superiors to take up this question with a view to having available in time of necessity "a completely prepared and organized agency for this purpose." No attention was paid to that advice then, and it has not been heeded since. With no previous formal preparation, if we are to be saved from repeating the blunders of our censorship efforts of World War I, the selection for censorship of men of broad interests, mentally and physically alert, who have been successful in their chosen fields of endeavor, and who are of unquestioned patriotism, will go far toward repairing any damage done by a censorship corps untrained and uninstructed prior to the time it enters upon its duties. Above all, these men should have the interest of the Republic so much at heart that they will not allow the censorship to be used to protect military and bureaucratic incompetents from needed public criticism. We must not expect too much omniscience from even these men of high calibre, for as Josephus Daniels once told the writer, "God never made a man who was wise enough to be a censor."

With a group of censors possessing these qualifications, the purposes of censorship would be kept to their legal limits. Their efforts would consist, largely, of keeping information from the enemy. Such men would realize that the purpose of censorship in a democracy should not be propagandistic. That is, the George Creels or the Byron Prices should not withhold information from the American citizens to produce a desired public reaction. In England, during the first phase of World War I, British censorship was used not only to prevent the publication of confidential war news, but also to shape public opinion through circulation of favorable news as well as through suppression of unfavorable items. However, recruiting being unsatisfactory, greater publicity of reverses in France was authorized early in September 1914; and in London the rate increased from 1,200 to nearly 5,000 recruits daily.

Such slanting of the news is not the real purpose of censorship. Influencing the public should be left to an intelligent ministry of information. Even that agency, it is worth noting, has its limits in a long war. The ministry of information must not deviate from the truth if it is to attain and to keep its effectiveness.

Unless the censors are able men who exercise rare common sense, the effect of censorship may be just the opposite of the effect desired. While there may be suppression of information at the source to keep the enemy in ignorance, the eventual effect of that action may be to keep our own citizens unaware of reverses, the knowledge of which affects adversely public morale when those defeats finally become known. When long concealed information about disasters and poor leadership is released, the time has passed when the public can do much more than play the part of voluble but helpless back seat drivers.

As long as we are a democracy, the citizens have rights that no censorship should set aside. They are entitled to know at all times what their government and their armed forces have done.

Finally, there is a time limit that must be applied to all censorships except those under a dictatorship. Our censors should perform their duties only during the period of actual hostilities. After the war, in some instances before the treaty of peace has been signed, the public should be informed of the post-war aims and policies of this government. After this present struggle, not censorship but complete information must be insisted upon, in the hope that we shall not have a situation similar to that of post-World War I, in which partisan politics so jarred our aims as to make our future a blur.

Again, by limiting all censorship to the control of the Federal Government, another evil of this earlier period will be avoided when peace comes. There will be no reason, no excuse, and no basis for private persons and organizations, municipalities and states using the censorship against their political, social, or economic domestic foes under the cloak of protecting the American way of life.

Even in wartime, a democracy needs information rather than censorship—except censorship at the source as described above. Since we have been interested in the paths of peace rather than in the ways of war, we can expect reverses and blundering at the beginning of hostilities. These constitute the price we pay for being a democracy, but the value we receive from being, and from continuing to be, a democracy is greater than its cost.

APPENDIX

EXECUTIVE ORDER CREATING COMMUNICATIONS BOARD [1]

WHEREAS The Senate and House of Representatives of the United States of America in Congress assembled have declared that a state of war exists between the United States and the Imperial Japanese Government;

AND WHEREAS Section 606 of the Communications Act of 1934 (48 Stat. 1104; U.S.C., title 47, sec. 606) authorizes the President under such circumstances to cause the closing of any radio station and the removal therefrom of its apparatus and equipment, and to authorize the use or control of any such station and/or its apparatus and equipment by any agency of the government under such regulations as the President may prescribe upon just compensation to the owners, and further authorizes him to direct that communications essential to the national defense and security shall have preference or priority;

AND WHEREAS It is necessary to insure the national defense and the successful conduct of the war that the Government of the United States shall take over, operate, and have use or possession of certain radio stations or parts thereof within the jurisdiction of the United States, and shall inspect, supervise, control or close other radio stations or parts thereof within the jurisdiction of the United States, and that there should be priority with respect to the transmission of certain communications by wire or radio;

NOW, THEREFORE, by virtue of authority vested in me under the Constitution of the United States and under the aforementioned joint resolution of Congress dated December 8, 1941, and under the provisions of the aforementioned Section 606 of the Communications Act of 1934, I hereby prescribe that from and after this date the Defense Communications Board created by the Executive Order of September 24, 1940 (hereinafter referred to as the Board) shall exercise the power and authority vested in me by Section 606 of the Communications Act of 1934 pursuant to and under the following regulations

1. The Board shall determine and prepare plans for the allocation of such portions of governmental and non-governmental radio facilities as may be required to meet the needs of the armed forces, due con-

[1] Full text of Executive Order signed by President Roosevelt December 10, 1941.

sideration being given to the needs of other governmental agencies, of industry, and of other civilian activities.

2. The Board shall, if the national security and defense and the successful conduct of the war so demand, designate specific radio stations and facilities or portions thereof for the use, control, supervision, inspection or closure by the Department of War, Department of Navy or other agency of the United States Government.

3. The Board shall, if the national security and defense and the successful conduct of the war so demand, prescribe classes and types of radio stations and facilities or portions thereof which shall be subject to use, control, supervision, inspection or closure, in accordance with such prescription, by the Department of War, Department of Navy or other agency of the United States Government designated by the Board.

4. Every department and independent agency of the government shall submit to the Defense Communications Board, at such time and in such manner as the Board may prescribe, full information with respect to all use made or proposed to be made of any radio station or facility and of any supervision, control, inspection or closure which has been or is proposed to be effected pursuant to paragraph 3 hereof.

5. No radio station or facility shall be taken over and operated in whole or in part or subjected to governmental supervision, control or closure unless such action is essential to national defense and security and the successful conduct of the war. So far as possible, action taken pursuant to this Order shall not interfere with the procurement needs of civilian governmental agencies, the normal functioning of industry or the maintenance of civilian morale.

6. Until and except so far as said Board shall otherwise provide, the owners, managers, boards of directors, receivers, officers and employees of the radio stations shall continue the operation thereof in the usual and ordinary course of business, in the names of their respective companies, associations, organizations, owners or managers, as the case may be.

7. The head of any department or agency which uses or controls any radio station pursuant to the terms of this Order shall ascertain the just compensation for the use or control of such radio station and recommend such just compensation in each such case to the President for approval and action by him in accordance with the provisions of subsection (4) of Section 606 of the Communications Act of 1934 (U.S.C., title 47, sec. 606 (d)).

8. By subsequent order of the Board, the use, control, or supervision of any radio station or facility or class or type thereof assumed under the provisions of this Order may be relinquished in whole or in

part to the owners thereof and any restrictions placed on any radio station or facility pursuant hereto may be removed in whole or in part.

9. The Board is hereby designated, in accordance with the provisions of Section 606 (a) of the Communications Act of 1934, to make such arrangements as may be necessary in order to insure that communications essential to the national defense and security shall have preference or priority with any carrier subject to the Communications Act of 1934. The Board may issue any regulation which may be necessary to accomplish this purpose.

10. All terms herein used shall have the meanings ascribed to such terms in Section 3, as amended, of the Communications Act of 1934.

11. All regulations of general applicability issued by the Secretary of War, the Secretary of the Navy, or any other governmental agency under these Presidential regulations shall be published in the *Federal Register*.—FRANKLIN D. ROOSEVELT.

C.W.I. WAR NEWS POLICIES [2]

1. ACTION AT SEA

(a) News of the destruction and sinking of American combat vessels is published only when and if it is felt that such publication will be of no value to the enemy. Publication will be definitely delayed 48 hours from the time the navy has had opportunity to start notifying next of kin of casualties.

(b) The *fact* of damage to an American combat vessel through enemy action is released as soon as verified information is received, if there is reason to believe that such damage has occurred in sight of the enemy. The *extent* of damage to a combatant vessel will probably not be released until the vessel has been repaired as this information is valuable to the enemy.

(c) News of the destruction, sinking or damage to enemy surface vessels is released as soon as verified information is received.

(d) News of the sinking or the probable destruction of enemy submarines is ordinarily not released, for three reasons: (1) It is often difficult to verify the sinking of a submarine. (2) Experience has shown that the withholding of news of the sinking of submarines has an adverse phychological effect on the enemy. (3) If the enemy is

[2] From "Specific War News Policies Laid Down by the C.W.I.," newsstory. *Broadcasting.* 22:22. March 23, 1942. Reprinted by permission.

informed that one of his submarines has been destroyed, he knows it is necessary for him to replace it by another.

From time to time, it will be possible to give news on the sinking or probable sinking of enemy submarines over a past period.

(e) On merchant ship losses the following procedure is being followed: The Commandant of the District in which the sinking occurs notifies the Navy Department. The Navy Department in turn notifies the Maritime Commission, which notifies the owners so that next of kin of any casualties may be notified. As soon as the next of kin have had time to receive notice, the Maritime Commission advises the Navy Department which then releases the story of the sinking to the press and allows eyewitness accounts to be obtained from survivors. The names and precise tonnages will not ordinarily be released.

(f) It must be remembered that details of action at sea are rarely received until days or even weeks after the action has been concluded, because radio signals enable the enemy immediately to locate the position of our ships in combat areas. Full details on any significant action are released as soon as practicable, but these details are rarely available until the vessels involved have returned to port.

2. AIR ACTION

(a) A statement of the exact number of American planes lost in action in the air is made as soon as received (provided the loss has been apparently obvious to the enemy), but no statement of the number of planes lost on the ground is made until such time as it is believed that the statement will not be of value to the enemy. The reason for this is that enemy airmen are usually unable to tell the extent of damage to aircraft attacked on the ground.

(b) An exact statement of losses of enemy aircraft both in the air and on the ground is made as soon as verified information is received. No claim of the destruction of an enemy plane is made unless the authorities in charge are satisfied that the information furnished by the American pilot or other observer is correct.

(c) No statement of the loss of American aircraft in transit or through accident at air fields is made since such news would be of great value to the enemy. An exception is made in the case of aircraft lost through accident in the continental United States.

(d) News of the effect of bombing of enemy objectives is given as soon as verified information is received, in such detail as possible. This information is released only to the extent that the authorities are satisfied of the accuracy of observation by the American pilots or observers.

(e) News of the extent of damage to American objectives by enemy bombing is released as soon as verified information is received, if it is believed that such information will not be of value to the enemy. In no event is an untrue statement of the effect of enemy bombing made. Statements may, however, be incomplete for reasons given above. Such statements will be completed as soon as this can be done without aiding the enemy.

3. ACTION ON LAND

Information relative to action on land is issued during the progress of such action, or as soon as practicable after its termination. This information will be given in as much detail as possible immediately upon receipt and verification. Where possible, such information will include enemy casualties, a statement as to enemy forces engaged, and as to positions won or lost. It will not ordinarily include the strength or distribution of our forces, as this would give information of value to the enemy.

4. MOVEMENTS OF SHIPS AND TROOPS

Movement of ships and troops are among the most valuable forms of information which the enemy is constantly seeking to discover. Such information cannot possibly be published until after the movement is completed, and the enemy can no longer derive value from the knowledge of the movement. Similarly, identification of vessels or army units in action cannot be published until it is clear that such information will not be of value to the enemy. Sailings, routes, and cargoes of cargo ships are also withheld from publication.

5. PROSPECTIVE ACTION

It is obvious that information of what the army or navy intend or plan to do in action cannot possibly be released by the government. There is, of course, no objection to the publication of any private comment upon the future course of military or naval operations, but all such comments are wholly unofficial.

6. REVIEW OF MILITARY SITUATION

The Joint Chiefs of Staff will shortly begin the publication of bulletins from time to time which will furnish an authoritative general review of the military situation in various theaters of war.

7. CASUALTIES (Killed in action)

Lists of members of the armed forces killed in action will be given out subject to the stipulation that press and radio will not publish nationwide round-ups but that newspapers and radio stations will

confine themselves to the publication of casualties from their own localities.

Publication of such lists will be made subject also to the following
restrictions:

a. Release will be delayed until the accuracy of the lists is well
established and relatives notified, and until not giving aid or comfort
to the enemy.

b. The rank and ratings of navy officers and men will be withheld; likewise, designation of units to which army officers and men
have been assigned will be withheld.

Subject to these restrictions and to the above stipulation, the
names of those killed in action will be made available with all possible speed.

8. PRODUCTION INFORMATION

To provide essential public information as to the progress of the
production effort as a whole, the War Production Board will publish
at frequent intervals a production communique, which will enable the
public to judge whether the production program is progressing satis-
factorily or not.

With respect to the shipbuilding program, the Maritime Commission publishes information concerning the laying of keels, launchings and deliveries.

General publication of specific information as to contract awards,
site locations of war industries, and military installations, estimated
supplies of certain strategic and critical materials, specific production
schedules and detailed progress reports have been discontinued. General publication of such material can be most helpful to enemy spies and
saboteurs. Publication of certain information of this kind is necessary
to specific sections of the population, such as sub-contractors, suppliers
of labor, public utilities, and others. Therefore, information of a
non-detailed character with regard to plants and installations and the
placing of large contracts is released for local publication. Moreover, information regarding the letting of contracts, the construction of
factories and cantonments, and the like which are necessary for the
proper functioning of suppliers of labor, materials, facilities, and other
services, is given directly by appropriate agencies.

9. STATISTICAL INFORMATION

Certain statistics formerly published by the government have been
withheld from publication because they are likely to give valuable
information to the enemy, as, for example, information as to the utiliza-
tion of ship tonnage. Every attempt is being made to keep such re-

strictions to a minimum and to continue publication of all statistical information of value to business, labor, agriculture, and other elements of the population.

REVISED PRESS CODE [3]

(New or revised matter enclosed in parentheses. Excised matter struck through.)

(This revision of the code of wartime practices for the American press is based on the experience of the Office of Censorship and of the press during the weeks since the original code was issued on Jan. 15, 1942. But let it be repeated)

It is essential that certain basic facts be understood. The first of these facts is that the outcome of the war is a matter of vital personal concern to the future of every American citizen. The second is that the security of our armed forces and even of our homes and our liberties will be weakened in greater or less degree by every disclosure of information which will help the enemy.

If every member of every news staff and contributing writer will keep these two facts constantly in mind, and then will follow the dictates of common sense, he will be able to answer for himself many of the questions which might otherwise trouble him. In other words a maximum of accomplishment will be attained if editors will ask themselves with respect to any given detail: "Is this information I would like to have if I were the enemy?" and then act accordingly.

The result of such a process will hardly represent "business as usual" on the news desks of the country. On the contrary, it will mean some sacrifice of the journalistic enterprise of ordinary times. But it will not mean a news or editorial blackout. It is the hope and expectation of the Office of Censorship that the columns of American publications will remain the freest in the world and will tell the story of our national successes and shortcomings accurately and in much detail.

The highly gratifying response of the press so far proves that it understands the need for temporary sacrifice and is prepared to make that sacrifice in the spirit of the President's assurance that such curtailment as may be necessary will be administered "in harmony with the best interests of our free institutions."

Below is a summary covering specific problems. This summary repeats, with some modifications, requests previously made by various

[3] Text of the new code of wartime practices for the press issued by the Office of Censorship, June 25, 1942.

agencies of the Federal Government, and it may be regarded as superseding and consolidating all of these requests.

(Obviously it is impossible to anticipate every conceivable contingency. The Office of Censorship will make special requests from time to time covering individual situations in order to round out this outline of newspaper and magazine practices which the government feels are desirable for the effective prosecution of the war and the security of American citizens.)

Special attention is directed to the fact that all of the requests in the summary are modified by a proviso that the information listed may properly be published when authorized by appropriate authority. News on all of these subjects will become available from government sources; but in war, timeliness is an important factor, and the government unquestionably is in the best position to decide when disclosure is timely.

The specific information which newspapers, magazines and all other media of publication are asked not to publish except when such information is made available officially by appropriate authority falls into the following classes:

Troops

The general character and movements of United States Army, Navy, or Marine Corps units, within or without the continental limits of the United States—their location, identity, or exact composition, equipment, or strength; destination, routes, and schedules; assembly for embarkation, prospective embarkation, or actual embarkation. Any such information regarding the troops of friendly nations on American soil.

Note—The request as regards "location" and "general character" does not apply to troops in training camps in continental United States, nor to units assigned to domestic police duty. (Names and addresses of troops in domestic camps may be published, if they do not give the location of units disposed for tactical purposes or predict troop movements or embarkations. Names of naval personnel should not be linked with their ships or bases. Names of individuals, stationed in combat areas outside the United States may be published after there has been official announcement of the presence of American troops in such areas. No mention should be made of their military units. Possible future military operations should not be revealed by identifying an individual known for a specialized activity.)

Ship Movements, Cargoes, Etc.

(The identity, location and movements of United States naval or merchant vessels, of neutral vessels, or vessels of nations opposing the

Axis powers in any waters, unless such information is made public outside continental United States; the port and time of arrival or prospective arrival of such vessels, or the port from which they leave; the nature of cargoes of such vessels; the identity or location of enemy naval or merchant vessels in any waters, unless such information is made public outside continental United States; the identity, assembly, or movements of transports or convoys; the existence of mine fields or other harbor defenses; secret orders or other secret instructions regarding lights, buoys and other guides to navigators; the number, size, character and location of ships in construction, or advance information as to the date of launchings or commissions; the physical set-up or technical details of shipyards.

(Note—This has no reference to the movement of merchant vessels on the Great Lakes or other sheltered inland waterways, unless specific instances require special ruling.)

Ship Sinkings, Damage by Enemy Attacks, Etc.

(Information about the sinking or damaging from war causes of war or merchant vessels in any waters, unless such information is made public outside continental United States, and its origin stated.

(Note—The appropriate authority for the release of news about the sinking or damaging of American naval or merchant vessels in or near American waters is the Naval Office of Public Relations, Washington; for results of United States naval action against enemy vessels in or near American waters, the commanding officer of the district in which the action occurs, or the Naval Office of Public Relations, Washington.

(Information about damage to military objectives, including docks, railroads, airfields, or public utilities or industrial plants engaged in war work, through enemy land or sea attacks on continental United States or possessions.

(Note—In reporting such attacks, counter-measures or plans of defense should not be disclosed, except through appropriate military authorities.

(The appropriate authority for information about damage from enemy attacks to military objectives on land within continental United States or possessions is the commanding officer in the zone of combat or the Army Bureau of Public Relations, Washington. For the Hawaiian Islands, the Navy.)

Attacks by Air

(To the end that any air attack on continental United States may be reported in an orderly fashion, consistent with the highest requirements of national security, the following course of action before, during and after an air raid is suggested:

(Before a raid—It is desirable that no warning or report of an impending raid be published except as given out by designated representatives of the Army Defense Command.

(Note—It is suggested that newspapers write in advance to the appropriate defense commander to ascertain the location of the designated representatives of the defense command in their area.

(During a raid—It is requested that news dispatches transmitted or published at the beginning of a raid, prior to official announcement, be confined to the following: (1) the fact that a raid has begun, without estimating the number of planes; (2) the fact that some bombs have been dropped, if fully established, but without effort to estimate the number; (3) the bare fact that anti-aircraft guns have gone into action.

(Thereafter, until the raid is ended and the all-clear sounded, it is requested that nothing be transmitted or published except communiqués, which will become available promptly and periodically from the designated representatives of the Army Defense Command.

(After a raid—There is no objection to publication of general descriptions of the action after the all-clear is given, provided such accounts do not (1) play up horror or sensationalism; (2) deal with or refer to unconfirmed versions or reports; (3) contain any estimate of the number of planes involved or the number of bombs dropped except as given in communiqués; (4) make any reference to damage to military objectives such as fortifications, docks, railroads, ships, airfields, public utilities, or industrial plants engaged in war work; (5) make any mention of the exact routes taken by enemy planes; (6) describe counter-measures of defense, such as troop mobilizations or movements, or the number or location of anti-aircraft guns or searchlights in action, except as officially announced.

(It is requested that no photographs showing damage or combat action be published or transmitted except upon clearance by military authorities.

(Nothing in this request is intended to prevent or curtail constructive reporting of such matters as feats of heroism, incidents of personal courage, or response to duty by the military or by civilian defense workers.)

Planes

(Disposition, movements, missions, new characteristics, or strength of military air units of the United States or the United Nations unless such information is made public outside continental United States and its origin stated; scope and extent of military activities and missions of the Civil Air Patrol; movements of personnel, material, or other activities by commercial air lines for the military services, including changes of schedules occasioned thereby.

(Activities, operations and installations of the air forces Ferrying Command, the R.A.F. Ferrying Command, or commercial companies operating services for or in cooperation with the Ferrying Command.

(Information concerning new military aircraft and related items of equipment or detailed information on performance, construction and armament of current military aircraft or related items now in service or commercial airline planes in international traffic.)

Fortifications

(The location of forts and other fortifications; the location of coast-defense emplacements, anti-aircraft guns, and other defense installations; their nature and number; location of bomb shelters; location of camouflaged objects; information concerning installations by American military units outside the continental United States.)

Production

(Specifications which saboteurs could use to gain access to or damage war-production plants.

(Exact estimates of the amount, schedules or delivery date of future production, or exact reports of current production.

(Exact amounts involved in new contracts for war production, and the specific nature or specifications of such production.

(Note—Information about the award of contracts is proper for publication when officially announced by the War Production Board, or by the government agency responsible for executing the contract, or when officially announced to the press by a member of Congress, or when disclosed in public records.

(Nature of production should be generalized as follows: tanks, planes, plane parts, motorized vehicles, uniform equipment, ordnance, munitions, vessels. Generalize all types of camps to "camps" or "cantonments."

(Any statistical information other than officially issued by a proper government department which would disclose the amounts of strategic or critical materials produced, imported, or in reserve—such as tin, rubber, aluminum, uranium, zinc, chromium, manganese, tungsten, silk, platinum, cork, quinine, copper, optical glass, mercury, high-octane gasoline.

(Any information indicating industrial sabotage. In reporting industrial accidents, no mention of sabotage should be made unless cleared with the appropriate military authority.

(Any information about new or secret military designs, formulas, or experiments; secret manufacturing processes or secret factory designs, either for war production or capable of adaptation for war production.

(Nation-wide or regional round-ups of current war production or war contract procurement data; local round-ups disclosing total numbers of war production plants and the nature of their production.)

Weather

Weather forecasts, other than officially issued by the Weather Bureau; the routine forecasts printed by any single newspaper to cover only the State in which it is published and not more than four adjoining States, portions of which lie within a radius of 150 miles from the point of publication.

Consolidated temperature tables covering more than twenty stations in any one newspaper.

(Note—Any news stories about weather occurrences within the State of publication, and outside the State for an area not to exceed 150 miles from the point of news stories about weather occurrences, especially extremes such as blizzards, snowstorms, hurricanes, tornadoes and floods for areas other than the foregoing will be appropriate for publication only when specifically cleared through the Office of Censorship. Effects of weather conditions on sports events are appropriate for publication when used briefly to describe the condition of the grounds, or as reasons for postponing matches, such as "Muddy Field," "Wet Grounds" or "Game Called Because of Weather." Specific mention of such conditions as "rain," "overcast," "windy," "clear," or "sudden temperature drop" should be avoided.)

Notes on Rumors

The spread of rumors in such a way that they will be accepted as facts will render aid and comfort to the enemy. (The same is true of enemy propaganda or material calculated by the enemy to bring about division among the United Nations. Enemy claims of ship sinkings, or of other damage to our forces should be weighed carefully and the sources clearly identified, if published. Equal caution should be used in handling so-called "atrocity" stories.

(Interviews with service men or civilians from combat zones should be submitted for authority to the Office of Censorship or to the appropriate Army or Navy Public Relations officer.)

Photographs and Maps

(Photographs conveying the information specified in this summary including ports of embarkation, embarking troops, harbor views of convoys, military air fields in continental United States completed after Dec. 7, 1941, or emergency airfields no matter when completed; harbor defenses; inland waterway locks.

(Special care should be exercised in the publication of aerial photos presumably of non-military significance, which might reveal military or other information helpful to the enemy; also care should be exercised in publishing casualty photos so as not to reveal unit identifications through collar ornaments, etc. Special attention is directed to the section of this summary covering information about damage to military objectives.

(Maps disclosing the location of military depots of any kind, such as air, quartermaster or ordnance depots; key war production plants; arsenals; ammunition or explosive plants of any kind.

(Note—This has no reference to maps showing the general theatre of war or large-scale zones of action, movements of contending forces on a large scale, or maps showing the general ebb and flow of battle lines; or maps showing locations of military camps, provided no indication is given of size or strength, or maps showing airfields, except those constructed since Dec. 7, 1941.)

General Casualty Lists

(Note—There is no objection to publication of information about casualties from a newspaper's local field, obtained from nearest of kin, but it is requested that in such cases, specific military units and exact locations be not mentioned.

(There is no objection to identifying naval casualties with their ships, after such ships have been officially reported damaged or lost.)

Information disclosing the new location of national archives, or of public (or private) art treasures.

(Names of persons arrested, questioned, or interned as enemy aliens; names of person moved to resettlement centers; location and description of places of internment and resettlement.

(Note—The Department of Justice or the Provost Marshal General is the appropriate authority for disclosing names of persons arrested, questioned, or interned as enemy aliens; the official in charge, for names of persons moved to resettlement centers; the Office of Censorship, for location and description of internment camps; the official in charge, for location and description of resettlement centers.

(Information about production, amounts, dates and method of delivery, destination or routes, of lend-lease war material.

(Premature disclosure of diplomatic negotiations or conversations.) Information about the movement of munitions or other war materials.

Information about the movements of the President of the United States or of official military or diplomatic missions of the United States or of any other nation opposing the Axis powers—routes, schedules, destination, within or without continental United States; movements of ranking Army or Navy officers and staffs on official missions; movements of other individuals or units (on military or diplomatic missions.)

(Note—All requests in the code apply to advertising matter, news letters, corporation reports, letters to the editor, personal and society news [which often discloses identity or movement of activity] columns, etc.)

If information concerning any phase of the war effort should be made available anywhere which seems to come from doubtful authority, or to be in conflict with the general aims of these requests; or if special restrictions requested locally or otherwise by various authorities seem unreasonable or out of harmony with this summary, it is recommended that the question be submitted at once to the Office of Censorship.

In addition, if any newspaper, magazine, or other agency or individual handling news or special articles desires clarification or advice as to what disclosures might or might not aid the enemy, the Office of Censorship will cooperate gladly. Such inquiries should be addressed to the Office of Censorship, Washington. Telephone Executive 3800.

Should further additions or modifications of this summary seem feasible and desirable from time to time, the industry will be advised.

The Office of Censorship,
Byron Price, Director.

June 15, 1942.

REVISED RADIO CODE [4]

Five months have passed since the Office of Censorship issued the Code of Wartime Practices for American Broadcasters. This is a revision of that Code, combining original provisions with supplemental suggestions and interpretations which have developed out of our experience in working with the broadcasting industry.

The broad approach to the problem of voluntary censorship remains unchanged. In sum, this approach is that it is the responsibility of

[4] Text of "Code of Wartime Practices for American Broadcasters," as revised June 15, 1942; released June 24, 1942 by the Office of Censorship.

every American to help prevent the dissemination of information which will be of value to the enemy and inimical to the war effort. It is true now, as it was five months ago, that the broadcasting industry must be awake to the dangers inherent in (1) news broadcasts and (2) routine programming.

To combat these dangers effectively, broadcast management must be in complete control of all programming every minute of every day of operation. That accomplished—the broadcasting industry will have fulfilled an important wartime obligation.

Radio station managements will continue to function as their own censors. The facilities of the Office of Censorship are at their disposal 24 hours a day to assist them with consultation and advice when any doubt arises as to the application of this Code. The following are the principal advisory guideposts which are intended to aid them in discharging their censorship responsibilities.

1. NEWS BROADCASTS

Radio, because of the international character of its transmissions, should edit all news broadcasts in the light of this Code's suggestions, and of its own specialized knowledge, regardless of the medium or means through which such news is obtained.

It is requested that news in any of the following classifications be kept off the air, *unless released or authorized for release by appropriate authority.*

(a) Weather

ALL weather data, either forecasts, summaries, recapitulations, or any details of weather conditions.

Stations should refrain from broadcasting any news relating to the results of weather phenomena such as tornadoes, hurricanes, storms, etc., unless it is specifically authorized for broadcast by the Office of Censorship. Occasionally, it is possible to clear such news, but for security reasons this office cannot authorize blanket clearance in advance. Each case must be considered individually in the light of the extent to which the enemy will be benefitted if such information is broadcast. Confusion and inequalities of competition can be avoided if stations will consult the Office of Censorship promptly in all such cases, either directly or through their news service.

Exceptions: Emergency warnings when specifically released for broadcast by Weather Bureau authorities.

Announcements regarding flood conditions may be broadcast provided they contain no reference to weather conditions.

Information concerning hazardous road conditions may be broadcast when requested by a Federal, State or Municipal source, if it avoids reference to weather.

(Note: Special events reporters covering sports events are cautioned especially against the mention of weather conditions in describing contests, announcing their schedules, suspensions, or cancellations.)

(*b*) *Troops*

Type and movements of United States Army, Navy and Marine Corps Units, within or without continental United States, including information concerning

> Location
> Identity
> Composition
> Equipment
> Strength
> Routes
> Schedules
> Assembly for Embarkation
> Prospective Embarkation
> Actual Embarkation
> Destination

Such information regarding troops of friendly nations on American soil.

Revelation of possible future military operations by identifying an individual known for a specialized activity.

Exceptions: Troops in training camps in United States and units assigned to domestic police duty, as regards location and general character. Names, addresses of troops in domestic camps (if they do not give location of units disposed for tactical purposes or predict troop movements or embarkations). Names of individuals stationed in combat areas outside the United States (after presence of American troops in area has been announced and if their military units are not identified). Names of naval personnel should not be linked with their ships or bases.

(*c*) *Ships* (*Convoys, etc.*)

Type and movements of United States Navy, or merchant vessels, or transports, of convoys, of neutral vessels, of vessels of nations opposing the Axis powers in any waters, including information concerning

> Identity
> Location
> Port of Arrival

Time of Arrival
Prospect of Arrival
Port of Departure
Ports of Call
Nature of Cargoes
Assembly
Personnel
Enemy naval or merchant vessels in any waters, their
Type
Identity
Location
Movements
Secret information or instructions about set defenses, such as
Buoys, lights and other guides to navigators
Mine fields and other harbor defenses
Ship construction
Type
Number
Size
Advance information on dates of launchings, commissionings
Physical description, technical details of shipyards

Exceptions: Information made public outside United States and origin stated. Movements of merchant vessels on Great Lakes or other sheltered inland waterways unless specific instances require special ruling.

(d) Damage by Enemy Land or Sea Attacks

Information on damage to military objectives in continental United States or possessions, including
Docks
Railroads
Airfields
Public utilities
Industrial plants engaged in war work
Counter-measures or plans of defense.

(e) Action at Sea

Information about the sinking or damaging of navy, or merchant vessels or transports in any waters.

Exceptions: Information made public outside United States and origin stated.

Appropriate authority: For news about naval action AGAINST United States vessels in or near American waters: Naval Office of Public Relations; BY United States vessels or aircraft against the enemy in or near American waters: Naval commander in district where action occurs or Naval Office of Public Relations, Washington.

(f) Enemy Air Attacks

Estimates of number of planes involved; number of bombs dropped; damage to

> Fortifications
> Docks
> Railroads
> Ships
> Airfields
> Public Utilities
> Industrial plants engaged in war work
> All other military objectives

Warnings or reports of impending air raid; remote ad lib broadcasts dealing with raids, during or after action.

Mention of raid in the continental United States during its course by stations OUTSIDE the zone of action, unless expressly announced for broadcast by the War Department in Washington.

News which plays up horror or sensationalism; deals with or refers to unconfirmed reports or versions; refers to exact routes taken by enemy planes, or describes counter-measures of defense such as troop mobilization or movements, or the number and location of anti-aircraft guns or searchlights in action.

Exceptions: After an air raid, general descriptions of action after all-clear has been given. Nothing in this request is intended to prevent or curtail constructive reporting or programming of such matters as feats of heroism, incidents of personal courage, or response to duty by the military or by civilian defense workers.

(g) Planes

Air Units—Military air units of the United States and the United Nations as to

> Disposition
> Missions
> Movements
> New Characteristics
> Strength

Aircraft—New or current military aircraft or information concerning their

> Armament
> Construction

Performance
Equipment
Cargo

Civil Air Patrol—Nature and extent of military activities and missions.

Miscellaneous—Movements of personnel or material or other activities by commercial airlines for military purposes, including changes of schedules occasioned thereby.

Activities, operations and installations of United States and United Nations Air Forces Ferrying Commands, or commercial companies operating services for, or in cooperation with such Ferrying Commands.

Commercial airline planes in international traffic.

Exceptions: When made public outside continental United States and origin stated.

(h) Fortifications and Bases

The location of forts, other fortifications, their nature and number, including

Anti-aircraft guns
Barrage balloons and all other air defense installations
Bomb shelters
Camouflaged objects
Coast-defense emplacements

Information concerning installations by American military units outside the continental United States.

Exceptions: None.

(i) Production

Plants—Specifications which saboteurs could use to gain access to or damage war production plants.

Exact estimates of the amount, schedules, or delivery date of future production or exact reports of current production.

Contracts—Exact amounts involved in new contracts for war production and the specific nature or the specifications of such production.

Statistics—Any statistical information which would disclose the amounts of strategic or critical materials produced, imported or in reserve, such as tin, rubber, aluminum, uranium, zinc, chrominum, manganese, tungsten, silk, platinum, cork, quinine, copper optical glasses, mercury, high octane gasoline. Disclosure of movements of such materials and of munitions.

Sabotage—Information indicating sabotage in reporting industrial accidents.

Secret Designs—Any information about new or secret military designs, formulas or experiments, secret manufacturing, either for war production, or capable of adaptation for war production.

Roundups—Nation-wide or regional roundups of current war production or war contract procurement data; local roundups disclosing total number of war production plants and the nature of their production.

Type of Production—Nature of production should be generalized as follows: tanks, planes, parts, motorized vehicles, uniform equipment, ordnance, munitions, vessels.

Exceptions: Information about the award of contracts when officially announced by the War Production Board, the government agency executing the contract, a member of Congress, or when disclosed in public records.

(j) Unconfirmed Reports, Rumors

The spread of rumors in such way that they will be accepted as facts will render aid and comfort to the enemy. The same is true of enemy propaganda or material calculated by the enemy to bring about division among the United Nations. Enemy claims of ship sinkings, or of other damage to our forces should be weighed carefully and the sources clearly identified, if broadcast. Equal caution should be used in handling so-called "atrocity" stories. Interviews with Service men or civilians from combat zones should be submitted for authority either to the Office of Censorship or to the appropriate Army or Navy public relations officer.

(k) Communications

Information concerning the establishment of new international points of communication.

(1) General

Aliens—Names of persons arrested, questioned or interned as enemy aliens; names of persons moved to resettlement centers; location and description of internment camps; location and description of resettlement centers.

Art Objects, Historical Data—Information disclosing the new location of national archives, or of public or private art treasures.

Casualties—Mention of specific military units and exact locations in broadcasting information about casualties from a station's primary area, as obtained from nearest of kin. Indentification of naval casualties with their ships, unless such ships have been officially reported damaged or lost.

Diplomatic Information—Information about the movements of the President of the United States or of official, military or diplomatic missions or agents of the United States or of any nation opposing the Axis powers—routes, schedules, destinations within or without continental United States. Premature disclosure of diplomatic negotiations or conversations.

Lend-Lease War Material—Information about production, amounts, dates and method of delivery, destination or routes, of Lend-Lease war material.

Exceptions: None.

II. PROGRAMS

The following suggestions are made in order that broadcasters will have a pattern to follow in accomplishing the most important censorship function of program operation: keeping the microphone under the complete control of the station management, or its authorized representatives.

(a) Request Programs

Music—No telephoned or telegraphed requests for musical selections should be accepted.

No requests for musical selections made by word-of-mouth at the origin of broadcast, whether studio or remote, should be honored.

Talk—No telephoned or telegraphed requests for service announcements should be honored, except as hereinafter qualified. Such service announcements would include information relating to:

> Lost pets
> "Swap" ads
> Mass meetings
> Club meetings
> Club programs, etc.

No telephoned, telegraphed or word-of-mouth dedications of program features or segments thereof should be broadcast.

Exceptions: Emergency announcements (such as those seeking blood donors, doctors, lost persons, lost property, etc.) may be handled in conventional manner if the broadcaster confirms their origin. They should emanate from the police, the Red Cross, or similar recognized governmental or civilian agency.

Service announcements may be honored when source is checked and material is submitted in writing, subject to rewriting by station continuity staff. Requests for the broadcast of greetings or other programs to commemorate personal anniversaries may be honored on the anniversary date or at the time or on the date designated in the request.

These and ALL requests may be honored when submitted via mail, or otherwise in writing if they are held for an unspecified length of time and if the broadcaster staggers the order in which such requests are honored, rewriting any text which may be broadcast.

(b) Quiz Programs

It is requested that all audience-participation type quiz programs originating from remote points, either by wire, transcription or short wave, be discontinued, except as qualified hereinafter. Any program which permits the public accessibility to an open microphone is dangerous and should be carefully supervised.

Because of the nature of quiz programs, in which the public is not only permitted access to the microphone but encouraged to speak into it, the danger of usurpation by the enemy is enhanced. The greater danger here lies in the informal interview conducted in a small group—10 to 25 people. In larger groups, where participants are selected from a theater audience, for example, the danger is not so great.

Generally speaking, any quiz program originating remotely, wherein the group is small, wherein no arrangement exists for investigating the background of participants, and wherein extraneous background noises cannot be eliminated at the discretion of the broadcaster, should be discontinued. Included in this classification are all such productions as man-in-the-street interviews, airport interviews, train terminal interviews, and so forth.

In all studio-audience type quiz shows, where the audience from which interviewees are to be selected numbers less than 50 people, program conductors are asked to exercise special care. They should devise a method whereby no individual seeking participation can be guaranteed participation.

(c) Forums and Interviews

During forums in which the general public is permitted extemporaneous comment, panel discussions in which more than two persons participate, and interviews conducted by authorized employees of the broadcasting company, broadcasters should devise methods guaranteeing against the release of any information which might aid the enemy as described in Section I of the Code. If there is doubt concerning the acceptability of material to be used in interviews, complete scripts should be submitted to the Office of Censorship for reviews.

(d) Commentaries (ad lib)

Special events reporters should study carefully the restrictions suggested in Section I of the Code, especially those referring to interviews and descriptions following enemy offensive action. Reporters and commentators should guard against use of descriptive material which might be employed by the enemy in plotting an area for attack.

If special programs which might be considered doubtful enterprises in view of our effort to keep information of value from the enemy are planned, outlines should be submitted to the Office of Censorship for review.

Caution is advised against reporting, under the guise of opinion, speculation or prediction, any fact which has not been released by an appropriate authority.

(e) Dramatic Programs

Radio is requested to avoid dramatic programs which attempt to portray the horrors of war, and sound effects which might be mistaken for air raid alarms, or for any other defense alarms.

(f) Commercial Continuity

Broadcasters should be alert to prevent the transmission of subversive information through the use of commercial continuity in program or announcement broadcasts.

In this connection, the continuity editor should regard his responsibility as equal to that of the news editor.

(g) Foreign Language Programs

Broadcasters have recognized that the loyalty of their personnel is of supreme importance in voluntary censorship; they recognize the dangers inherent in those foreign language broadcasts which are not under the control at all times of responsible station executives. Station managements, therefore, are requested to require all persons who broadcast in a foreign language to submit to the management in advance of broadcast complete scripts or transcriptions of such material, with an English translation. It is further requested that such material be checked "on the air" against the approved script, and that no deviations therefrom be permitted. These scripts or transcriptions with their translations should be kept on file at the station.

Broadcasters should ask themselves, "Is this information of value to the enemy?" If the answer is "yes," they should not use it. If doubtful, they should measure the material against the Code.

If information concerning any phase of the war effort should be made available anywhere, which seems to come from doubtful authority, or to be in conflict with the general aims of these requests; or if special restrictions requested locally or otherwise by various authorities seem unreasonable or out of harmony with this summary, it is recommended that the question be submitted at once to the Office of Censorship.

THE OFFICE OF WAR INFORMATION [5]

Full text of the June 13 Executive Order consolidating certain war information functions into an Office of War Information follows:

In recognition of the right of the American people and of all other peoples opposing the Axis aggressors to be truthfully informed about the common war effort, and by virtue of the authority vested in me by the Constitution, by the First War Powers Act, 1941, and as President of the United States and Commander in Chief of the Army and Navy, it is hereby ordered as follows:

1. The following agencies, powers, and duties are transferred and consolidated into an Office of War Information which is hereby established within the Office for Emergency Management in the Executive Office of the President:

a. The Office of Facts and Figures and its powers and duties.

b. The Office of Government Reports and its powers and duties.

c. The powers and duties of the Coordinator of Information relating to the gathering of public information and its dissemination abroad, including, but not limited to, all powers and duties now assigned to the foreign information service, outpost, publications, and pictorial branches of the Coordinator of Information.

d. The power and duties of the Division of Information of the Office for Emergency Management relating to the dissemination of general public information on the war effort, except as provided in paragraph 10.

2. At the head of the Office of War Information shall be a Director appointed by the President. The director shall discharge and perform his functions and duties under the direction and supervision of the President. The director may exercise his powers, authorities, and duties through such officials or agencies and in such manner as he may determine.

3. There is established within the Office of War Information a Committee on War Information Policy consisting of the director as chairman, representatives of the Secretary of State, the Secretary of War, the Secretary of the Navy, the Joint Psychological Warfare Committee, and of the Coordinator of Inter-American Affairs, and such other members as the director, with the approval of the President, may determine. The Committee on War Information Policy shall formulate basic policies and plans on war information, and shall advise with respect to the development of coordinated war information programs.

[5] Full text of Executive Order of June 13 consolidating certain information functions into an Office of War Information.

4. Consistent with the war information policies of the President and with the foreign policy of the United States, and after consultation with the Committee on War Information Policy, the director shall perform the following functions and duties:

a. Formulate and carry out, through the use of press, radio, motion picture, and other facilities, information programs, designed to facilitate the development of an informed and intelligent understanding, at home and abroad, of the status and progress of the war effort and of the war policies, activities, and aims of the government.

b. Coordinate the war information activities of all federal departments and agencies for the purpose of assuring an accurate and consistent flow of war information to the public and the world at large.

c. Obtain, study, and analyze information concerning the war effort and advise the agencies concerned with the dissemination of such information as to the most appropriate and effective means of keeping the public adequately and accurately informed.

d. Review, clear and approve all proposed radio and motion picture programs sponsored by federal departments and agencies; and serve as the central point of clearance and contact for the radio broadcasting and motion picture industries, respectively, in their relationships with federal departments and agencies concerning such government programs.

e. Maintain laison with the information agencies of the United Nations for the purpose of relating the government's informational programs and facilities to those of such nations.

f. Perform such other functions and duties relating to war information as the President may from time to time determine.

5. The director is authorized to issue such directives concerning war information as he may deem necessary or appropriate to carry out the purposes of this order, and such directives shall be binding upon the several federal departments and agencies. He may establish by regulation the types and classes of informational programs and releases which shall require clearance and approval by his office prior to dissemination. The director may require the curtailment or elimination of any federal information service, program, or release which he deems to be wasteful or not directly related to the prosecution of the war effort.

6. The authority, functions, and duties of the director shall not extend to the Western Hemisphere exclusive of the United States and Canada.

7. The formulation and carrying out of informational programs relating exclusively to the authorized activities of the several departments and agencies of the government shall remain with such depart-

ments and agencies, but such informational programs shall conform to the policies formulated or approved by the Office of War Information. The several departments and agencies of the government shall make available to the director, upon his request, such information and data as may be necessary to the performance of his functions and duties.

8. The director of the Office of War Information and the Director of Censorship shall collaborate in the performance of their respective functions for the purpose of facilitating the prompt and full dissemination of all available information which will not give aid to the enemy.

9. The director of the Office of War Information and the Defense Communications Board shall collaborate in the performance of their respective functions for the purpose of facilitating the broadcast of war information to the peoples abroad.

10. The functions of the Division of Information of the Office for Emergency Management with respect to the provision of press and publication services relating to the specific activities of the constituent agencies of the Office for Emergency Management are transferred to those constituent agencies respectively, and the Division of Information is accordingly abolished.

11. Within the limits of such funds as may be made available to the Office of War Information, the director may employ necessary personnel and make provision for the necessary supplies, facilities and services. He may provide for the internal management and organization of the Office of War Information in such manner as he may determine.

12. All records, contracts, and property (including office equipment) of the several agencies and all records, contracts, and property used primarily in the administration of any powers and duties transferred or consolidated by this order, and all personnel used in the administration of such agencies, powers, and duties (including officers whose chief duties relate to such administration) are transferred to the Office of War Information, for use in the administration of the agencies, powers, and duties transferred or consolidated by this Order; provided, that any personnel transferred to the Office of War Information by this Order, found by the director of the Office of War Information to be in excess of the personnel necessary for the administration of the powers and duties transferred to the Office of War Information, shall be retransferred under existing procedure to other positions in the government service, or separated from the service.

13. So much of the unexpended balances of appropriations, allocations, or other funds available for the use of any agency in the exercise of any power or duty transferred or consolidated by this order or for the use of the head of any agency in the exercise of any power or duty so

transferred or consolidated, as the Director of the Bureau of the Budget with the approval of the President shall determine, shall be transferred to the Office of War Information, for use in connection with the exercise of powers or duties so transferred or consolidated. In determining the amount to be transferred, the Director of the Bureau of the Budget may include an amount to provide for the liquidation of obligations incurred against such appropriations, allocations, or other funds prior to the transfer or consolidation.

Full text of the Military Order accompanying the Executive Order follows:

By virtue of the authority vested in me as President of the United States and as Commander-in-Chief of the Army and Navy of the United States, it is ordered as follows:

1. The office of Coordinator of Information established by Order of July 11, 1941, exclusive of the foreign information activities transferred to the Office of War Information by Executive Order of June 13, 1942, shall hereafter be known as the Office of Strategic Services, and is hereby transferred to the jurisdiction of the United States Joint Chiefs of Staff.

2. The Office of Strategic Services shall perform the following duties:

a. Collect and analyze such strategic information as may be required by the United States Joint Chiefs of Staff.

b. Plan and operate such special services as may be directed by the United States Joint Chiefs of Staff.

3. At the head of the Office of Strategic Services shall be a Director of Strategic Services who shall be appointed by the President and who shall perform his duties under the direction and supervision of the United States Joint Chiefs of Staff.

4. William J. Donovan is hereby appointed as Director of Strategic Services

5. The Order of July 11, 1941 is hereby revoked.

THE FIRST N.A.B. WAR SERVICE BULLETIN [6]

STATION SILENCES

The Federal Communications Commission announces that at the request of the army, it has assigned field inspectors to perform liaison duties between the Interceptor Command and the commercial radio

[6] Excerpts from "War Service," the first of the N.A.B. War Service Bulletins, issued to all broadcasters December 9, 1941.

stations in each area where radio silence may be required. When the inspector directs a station to maintain radio silence, it should be understood that the order originated with the Interceptor Command of the Army and carries with it the authority of the Federal Communications Commission.

Radio stations will be advised as promptly as possible when radio silence is no longer required so that they may resume normal operations. In this connection, plans are being made to effect a more rapid system of communication between the Commission's inspectors and the radio stations which may be required to go off the air. . . .

WAIT FOR FACTS

Don't broadcast "unconfirmed reports."
Don't broadcast rumors.

This should apply whether your own news staff has gathered these "unconfirmed reports" or *whether they come from the news services.*

Wait for the facts. This is part of your responsibility for civilian morale.

PROGRAM CAUTIONS

The War Department has pointed out the need for the exercise of extreme care in the handling of all news and the opportunities for facts to reach the air, and this involves even the innocent looking quiz type show or man on the street broadcast. For example, in a seaport city a man on the street announcer on the air noticed a little girl in the crowd. He asked her her name and she told him. He asked her where she was going and this is what she said. "I am going to the Navy Yard. My Mummy just got a call from my brother," and the announcer said, "What is that package you have under your arm?" She replied, "Mummy is sending some cakes and cookies to my brother before he leaves." The announcer then asked, "Where is he going?" and she said immediately to be heard by the entire radio audience, "He is going to Iceland and I'd better hurry because he told Mummy the boat was leaving in an hour."

The War Department points out that this information could have led to the loss of American lives on a transport for it would be relayed by any enemy agents who were monitoring the station.

This is what we mean when we say that caution should be exercised not only in what we ourselves do but in permitting an opportunity, however inadvertent, for such information to reach the air.

The War Department points out that with the establishment of a system of daily communiques stations will no doubt find it possible and desirable to bring about a more orderly handling of the war news at definite periods of time rather than the constant interruption of program service which has the effect of keeping people (who should be working) listening to the radio all day long. If these people knew that at stated intervals of time they could hear the latest war news it would materially assist the establishment of a stable and orderly civilian morale.

The N.A.B. is in hearty agreement with this.

WAR DEPARTMENT POINTERS

The following memorandum went out December 8 from the War Department to all broadcasters. On December 9, Point 1, regarding casualty lists, and Point 3, regarding station protection, were modified. Be sure to read the modifications, following this memorandum.

In line with the cooperation of Radio News Wire Services with the Radio Branch of the War Department, the following is for your information and we request immediate transmission to your radio clients:

1. Broadcast of casualty lists.

No casualty lists will be released until nearest of kin have been notified; they will be available for immediate broadcast, upon release, from this wire. To eliminate undue anxiety, however, it is suggested that only names of persons in your immediate listening area be broadcast. No network will broadcast complete lists, although newspapers will publish them. Names of casualties, when released, should be broadcast in regular newscast periods or in groups in time set aside for that purpose and NOT as flashes, interrupting regular program service. Rumors of casualties should NOT be broadcast. No surmises of persons believed to be on casualty lists should be broadcast until officially confirmed in official releases from the War Department.

2. Broadcasting secret information.

Reemphasizing the statement of Secretary Stimson made Sunday concerning restriction on the broadcast or publication of information regarding the strength, positions, or movements of United States troops, outside the continental limits of the United States. This statement also covers all troop movements in the United States or to outlying posts unless same is officially announced.

3. Transmitter protection.

Station managers desiring military protection of transmitters should immediately contact the Commanding Officer of the Corps Area in which transmitter is located. (Consult map in relation to Radio Stations and Corps Areas, distributed by N.A.B.)

4. State news editor's groups.

District N.A.B. directors are requested to send to E. M. Kirby, Chief, Radio Branch, War Department, immediately names of state chairmen of news editors and program directors as set up at recent district N.A.B. meetings.

5. News releases.

The War and Navy Departments soon will establish a regular schedule of official communiques, possibly for release twice daily so that broadcasters may present war news in a more orderly scheduled manner.

As to Casualties

We are requested to transmit the following statement signed by Ed Kirby, Radio Branch, War Department, and addressed to all radio stations:

"We have just been informed by the National Association of Broadcasters that it is advising radio stations NOT to broadcast the names of casualties. This is deeply appreciated as broadcast of casualty lists would, in effect, set up obituary columns on the air when such time can be used to elevate morale rather than depress it. Because of opportunity for mispronunciation of names it is felt that such lists should appear in print rather than uttered over the air. No objection to mentioning, however, occasional newsworthy names or, of course, broadcast of numbers of casualties."

Signed: ED KIRBY, Chief,
Radio Branch, War Department.

Watch Requests Carefully

Whenever a station receives a request, ostensibly originating with one of the branches of the armed forces, to make an announcement of any kind be sure to authenticate it. Broadcasters are cautioned not to put any announcements on the air notifying military or naval personnel to return to posts or stations unless they are absolutely certain that the person requesting the announcement has proper authority.

Help Recruiting

Manpower is our first need right now. Army, navy and marines have asked for more recruiting help. Suggestions for your help will be outlined in letters mailed this week.

N.A.B. WARTIME GUIDE [7]

This is a different war. It affects all phases of the nation's activity and reaches into every home. This is total war and victory requires the combined efforts of all our people. While we have learned much, from broadcasting war news since 1939, we now have new responsibilities and new opportunities. The relationship between broadcasting and government and the manner in which it will perform its function as the chief source of news and information requires careful appraisal. Upon the judgments and policies now formulated will depend our effectiveness.

The broad outlines of the policies to be followed in dealing with news and radio were given by the President in his speech of December 9. . . .

The National Association of Broadcasters after careful consultation with the military branches of the government as well as other agencies has attempted to make more detailed and specific the broader principles as enunciated by the President. With the objective of setting forth certain basic requirements your Association offers to broadcasters this pamphlet of recommendations as a guide to wartime broadcasting.

In general accept the fact that this is likely to be a long war— with both reverses and triumphs. Avoid broadcasting the news in a manner that is likely to cause exaggerated optimism. Likewise avoid creating an atmosphere of defeatism and despair. At all times practice moderation in the writing, delivering and scheduling of news broadcasts.

The writing should avoid sensationalism.

The delivery should be calm, accurate, factual.

There should be a minimum of production trappings surrounding news broadcasts. The news of America at war is sufficiently exciting; do not try to make it more so by presenting it with sound-effects. The tension needs to be lessened, not increased.

Newcasts should be scheduled at regular intervals, and, in the absence of news of extreme importance, this regular schedule should be followed.

Artificial efforts to stimulate listening audience by promises of immediate interruption of regular programs for important news broadcasts should not be attempted. Let the events speak for themselves.

Extreme care should be used in the handling and broadcasting of any communiques or radio reports from our enemies.

They should not be used unless coupled, by careful editing, with known facts or an official statement on the same subject by our government. If you don't have the facts or an official statement on the same subject, don't broadcast the enemy communique until you get them.

[7] From "N.A.B. Wartime Guide," released to American radio stations by the National Association of Broadcasters, December 18, 1941.

In this connection, broadcasters should remember that extraordinary care must be taken to insure that those who tune in late do not get a wrong impression. *Remember the Men from Mars!*

Remember we are at war with other Axis countries as well as Japan. Their communiques should be considered in the same light as those of the Japs.

The broadcasting industry has been given to understand that it can use news from recognized press services because responsibility for that news rests with the press services. News gathered from other sources must be thoroughly checked and verified before broadcasting.

Do NOT broadcast rumors, "hot tips" or "unconfirmed reports," no matter what their source. "Hot tips" and rumors may burn your fingers.

If you have the slightest doubt on any story, check with your press association. It is better to have no news than to broadcast false or harmful news.

In this connection, a word of caution on news flashes. A good practice is to wait a few minutes after the first flash until you are perfectly satisfied from the following story that the flash is borne out. Radio's speed of light is cause for caution.

Do NOT broadcast news which concerns war production figures unless such news is *officially* released by the government.

Do NOT broadcast the movement of naval or any other vessels.

Do NOT broadcast news about the movement of troops or personnel either outside or within the continental limits, unless it has been released *officially* by the War or Navy Departments.

Do NOT broadcast the location of vessels, either under construction or about to be launched.

Do NOT broadcast figures of Selective Service enrollments and inductions.

Do NOT broadcast personal observations on weather conditions. Watch sports broadcasts for this. A late night or early morning comment that "it's a fine, clear night (or morning)" might be invaluable information to the enemy. Stick to official weather reports your station receives from your local weather bureau.

Do NOT broadcast such imperatives as "Attention all men! Report to your local Civilian Defense headquarters tonight at eight." Announcements may be requested in that manner. They should be changed to qualify the source at the beginning, such as: "The local Civilian Defense Committee requests all men, etc." Reserve such "attention compellers" for important war purposes.

Do NOT overestimate American power nor underestimate the enemy strength and thereby tend to create complacent confidence. Stick to the facts as presented in official releases.

Do NOT allow sponsors to use the news as a springboard for commercials. Such practices as starting commercials with "Now some good news, etc." should NEVER be permitted. Also, it is important that such news-phases as "Bulletin," "Flash," "News" and the like be used only in their legitimate functions. Do NOT permit, "Here's good news! The Bargain Basement announces drastic reductions, etc."

Do NOT use any sound-effects on dramatic programs, commercial announcements or otherwise which might be confused by the listener with air raid alarms, alert signals, etc.

Do NOT try to second-guess or master-mind our military officials. Leave this for established military analysts and experts, who are experienced enough to await the facts before drawing conclusions.

Do NOT broadcast any long list of casualties. This has been specifically forbidden.

Do NOT permit speakers, in discussions of controversial public issues, to say anything of aid to the enemy.

Do NOT broadcast the location of plants engaged in the manufacture of war materials unless approved by the government. This applies to emergencies such as explosions, sabotage, etc., unless such reports have been approved by government or cleared at the source by press associations.

Do NOT take chances with ad lib broadcasts, on the street or in the studio. An open microphone accessible to the general public constitutes a very real hazard in times of war. Questions should be prepared and approved in advance, and extreme care should be exercised to avoid the asking of questions which would draw out any information of value to the enemy. Any questions regarding the war or war production might make trouble.

Do—Maintain constant vigil over the news machines. Be sure to designate a responsible staff member in charge of the news at all hours of your operation. That person should be the one to determine the advisability of breaking programs for news bulletins, flashes, etc., and should be responsible for all news during the period he is designated in charge of the news machines.

Look for further instructions on the press wires, from the National Association of Broadcasters, the War Department, the Navy, or other official sources.

See that every member of your staff knows and understands these guides. *Let your entire news staff and announcers know your policy.*

File a complete script of all your news broadcasts. Keep the file until the war ends.

Prepare and present your news factually, authentically, calmy. This is repetition, but this caution cannot be repeated too much.

Do your job as best you can, knowing it is one of the significant jobs in this all-out war in which America is engaged. Do your job measured to even stricter standards than we have set. Do your job in a manner that will satisfy yourself, advance the cause of free radio and serve the best interests of your country.

BIBLIOGRAPHY

An asterisk (*) preceding a reference indicates that the article or a part of it has been reprinted in this book.

Books, pamphlets, etc.

Angell, James R. War propaganda and the radio. U. of Pa. Press. Philadelphia. '40.

Antheil, George. The shape of the war to come. Longmans, Green. N.Y. '40.

Beman, Lamar T. Censorship of speech and the press. H. W. Wilson Co. N.Y. '30.

Censorship. Democracy in Action series, no. 10. Council for Democracy. N.Y. '42.

Censorship and Trade. Eyre & Spottiswoods. London. '16

Chafee, Zechariah, Jr. Free speech in the United States. Harvard U. Press. Cambridge. '41.

Childs, Harwood L. An introduction to public opinion. Wiley. N.Y. '40.

FYI. Time, Inc. house organ. Issue of Ja. 26, '42. lttr announcing appointment of Eric Hodgins as editorial vice president of Time to act as contact with Office of Censorship.

*FYI. Time, Inc. house organ. Issue of My. 18, '42. Discussion of Time's relations with the problem of censorship.

Great Britain. Foreign Office. Secret German documents—instructions to the army on control of press. Norway no. 1. '41.

Great Britain. General Staff. Censorship orders and regulations for troops in the field. '17.

Hargrave, John. Propaganda the mightiest weapon of them all. W. Gardner, Darton. London. '40.

Holmes, J. H. What is happening to our bill of rights? American Unitarian Assoc. Boston. '42.

Howe, Quincy. The news and how to understand it. Simon & Schuster. N.Y. '40.

Ickes, Harold L. America's House of Lords. Harcourt, Brace. N.Y. '39.

Ickes, Harold L., compiler. Freedom of the press today: a clinical examination by 28 specialists. Vanguard. N.Y. '41.

Lavine, Harold, and Wechsler, James. War propaganda and the United States. Institute for Propaganda Analysis. Yale U. Press. New Haven, Conn.

Lee, Alfred McLung: Elizabeth Bryant. The fine art of propaganda: a study of Father Coughlin's speeches. Institute for Propaganda Analysis. Harcourt, Brace. N.Y. '39.

Lippman, Walter. Liberty and the news. Harcourt, Brace. N.Y. '20.

*MacArthur, General Douglas. The statement issued at his first press conference in Australia, March 23, '41.

McLeish, Archibald. Talk before the N.A.B. convention, Cleveland, O., My. 11, '42.

McCamy, James L. Government publicity. U. of Chicago Press. Chicago. '39.

Miller, Neville. Let's keep radio free. Testimony before House Interstate and Foreign Commerce Committee, Ap. 16, '42, at a hearing on Sanders Bill (HR 5497) to amend the Federal Communications Act of 1934. Pamphlet issued by N.A.B. Washington, D.C. '42.

Mock, James R., and Larson, Cedric. Words that won the war: the story of the Committee on Public Information, 1917-1919. Princeton U. Press. Princeton. '39.

*Mock, James R. Censorship 1917. Princeton U. Press. Princeton. '41.

Office of Censorship. Code of wartime practices for American broadcasters. Ja. 15, '42. U.S. Gov. Printing Office. Washington, D.C. '42.

Office of Censorship. Code of wartime practices for the American press. Ja. 15, '42. U.S. Gov. Printing Office. Washington, D.C. '42.

Office of Censorship. Statement regarding clarification of naval news, released by Byron Price, Feb. 4, '42, to managing editors and marked "confidential—not to be published." Washington, D.C. '42.

Office of Censorship. Statement regarding news of enemy attacks, released by Byron Price F. 25, '42, as a note to managing editors marked "not for publication." Washington, D.C. '42.

Office of Censorship. Release describing functions, accomplishments of Mr. 3, '42. Washington, D.C. '42.

*Office of Censorship. Statement regarding amateur photography issued Mr. 12, '42. Washington, D.C. '42.

*Office of Censorship. Statement regarding export publications issued Mr. 18, '42. Washington, D.C. '42.

*Office of Censorship. Statement regarding regulation of maps, released Mr. 31, '42. Washington, D.C. '42.

Office of Censorship. Statement regarding news of air raids, issued by Byron Price, My. 13, '42, to newspapers and radio stations, and marked "confidential—not for publication."

*Office of Censorship. Code of wartime practices for the American press, as revised Je. 15, '42, released Je. 25, '42. Washington, D.C. '42.

*Office of Censorship. Code of wartime practices for American broadcasters, as revised Je. 15, '42, released Je. 25, '42. Washington, D.C. '42.

Phelps, Edith M., compiler. Regulation of the American press, p. 281-344. Univ. Debaters Annual. 1940-41. H.W. Wilson Co. N.Y. '41.

Price, Byron. Address before N.A.B. convention, Cleveland, O., My 11, '42.

Scanlon, H. L., compiler. Freedom of communication in wartime. Carnegie Endowment for International Peace Library. Washington, D.C.

Seldes, George. You can't print that! Payson & Clark. N.Y. '29.

Seldes, George. Freedom of the press. Bobbs-Merrill. N.Y. '35.

Sharp, Eugene. The censorship and press laws of 60 countries. Mo. U. Journalism series, no. 77. Columbia, Mo. '36.

Sherly, Swagar. Argument in connection with issues raised by the International Shortwave broadcasting rule 42.03 (a) in hearings before the F.C.C., Jl. 14, 15 and 17, '39. Pamphlet issued by the N.A.B. Washington, D.C. '39.

Steed, Henry Wickham. The press. Penguin Books, Ltd. Harmondsworth, Middlesex, England. '39.

Steed, Henry Wickham. The fifth arm. Constable. London. '40.

United States Espionage Act. Extract from "The Code of the Laws of the United States of America in force Ja. 3, '35." Title 50—War. Chapter 4—Espionage. Sections 31-42. Pamphlet issued to employees of the networks in cooperation with the government. N.Y. '42.

United States War College Division. The proper relations between the army and the press in war. N. '15. United States Government Printing Office. Washington, D.C. '16.

War Service Bulletin. Commercial News Programs. Release of F. 6, '42. National Association of Broadcasters. Washington, D.C. '42.

War Time Code for Broadcasters, as issued by the Office of Censorship, Ja. 15, '42. National Association of Broadcasters. Washington, D.C. '42.

War Time Restraints. Texts of the federal laws and regulations affecting utterances, communication, enemy aliens, labor, etc. American Civil Liberties Union. N.Y. Mr. '42.

PERIODICALS

Advertising Age. 13:6. Ja. 19, '42. Office of censorship announces code of practices, for magazines, newspapers & other periodicals.

*Advertising Age. 13:8. Ja. 19, '42. Censors tighten rules on radio audience shows.

*Advertising Age. 13:12. F. 2, '42. What about censorship?

*Advertising Age. 13:16. F. 16, '42. Clear ads through army and navy, Shaner counsels.

Advertising Age. 13:30. F. 23, '42. Special newspaper sections or editions on war production activities banned by War Dept. unless previously okayed by Army censors.

Advertising Age. 13:26. Mr. 2, '42. Customs officers will review all advertising prepared for exploiting movies in foreign markets.

Advertising Age. 13:27. Mr. 9, '42. Washington doesn't like psychological effect of too much after the war is over in copy; mfrs. asked not to use it.

Advertising Age. 13:7. Mr. 23, '42. Col. Ennis, public relations branch, Army Air Corps, explains why ad copy & photos must be reviewed.

*Advertising Age. 13:25. Mr. 23, '42. U.S. Steel issues first "censored" annual report.

Advertising Age. 13:26. Mr. 30, '42. Board of Economic Warfare to license, Apr. 1, business papers containing technical data before their export to foreign countries.

*Advertising Age. 13:25. Ap. 20, '42. What to do with foreign press puzzles officials.

Advertising Age. 13:6. Ap. 27, '42. Business paper editors meet to discuss censorship plans.

Advertising Age. 13:12. My. 11, '42. U.S. News solves foreign copy censorship with announcement that hereafter no copies will be sent outside the jurisdiction of U.S. and Canada, and that none of its content is to be broadcast in any way.

American Forum of the Air. 4:1-12. Mr. 8, '42. Free speech and censorship in wartime. A symposium by Byron Price and others.

American Historical Review. 23:303-23. 1918. Newspaper problem in its bearing upon military secrecy during the Civil War. James G. Randall.

American Historical Review. 39:284-97. 1934. Federal generals and a good press. James Gordon Bennett.

American Mercury. 54:666-71. Je. '42. Wanted: Opposition. George Creel.

Atlantic Monthly. 169:156-61. F. '42. Newspapers on guard. Gerald W. Johnson.

Bill of Rights Review. 1:293-302. Summer, '41. Mars with a blue pencil. H. C. Shriver and Cedric Larson.

*Broadcasting. 21:20. Ag. 4, '41. The press must be free. Raymond Clapper.

*Broadcasting. 21:52. S. 22, '41. Proposals to censor communications are told to Congress by army and navy.

*Broadcasting. 21:14. O. 20, '41. Navy proceeding with censorship plan, possibly conflicting with Donovan unit.

*Broadcasting. 21:21. O. 20, '41. Free press, air viewed as vital.

*Broadcasting. 21:7. D. 15, '41. Industry takes its place in war program.

*Broadcasting. 21:12. D. 15, '41. President issues executive order on radio.

*Broadcasting. 21:26. D. 15, '41. Broadcasts of casualty lists are restricted in army plan.

*Broadcasting. 21:38. D. 15, '41. Radio goes to war.

*Broadcasting. 21:51. D. 15, '41. Care in news broadcasts and measures to safeguard nation advised by N.A.B.

*Broadcasting. 21:7-8. D. 29, '41. J. Harold Ryan named broadcast censor.

*Broadcasting. 22:10. Ja. 5, '42. Industry cooperates in censorship plan.

*Broadcasting. 22:45. Ja. 5, '42. Calling all calls.

*Broadcasting. 22:44. Ja. 19, '42. Federal bureaus on censor board.

*Broadcasting. 22:55. Ja. 19, '42. Censorship rules bring net praise.

*Broadcasting. 22:24. Ja. 26, '42. It could be worse.

*Broadcasting. 22:8. F. 2, '42. Ryan denies Shepard's appeal to ease open-mike decision.

*Broadcasting. 22:10. F. 9, '42. N.A.B. code committee's news control suggestions.

*Broadcasting. 22:10. F. 9, '42. N.A.B. code group votes news control plan.

*Broadcasting. 22:15. F. 16, '42. The test—can the enemy utilize it? John Harold Ryan.

*Broadcasting. 22:32. F. 16, '42. Censorship loopholes.

*Broadcasting. 22:14. F. 23, '42. "Town Hall' adopts rule to abide by censorship.

*Broadcasting. 22:14. F. 23, '42. Controlled remote interview allowed.

*Broadcasting. 22:14. F. 23, '42. Army command on West Coast forbids net testimonials and request programs.

*Broadcasting. 22:20. F. 23, '42. Commercials cut on news by CBS.

*Broadcasting. 22:36. Mr. 9, '42. Censor formulas given advertising.

*Broadcasting. 22:22. Mr. 23, '42. Official policy issued by O.F.F. as guide to handling of news.

*Broadcasting. 22:22. Mr. 23, '42. Specific war news policies laid down by the C.W.I.

*Broadcasting. 22:48. Ap. 13, '42. Censorship bans news of race riot.

*Broadcasting. 22:7. Je. 29, '42. Revised radio code clears many problems.

Business Week. p. 48+. Ja. 24, '42. Censor over ads.

Can. J. Econ. & Pol. Sci. 7:313-23. Ag. '41. Press censorship. Wilfrid Eggleston.

Christian Century. 59:412. Ap. 1, '42. Censorship policy changing?

Colliers. 107:82. Je. 28, '41. Creel on censorship.

Colliers. 107:13+. My. 24, '42. The plight of the last censor. George Creel.

Commonweal. 35:547-8, 561, 617. Mr. 27-Ap. 10, '42. Views and reviews. M. Williams.

Congressional Digest. 21:36-7. F. '42. What can and cannot be printed in wartime. Byron Price.

*Editor & Publisher. 74:64. D. 13, '41. J. E. Hoover coordinator of U. S. war censorship.

*Editor & Publisher. 74:36. D. 20, '41. Shop talks at thirty. Arthur Robb.

*Editor & Publisher. 75:22. Ja. 3, '42. Vagaries of censorship.

*Editor & Publisher. 75:27. Ja. 10, '42. Coordination of censorship with Allies is seen.

*Editor & Publisher. 75:5. Ja. 17, '42. Price issues censorship rules: promises "no news blackout".

*Editor & Publisher. 75:32. Ja. 17, '42. Shop talks at thirty. Arthur Robb.

*Editor & Publisher. 75:26. Ja. 24, '42. No curb on opinion.

*Editor & Publisher. 75:26. Ja. 24, '42. Uneven censorship.

*Editor & Publisher. 75:36. Ja. 24, '42. Promotion men must obey censorship code. T. S. Irwin.

*Editor & Publisher. 75:38. Ja. 24, '42. Shop talk at thirty. Arthur Robb.

*Editor & Publisher. 75:7. Ja. 31, '42. Navy apologizes for confusion on "Coimbra" sinking.

*Editor & Publisher. 75:7. Ja. 31, '42. Navy working on plan for news releases.

*Editor & Publisher. 75:22. Ja. 31, '42. Censorship, not strangulation.

*Editor & Publisher. 75:8. F. 7, '42. Army lists regulations for war correspondents.

*Editor & Publisher. 75:9. F. 7, '42. New army rule.

*Editor & Publisher. 75:32. Admiral Andrews tells his part in navy news. Adolphus Andrews.

*Editor & Publisher. 75:7. F. 14, '42. O.F.F. to censor speeches of cabinet officers.

*Editor & Publisher. 75:9. F. 14, '42. Editors decry "Normandie" censorship: Navy acts. W. E. Schneider.

*Editor & Publisher. 75:6. F. 21, '42. Censors clip L. A. Times at post office.

*Editor & Publisher. 75:40. F. 21, '42. Shop talk at thirty. Arthur Robb.

Editor & Publisher. 75:22. F. 28, '42. Official secrets.

*Editor & Publisher. 75:7. Mr. 7, '42. Open censorship started in New York on foreign file.

*Editor & Publisher. 75:36. Mr. 7, '42. Shop talk at thirty. Arthur Robb.

*Editor & Publisher. 75:9. Mr. 14, '42. Navy unifies news rules on U. S. ship sinkings.

*Editor & Publisher. 75:5. Mr. 21, '42. O.F.F. instructing government services to issue propaganda. J. J. Butler.

*Editor & Publisher. 75:8. Mr. 28, '42. Release from Office of Censorship to editors inquiring for information on identification of servicemen for use in local papers.

Editor & Publisher. 75:8. Mr. 28, '42. Hit Canadian dailies.

*Editor & Publisher. 75:18. Ap. 4, '42. Editorial.

Editor & Publisher. 75:22. Ap. 4, '42. Bracken reassures U. S. correspondents.

*Editor & Publisher. 75:37. Ap. 18, '42. Social Justice barred from the mails for war criticism.

*Editor & Publisher. 75:86. Ap. 25, '42. Statement at Founders' Day meeting, Sigma Delta Chi fraternity. Palmer Hoyt.

*Editor & Publisher. 75:8. My. 2, '42. Biddle reassures "loyal" newspapers.

*Editor & Publisher. 75:6. My. 9, '42. Three publications denied 2nd class mail privileges.

*Editor & Publisher. 75:20. My. 16, '42. A present danger.

*Editor & Publisher. 75:9. F. 21, '42. Censor's office works smoothly on war news. James J. Butler.

Export Trade & Shipper. p. 3-5. Mr. 3, '41. How Britain's blacklists and censorship affect American traders. Franklin Johnson.

Forbes. 49:10-11. Mr. 1, '42. How to weigh the war news. William F. Brooks.

Forbes. 49:11. My. 15, '42. Washington Wonderland. Potomacus.

*Fortune. 23:88+. Je. '41. Censorship.

*Harper's. 180:187-95. Ja. '40. Wartime censorship in the United States. Lucille B. Milner & Groff Conklin.

Industrial Marketing. p. 13-16+. Mr. '42. Application of censorship and military regulations to advertising copy.

Journalism Quarterly. 19:34-9. Mr. '42. Editorial pages in wartime. W. W. Waymach.

Journalism Quarterly. 19:51-7. Mr. '42. Relationship of press to government and to the people. Gideon Seymour.

Life. 12:71-4. Mr. 16, '42. Wartime censorship; how England keeps its freedom of the press. Brenden Bracken.

Magazine Art. 35:74. F. '42. Censorship and common sense.

Journal of the Military Service Institution of the U. S. 56:9-23. Ja.-F. '15. The press in time of war. Capt. Frank Geere.

*Modern Industry. 3:60. F. 14, '42. How censorship affects industry.

*Modern Industry. 3:80-1. Ap. 15, '42. Censorship rules affect industry.

Nation. 154:86. Ja. 24, '42. The limits of liberty. Reinhold Niebuhr.

Nation. 154:175. F. 7, '42. Liberty in wartime. Roger Baldwin.

*Nation. 154:180. F. 14, '42. The rake's progress.

National Educational Association of United States Proceedings: 1941. p. 176-9. Press as a safeguard of freedom in a democracy. E. D. Canham.

National Educational Association of United States Proceedings: 1941. p. 170-3. Radio as a safeguard of freedom in a democracy. J. R. Angell.

Nation's Business. 29:28. Ag. '41. Read but not dictated.

New Masses. p. 9-11. My. 20, '41. Conscripting the news. Julian Webb.

New Republic. 105:860. D. 22, '41. Freedom of press in wartime.

New York Times. 90:1. D. 10, '42. Roosevelt says adverse war news to be published only if non-informative to enemy, radio speech—text.

New York Times. 90:5. D. 10, '42. Roosevelt press conference—news to come only from the executive, army and navy offices.

New York Times. 90:23. D. 16, '42. Commissioner Fly holds neither F.C.C. nor Defense Communications Board will censor radio or press.

New York Times. 90:1. D. 17, '42. Roosevelt names Price director of censorship—text of appointment speech.

New York Times. 90:9. D. 20, '42. Roosevelt creates office of censorship—text of order.

New York Times. 90:IV, 5. D. 28, '42. Censorship set-up reviewed.

New York Times. 91:10. Ja. 12, '42. Price appoints 16 government employees to censorship board.

*New York Times. 91:18. Ja. 13, '42. A summary of censorship. Arthur Krock.

New York Times. 91:5. F. 6, '42. Lt. Gen. A. G. L. McNaughton on secrecy need.

New York Times. 91:IV, 3. F. 8, '42. Krock comments on government system of withholding news.

New York Times. 91:18. F. 10, '42. Krock comments on news policy.

New York Times. 91:14. F. 13, '42. Sen. Taft scores censorship.

New York Times. 91:8. F. 18, '42. Gov. Lehman on news withholding.

New York Times. 91:7. F. 19, '42. A. W. Baldwin on need for facts.

New York Times. 91:18. F. 24, '42. Sen. Barbour scores withholding of adverse news.

New York Times. 91:14. Mr. 1, '42. J. G. McDonald warns commentators and editors on attitude.

New York Times. 91:4. Mr. 3, '42. Adm. King says public will get non-information news.

New York Times. 91:IV, 5. Mr. 22, '42. O.F.F. promises more news, general problems reviewed.

New York Times. 91:3. Mr. 25, '42. Gen. MacArthur promises no censorship.

New York Times. 91:13. Ap. 18, '42. Arthur Robb criticizes voluntary system.

New York Times. 91:1. Ap. 20, '42. Willkie drafts resolution for Republican party urging that bad news not be withheld—text.

New York Times. 91:1. Ap. 21, '42. Willkie resolution adopted by National Committee—text.

New York Times. 91:11. Ap. 25, '42. Price lauds cooperation.

*New York Times. 91:14L. My. 25, '42. Knowledge and morale.

*New York Times. 91:5E. Je. 21, '42. War news system reshaped. F. L. Kluckhohn.

*New York Times. 91:3E. Je. 28, '42. Washington publicity due for improvement. E. L. James.

Newsweek. 18:22. D. 29, '41. Basic pattern for the news censor's shears. E. K. Lindley.

Newsweek. 19:56. Ja. 5, '42. Living with censorship. Ramond Moley.

*Newsweek. 19:29. F. 16, '42. Report on growing pains of censorship. E. K. Lindley.

Princeton U. Library Chronicle. 2:97-104. Ap. '41. Nazi domination of the press—France. H. A. Grubbs.

Printers Ink. p. 35+. Mr. 20, '42. Commercial wartime news standards are fixed by networks. G. W. Johnstone.

*Public Opinion Quarterly. 6:3-26. Spring, '42. The limits of censorship, a symposium. Arthur Krock, Ralph D. Casey, Zechariah Chafee, Jr., James R. Mock and George Creel.

Radio Retailing. p. 18-19. Mr. '42. Radio's battleground.

*Redbook. 79:54-6. Jl. '42. Getting the news. Charles Hurd.

Saturday Evening Post. 213: . Ja. 5, '41. How your news is censored. Joe Alex Morris.

*Saturday Evening Post. 214:26. Ja. 24, '42. Censorship.

Saturday Review of Literature. 25:3-14+. Mr. 7, '42. Censorship and propaganda. E. L. Bernays.

Scribner's Commentator. p. 85-90. S. '41. Censorship now: no! Arthur Levin.

Social Education. 5:176-81. Mr. '41. A study in censorship. Harold Rugg.

Social Research. 8:238-46. My. '41. German censorship instructions for the Czech press.

Social Research. 8:399-418. Je. '41. Radio communication of war news in Germany. Hans Speir.

Sociology & Social Research. 22:57-66. '37. Censorship as a medium of propaganda. James E. Foster.

Special Libraries. 32:205-8. What is freedom of the press? E. R. Stevenson.

*Tide. 16:12. Ap. 15, '42. Export magazines.

Time. 38:54. S. 29, '41. Censorship changes: Navy's move.

Time. 39:56+. Ja. 26, '42. Censorship ground rules.

Time. 39:48-50. Mr. 30, '42. Churchill's men get touchy.

Time. 39:51-3. Ap. 6, '42. Censorship grows bold.

Time. 39:75. Ap. 13, '42. 35 day's ignorance.

*Time. 39:90. My. 11, '42. Science hush-hushed.

*Time. 39:64. Je. 8, '42. Censorship fantasia.

*Time. 39:58-60. Je. 22, '42. What sense censorship?

Town Meeting. 7:1-29. D. 15, '41. Propaganda and censorship in wartime. Roger Baldwin and others.

Town Meeting. 8:1-24. My. 4, '42. The role of criticism in wartime. William Deane Fuller and others.

*U. S. News. 12:17. F. 6, '42. Censorship of the news: effect on press and reader.

*U. S. News. 12:12. F. 13, '42. U-Boat attacks: press view.

U. S. News. 12:13-14. Mr. 6, '42. Threat to freedom of the press.

U. S. News. 12:21. Mr. 6, '42. Official secrets bill: widespread press opposition.

UNIVERSITY DEBATERS' ANNUALS

E. M. PHELPS, ED. *Cloth. Price* $2.25

Series of year books, each a collection of representative intercollegiate debates on important questions of the day. Constructive and rebuttal speeches for both sides. Each debate is accompanied by selected bibliography and briefs.